COBOL
Programming

COBOL Programming

A Structured Approach

ROBERT C. NICKERSON
California State University, Hayward

WINTHROP PUBLISHERS, INC., Cambridge, Massachusetts

Library of Congress Cataloging in Publication Data

Nickerson, Robert C
   COBOL programming.

   Includes bibliographical references and index.
   1.   COBOL (Computer program language)   2.   Structured
programming.   I.   Title.
QA76.73.C25N5   001.6'424   76-58884
ISBN 0-87626-129-2

Cover design by David Ford

© *1977 by Winthrop Publishers, Inc.*
   17 Dunster Street, Cambridge, Massachusetts 02138

10   9   8   7   6   5   4   3   2

For Betsy and Lisa
and their happiness

Contents

Preface

This textbook is a carefully paced introduction to the COBOL programming language with an emphasis on good programming procedures. More specifically, the book has the following four main objectives:

1. To introduce basic concepts about computers, programming, and data.
2. To describe the COBOL programming language at a level of detail that allows the student to gain a working knowledge of the fundamentals of the language.
3. To explain and demonstrate the process of preparing programs with an emphasis on "structured" programming principles.
4. To explore programming techniques and computer applications.

The first objective is accomplished by providing introductory material on computers and data processing. No previous exposure to these topics is assumed. Chapters 1 and 2 present the essential background material necessary to begin studying COBOL.

The majority of the book is devoted to the second objective. The COBOL language is described carefully, and many examples are provided. The approach is to develop the concepts informally so that the student gains an intuitive feeling for the language. Sufficient material for coding simple programs is presented as early as possible in the book (Chapter 3). This material then is expanded in logical steps in subsequent chapters.

The version of COBOL that is emphasized is mainly a subset of the 1974 American National Standard (ANS) COBOL. The subset is compatible for the most part with the 1968 version of ANS COBOL. Where differences exist they are pointed out in the text and the reader is referred to Appendix A for further explanation. This appendix also summarizes implementation differences for several common computers. The machines discussed are the IBM System/360 and System/370, the IBM System/3, and the IBM 1130.

The third objective provides the most unique feature of the book. The process of developing a computer program that is understandable and correct is emphasized from the beginning. Sample programs with text discussion of the development process are used to demonstrate these ideas. The programming process is summarized in Chapter 8.

The approach to programming that is emphasized is commonly called "structured" programming. There is a lot of disagreement and misunderstanding about what structured programming means. In this book we use the definition that structured programming is a systematic process that results in programs that are easily understood, maintained, and modified, and that can be shown to be correct. We emphasize designing programs in a top-down manner. This approach leads to modular programs that are easy to understand and to change. In addition, top-down design helps us show the correctness of the program. We discuss program structure and style rules throughout the book and emphasize their importance in producing readable and correct programs.

COBOL is not the most ideally suited language for implementation of structured programming concepts. However, with some degree of care, it is possible to produce well-structured COBOL programs. One purpose of this book is to demonstrate the care that is required to accomplish this.

A problem that often occurs when attempting to use structured programming principles with a particular language is what to do with the GO TO statement. While some may feel that it is ideal to eliminate this statement completely from all programs, it is not always practical. The principle that is used in this book is to avoid using the GO TO statement unless the resulting structure is more complicated than it would be with a GO TO. For didactic reasons, the GO TO statement is introduced as the first control statement (Chapter 3). However, the PERFORM statement is presented shortly afterward (Chapter 5) to give the student an alternative and to allow better structuring of programs.

The final objective of the book is accomplished through examples and programming problems. Examples that demonstrate various programming techniques and applications are included throughout the text. Programming problems that require the use of these and other techniques are included in Appendix D. These problems range in difficulty from simple list-producing programs to complex disk, tape, and table-processing programs.

This book is oriented to business and data processing students at two-year and four-year colleges, and to students in business schools and specialized computer schools. In addition, practitioners in industry may find many of the structured programming topics of interest. The book assumes no mathematical or accounting prerequisites, and no previous exposure to computers and data processing is required.

The text may be used in a one- or two-semester (quarter) course. The amount of material that can be covered in a term depends to a large extent on the students' previous exposure to programming. If the course for which the book is used has no prerequisites, then eight to ten chapters can be covered in depth in one term. During the second term the remainder of the book can be covered, along with supplementary material from the references and from the manufacturer's manual. If the student audience has had previous exposure to another programming language, then most of the material in the book can be covered in one term.

The book is divided into three parts. Part One (Chapters 1 and 2) introduces the background material necessary to begin studying the details of COBOL. Part Two (Chapters 3 through 8) presents the fundamental elements of COBOL and develops the programming process. Part Three (Chapters 9 through 13) discusses advanced COBOL features. Parts One and Two are prerequisite to Part Three and should be read in sequence. The chapters in Part Three may be taken in any order after completing Part Two.

Four appendices are provided. Appendix A summarizes the important differences between 1968 ANS COBOL, 1974 ANS COBOL, and the versions of COBOL implemented on several popular computers. Appendix B is a list of COBOL reserved words. Appendix C provides instructions for the operation of the IBM 029 keypunch. Appendix D contains the programming problems.

Finally, there is a list of COBOL reference manuals and an annotated bibliography of readings dealing with the programming process and structured programming.

As is always true, the ideas in this book come from many sources. I cannot begin to thank the professors, writers, colleagues, and students who have contributed in some way to this book. The original idea for the book came from discussions with Mike Meehan, editor at Winthrop Publishers. During the book's development, Dennie Van Tassel gave me his unbiased opinion of many of my ideas. The final manuscript could not have been prepared without the diligent typing of Jay Munyer.

Perhaps the most significant contributions came from my wife, Betsy. She is decidedly my best typist, editor, critic, and friend.

Robert C. Nickerson
Aptos, California

Acknowledgment

The following information is reprinted from *COBOL Edition 1965*, published by the Conference on Data Systems Languages (CODASYL) and printed by the U.S. Government Printing Office.

Any organization interested in reproducing the COBOL report and specifications in whole or in part, using ideas taken from this report as the basis for an instruction manual or for any other purpose, is free to do so. However, all such organizations are requested to reproduce this section as part of the introduction to the document. Those using a short passage, as in a book review, are requested to mention "COBOL" in acknowledgment of the source, but need not quote this entire section.

COBOL is an industry language and is not the property of any company or group of companies, or of any organization or group of organizations.

No warranty, expressed or implied, is made by any contributor or by the COBOL Committee as to the accuracy and functioning of the programming system and language. Moreover, no responsibility is assumed by any contributor, or by the committee, in connection therewith.

Procedures have been established for the maintenance of COBOL. Inquiries concerning the procedures for proposing changes should be directed to the Executive Committee of the Conference on Data Systems Languages.

The authors and copyright holders of the copyrighted material used herein

FLOW-MATIC (Trademark of Sperry Rand Corporation), Programming for the Univac® I and II, Data Automation Systems copyrighted 1958, 1959, by Sperry Rand Corporation; IBM Commercial Translator Form No. F28-8013, copyrighted 1959 by IBM; FACT, DSI 27A5260-2760, copyrighted 1960 by Minneapolis-Honeywell

have specifically authorized the use of this material in whole or in part in the COBOL specifications. Such authorization extends to the reproduction and use of COBOL specifications in programming manuals of similar publications.

COBOL
Programming

PART ONE

Introductory Concepts

CHAPTER 1
Computers, Programming, and Data

To understand computer programming it is first important to be familiar with a few general ideas about computers, programming, and data. In this chapter, we discuss the basic background material that is necessary to begin studying programming. In subsequent chapters we will use this background information in our detailed discussions of computer programming.

1-1. BASIC CONCEPTS

Any calculating device can be called a "computer." For example, adding machines, slide rules, and desk calculators are all "computers" because each calculates or computes. However, the word "computer" usually is not used for such devices. Instead we restrict its use to a particular device that has three distinguishing characteristics.

First, computers are always electronic; that is, computers calculate by electrical means. The consequence of this characteristic is that computers can operate at very high speeds — electronic speeds.

The second important characteristic of computers is that they have the ability to retain facts and figures, called *data*, for future use; that is, the computer has a "memory," or, more correctly, an *internal storage* in which it can hold information. Internal storage is not the same as human memory. However, like human memory, data can be placed in the computer's internal storage and then can be recalled at some time in the future.

Third, computers have the ability to retain in their internal storage a set of instructions that tells the computer what it is to do. Such a set of instructions is called a *program*. This program is prepared in advance by a person, called a *programmer*, who is familiar with the different things that the computer can do. The program that is prepared by the programmer is stored in the internal storage of the computer and is performed, or *executed*, automatically by the computer.

In this text we are concerned with the preparation of computer programs. The preparation process is called *programming*, and this book discusses a particular type of computer programming. However, before we can examine programming in detail, we must understand the physical organization of a computer.

1-2. ORGANIZATION OF A COMPUTER

Computers are distinguished from other devices by the characteristics described above. However, a computer requires a number of parts that have not been mentioned. For example, besides internal storage, there must be some unit in the computer that can interpret and execute instructions. In addition, there must be units to perform arithmetic, to make logical decisions, to put data into internal storage, and to retrieve data from storage.

We can view a computer as a system composed of several components. Figure 1-1 illustrates the important components of a computer and the relationship between them. Basically, a computer has three main parts — the input device, the central processing unit, and the output device.

An *input device* is a unit that accepts data from some source outside of the computer and transforms this data into electronic impulses. The data that is accepted is called *input data*, or simply *input*. One of the most common means of conveying input data to the computer is the punched card (see Figure 1-2). Data is recorded on the card by punching various patterns of holes into the card. (Details of punched card data are discussed later.) An input device for punched cards is designed to recognize what the patterns represent and to transform them into electronic impulses that are sent to the central processing unit. Such a device is called a *card reader* (see Figure 1-4).

An *output device* performs the opposite function of an input device. An output device transforms computer-created electronic

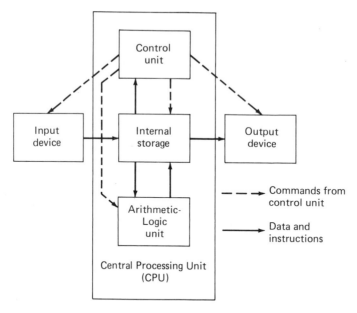

FIGURE 1-1. The Organization of a Computer

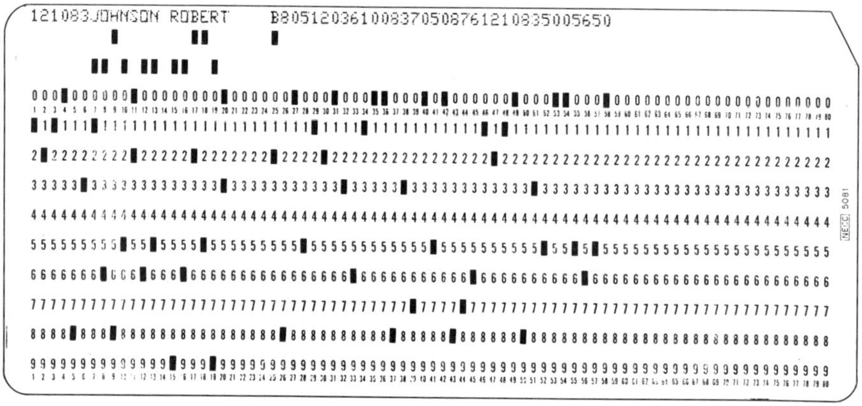

FIGURE 1-2. Punched Card Input

impulses from the central processing unit into a form that can be stored outside of the computer. The result is the *output data*, or simply the *output*, from the computer. A common form of output is a printed document or report (see Figure 1-3). Data from the central processing unit is transmitted by electronic impulses to a device called a *printer* (see Figure 1-4). In the printer these impulses are transformed into printed symbols, and a paper copy of the output data is produced.

Between the input device and the output device is the component that does the actual data processing and computing. This is the *central*

YEAR-TO-DATE SALES REPORT

SALESPERSON NUMBER	SALESPERSON NAME	SALES	RETURNS	NET
0005	BENNETT ROBERT	2,850.35	38.00	2,812.35
0016	LOCK ANDREW S	382.72	95.35	287.37
0080	PARKER JAMES E	30,700.14	555.00	30,145.14
0239	HAINES CYNTHIA L	101,000.00	2,200.00	98,800.00
0401	REDDING OLIVIA	156,159.15	24,052.64	132,106.51
0477	SMITH RICHARD A	1,450.00	510.00	940.00
0912	EMERY ELIZABETH G	36,200.35	1,730.15	34,470.20
1060	ROBINSON WILLIAM L	60,350.00	25.00	60,325.00
1083	JOHNSON ROBERT	63,311.96	893.55	62,418.41
1111	FREDERICKS RICHARD	52,600.00	483.50	52,116.50
1133	MARSHALL M S	210,000.00	.00	210,000.00
1205	HOLT BENTLEY	14,881.74	413.52	14,468.22
1374	BENTON ALEX J	2,600.13	267.50	2,332.63
1375	TAYLOR EVERETT	12,250.00	1,125.00	11,125.00
1420	EHRHARDT ELISE	4,890.64	981.00	3,909.64
1442	ADAMS JUNE R	96,771.46	1,572.36	95,199.10
1612	LOCATELLI FRANK	14,750.00	1,505.00	13,245.00
1698	GUZMAN JOSE	2,460.00	183.00	2,277.00
1842	COLE ROBERT N	306,650.39	81,637.92	225,012.47
	TOTALS	1,170,259.03	118,268.49	1,051,990.54

FIGURE 1-3. Printed Output

processing unit, or *CPU*. Input data is transformed into electronic impulses by the card reader or similar device, and this electronic representation of the input data is sent to the central processing unit. In the CPU the input data is stored and used in calculations and to help make decisions. After processing, the results are sent to the printer or other output device where the data is transformed into the final output.

Within the central processing unit, three important units work together to perform the functions of the computer. These are the internal storage, the arithmetic-logic unit, and the control unit. Internal storage, as we have seen, stores data to be processed and instructions (the program) to be executed by the computer.

The *arithmetic-logic* unit performs arithmetic and makes logical decisions. The basic arithmetic that a computer can do is addition, subtraction, multiplication, and division. Any complex arithmetic processing, such as finding a square root, is built up from these basic operations. Logical decisions are limited mainly to deciding if one item is greater than, less than, or equal to another. Complex logical decisions are merely combinations of these simple decisions.

The *control unit* tells the other computer units what to do. The control unit accomplishes this by following the instructions in the program. The program, as we have seen, is prepared in advance by the programmer and is placed in the computer's internal storage. During processing each programmed instruction is brought from the internal storage to the control unit. The control unit analyzes the instruction, then gives commands to the other units based on what the instruction tells the control unit to do. The execution of one instruction may involve actions in any of the other components of the computer. After executing an instruction, the next instruction in the programmed sequence is brought to the control unit and executed. This continues until all the instructions in the program have been executed.

For example, a simple computer program may include three instructions:

1. Read two numbers
2. Add the numbers
3. Write the result

These three instructions are prepared in a form recognizable to the computer and are placed in the computer's internal storage. On a signal to begin, the first instruction is brought from internal storage to the control unit. Execution of the instructions then proceeds as follows:

1. Read two numbers: The control unit examines this instruction and issues commands to the other units that cause the instruction to

be executed. For this instruction, the control unit issues a command to the input device that causes two numbers to be read and placed in the internal storage unit. The second instruction is then brought to the control unit.

2. Add the numbers: This instruction causes the control unit to issue three commands. The first, to the internal storage, causes the two numbers to be sent to the arithmetic-logic unit. Then a command is given to the arithmetic-logic unit to add the two numbers. Finally, the arithmetic-logic unit is commanded to return the result to the internal storage. The last instruction is then brought to the control unit.

3. Write the result: This instruction causes the control unit to issue a command to the internal storage to send the result to the output device and a command to the output device to write the result.

So far the only input device that we have considered is the card reader, and the only output device we have discussed is the printer. Many computers use other types of input/output (or I/O) devices. Sometimes several input and output devices are attached to the computer at one time.

In addition to the printer, a common output device is the *card punch* (Figure 1-4). This unit punches the results of computer proces-

FIGURE 1-4. A Typical Computer System, the IBM System/370 (Courtesy of IBM Corp.)

sing into cards. Other input/output devices include magnetic tape and disk drives.

Magnetic tape is much like tape recorder tape; data is recorded on the surface of the tape by patterns of magnetic spots. A *magnetic tape drive* is a device that records data on magnetic tape and also retrieves data from the tape (Figure 1-4).

A *magnetic disk* resembles a phonograph record. However, like tape, the disk surface records data by magnetic spot patterns. A *magnetic disk drive* is a device for recording data on magnetic disks and for retrieving data from disks (Figure 1-4).

Tape and disk drives are both input and output devices; that is, they can both retrieve input data and record output data. A card reader can be used only as an input device; printers and card punches are used only as output devices. No matter what device is used, we always say that the input device *reads* input data and the output device *writes* the output.

Figure 1-4 illustrates a typical computer with the components described in this section. This computer has a card reader, a card punch, a printer, and a number of magnetic tape drives and disk drives. Other types of computers have different configurations of I/O devices. The central processing units of different computers also vary, especially in their speed, size, and cost. Although there are many models and types of computers, the way they are programmed is often very similar. In this book we discuss a type of programming that is common to many different computers.

1-3. COMPUTER LANGUAGES

The basic issue of computer programming is communication between man and machine. In the last section we saw how a computer is told what to do by a set of instructions called a program. The program must specify precisely every operation that the computer is to perform. The instructions must be prepared so that the computer can understand them. The preparation of the instructions must follow certain rules. If the rules are not followed, then the computer does not do what we want it to do.

In general, communication is effected by languages that are understood by those who wish to communicate. Humans use *natural languages* such as English or Spanish to communicate with each other. The purpose of a *computer programming language* is to provide an effective means by which humans can communicate with computers.

Like natural human languages, computer programming languages are composed of symbols that are combined into patterns that have meaning. The rules that describe how these symbols may be combined into recognizable patterns are called the *syntax* of the language. The meanings of the patterns of symbols are called the *semantics* of the language. For example, the syntax of a language may say that a particular instruction has the form:

```
ADD data-name-1, data-name-2 GIVING data-name-3.
```

The semantics of the language tells us that this instruction means to add the values referred to by the first two data names and to assign the result to the third.

In this book we discuss the syntax and semantics of the COBOL programming language. COBOL is just one of many programming languages. In fact, there are several groups of languages and many different languages in each group.

One group of languages is called *machine language*. A machine language is the language in which a computer actually does its processing. To a computer, this type of language is a series of electronic impulses. The programmer expresses this language in the binary mode — that is, as a series of 1s and 0s. Each type of computer has its own machine language. There are many different types of computers, hence many machine languages. However, the most important characteristic of machine language is that, for any particular computer, the machine language for that computer is the *only language that it can understand. Every program for that computer must either be written in its machine language or written in another language, and then translated into its machine language.*

Machine language is considered low-level language because it is the basic language of a computer. Several higher levels of computer programming languages exist. These languages are called "higher level" because they are closer to natural human or mathematical language than to machine language. All high-level languages have one characteristic in common — any program that is written in a high-level language must first be translated into machine language before it can take control of the computer. (The translation process differs for each language, but fortunately for the programmer it can be done automatically by the computer.)

Another characteristic common to many, but not all, high-level languages is that they are independent of the computer being used. That is, a program written in a high-level machine-independent language can ordinarily be used on a wide variety of computers. However, it is still true that, for any *specific* computer, the high-level program must *first* be translated into the machine language of that particular computer. The same high-level program can be processed on a different type of computer by first translating it into the machine language of that computer.

One of the most widely used machine-independent high-level languages is *COBOL*. COBOL stands for COmmon Business Oriented Language. As the name implies, it is designed to be *common* to many different computers. In addition, it is most effectively used for *business-oriented* data processing rather than scientific or mathematical computing.

COBOL was one of the earliest high-level languages. It was developed originally in 1959 by a group of computer professionals called the Conference on Data Systems Languages (CODASYL). Since 1959 it has undergone a number of modifications and improvements.

Although COBOL was designed to be common to many types of computers, each computer manufacturer implemented a slightly different form of the language for use with its computers. For example, the version of COBOL on computer A might have some characteristics different from the version of COBOL for computer B. Thus, although a program was written in what was supposed to be a common language, it usually could not be processed on a different computer without some modification.

In an attempt to overcome this problem of incompatibility, the American National Standards Institute (ANSI) developed American National Standard (ANS) COBOL in 1968 and a revised version in 1974. Programs written in ANS COBOL should be able to be processed on any computer that implements the standard. In this text we describe mainly elements and features of COBOL that adhere to the 1974 standard.

Even though ANS COBOL is a standardized version of the language, there are still slight variations in the form of the language between different types of computers. Appendix A summarizes the important differences between ANS COBOL and several common implementations of the language. For further clarification of a language feature the references listed at the end of the book should be consulted.

1-4. PROGRAM COMPILATION AND EXECUTION

As we have seen, a program written in a high-level language must be translated into machine language before it can take control of the computer. For COBOL, as well as for most other high-level languages, this translation process is called *compilation*. The translation is performed by a special machine-language program called a *compiler program*, or simply a *compiler*. First a program is written in COBOL. Then the COBOL program is translated into an equivalent machine-language program by the compiler. Finally the machine-language program is executed.

The steps in the compilation and execution of a COBOL program are shown in Figure 1-5. After the program is prepared by the programmer, it is usually punched into cards. The resulting deck of cards is called the *source program*. The source program is in COBOL, a high-level language, and therefore cannot be executed until it is translated into machine language. To accomplish this, the COBOL compiler program is brought into the computer's internal storage. Outside of the computer the compiler can be stored in one of several forms. With some computers the compiler is punched on cards, while with others it is stored on magnetic tape or disk. No matter which form the compiler takes outside of the computer, it must first be stored in the computer's internal storage. After this is done, the compiler takes control of the computer and reads the COBOL source program, translating it into machine language. The resulting machine language equivalent of the COBOL source program is called the *object program*.

After compilation, the object program can take one of several forms. On some systems it is punched into cards; on others it is stored on magnetic tape or disk. In any case, it can be stored for future processing or executed immediately. If the program is to be executed, it is placed first in the computer's internal storage. The program then takes control of the computer and performs the tasks specified by the programmer. This often involves reading data from punched cards, using these data in calculations and in decision making, and producing printed output.

Although the translation of COBOL into the object program may seem complicated, it is handled to a large extent automatically by the computer. Most programmers need never see their object pro-

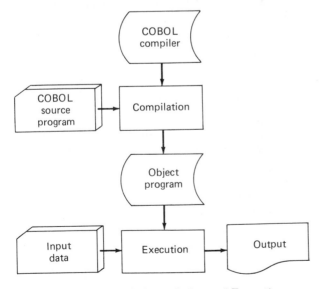

FIGURE 1-5. COBOL Compilation and Execution

grams. Instead, the programmer prepares the COBOL source program and the data, and everything else is handled automatically by the computer system. However, it is important to remember that it is not the source program that is executed; rather, it is the object program that results from the compilation process that is executed.

1-5. PUNCHED CARD DATA

As we have seen, one of the most common ways of conveying data and programs to a computer is by using *punched cards.* In this section we discuss the important characteristics of punched cards and see how information is recorded on cards.

There are several different types of punched cards; the most common is the type shown in Figure 1–6. This card is made of high quality paper to resist moisture and comes in a standard size. Its four corners may be square, cut or rounded and it may be any color. It has 80 vertical *columns* numbered 1 to 80 beginning at the left. In each column a pattern of rectangular holes may be punched to represent a letter, number, or special character. Thus, the card has a maximum capacity of 80 characters.

The punched card is divided horizontally into 12 *rows* or *punch positions.* The top row is called the 12-row. The next row down is the 11-row. Next comes the 0-row, the 1-row, and so forth until the bottom row which is the 9-row. Notice in Figure 1–6 that the 0- through 9-rows are numbered on the card while the 12- and 11-rows are not. Punches are made in the card in a particular row. For example, a punch in the 3-row is called a "3-punch"; a punch in the 12-row is called a "12-punch." A punch in one of the top three rows (12, 11,

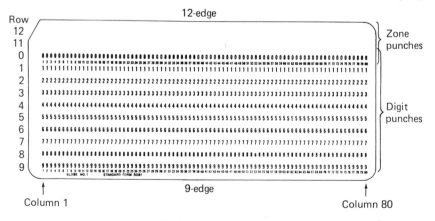

FIGURE 1-6. The Punched Card

or 0) is called a *zone punch* while a punch in the 0- through 9-row is called a *digit punch*. Note that a 0-punch is both a zone punch and a digit punch.

The top edge of the typical punched card is called the *12-edge*; the bottom edge is the *9-edge*. Again, these are shown in Figure 1–6. The front of the card is called the *face* of the card. These terms are important because all of the cards in a deck must be oriented in the same way. Instructions on how to orient the cards are usually expressed in these terms. For example, instructions for inserting cards into a particular type of card reader may say "9-edge first, face down." This means that all cards must be inserted into the machine with the bottom edge first and the front of the card facing down. If this is not done correctly, the data will not be read properly by the machine.

Data is recorded on a card in a special code known as the *Hollerith code*, which is named after Dr. Herman Hollerith, the inventor of the punched card. It is not necessary to memorize this code because it is recorded automatically when the card is punched with a *keypunch* machine. However, some degree of familiarity with the Hollerith code is useful. (See Appendix C for keypunch operating instructions.)

The basic principle of the Hollerith code is that any character — that is any number, letter, or special symbol — can be recorded in any of the 80 columns of a card by a unique combination of punches (see Figure 1–7). Numbers, or, more correctly, *numeric characters* or *digits*, are recorded by a single digit punch in the row that corresponds to the character. For example, the numeric character 5 is a 5-punch; the digit 0 is a 0-punch.

Alphabetic characters (letters) require two punches in a column, one zone punch and one digit punch. The letter A is a 12-punch and a 1-punch; B is a 12-punch and a 2-punch; P is an 11-punch and a 7-punch; U is a 0-punch and a 4-punch. As shown in Figure 1–7, the

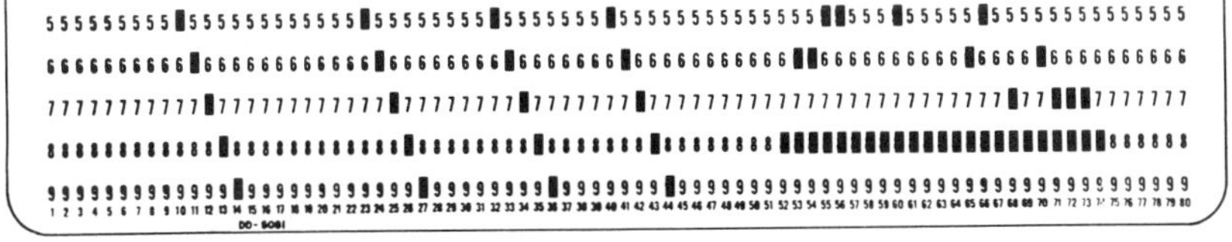

FIGURE 1–7. Punched Card Data

code for alphabetic characters follows a clear logical pattern. Notice that these are capital letters; lower case letters are not usually used on punched cards.

The coding of *special characters* does not follow an easy pattern like numeric and alphabetic characters. A special character can be coded with one, two, or three punches or even no punches. No punches in a column stands for a *blank* or *space*, which is a valid and often important special character in computer programming. A single 12-punch signifies the ampersand (&), while a single 11-punch stands for the minus sign. As can be seen in Figure 1–7, other special characters require two or three punches.

So far we have considered only the coding of individual characters. Although a single character can represent data, more often groups of characters convey information. Such a related group of characters is called a *field*. For example, a person's name is a field; it is a group of characters that conveys specific information. One's social security number is another field. Punched cards are organized into fields. Figure 1–8 illustrates one way that a card containing information about sales in a business could be divided into fields. For a particular problem, all cards of the same type are organized in the same manner. Thus, the salesperson-name field must be in the same columns on all cards of the type illustrated in Figure 1–8. For a different problem, the name field may be in different columns, but for any one problem, all cards must be arranged similarly.

Fields are grouped together to convey a variety of information about a single unit. Such a related group of fields is called a *record*. For example, the fields on the card shown in Figure 1–8 constitute a record of information about one salesperson. Note that a punched card is just one means of recording a record of information. Other

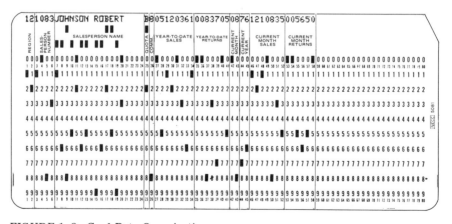

FIGURE 1–8. Card Data Organization

means may be used. For example, a line of print produced by a computer on its printer is a group of fields and hence is a record.

Finally, all of those records that serve a specific application are called a *file*. For example, all the records of the sales in one business constitute that business' sales file.

In summary, individual characters are the basic elements of data that are recorded on punched cards. Groups of characters, whether punched in cards, printed on paper, or recorded in some other manner, are called fields. Records are groups of fields, and a file is a group of records.

1-6. CARD AND REPORT LAYOUT

The programmer must know the arrangement of data in the file if he or she is to prepare a program to process the data. Usually this involves knowing the arrangement or *layout* of the fields in the records of the file. Sometimes these layouts are given to the programmer by the person who requires the program. At other times, it is the programmer's responsibility to design his or her own layouts. In this section we discuss convenient ways of showing the arrangement of punched cards and printed reports.

Card Layout

The layout of a punched card is often shown on a *multiple-card layout form*. An example of such a form is shown in Figure 1-9. Each band on the form (there are six) is used to show the layout of one card. Notice that each band looks like the bottom of a punched card with the row of nines and the card column numbers from 1 to 80.

The layout of a punched card is shown on the form by drawing vertical lines between columns to separate fields and by providing names for the fields. In Figure 1-9 the layout of one card is shown. This card contains data about salespeople in a business. All of the fields are separated by vertical lines. For example, the salesperson name is shown in columns 7 through 24; the year-to-date sales appears in columns 27 through 34; the current month is in columns 42 and 43. Notice that a field can be only one column if necessary. The quota class, in column 25, and the commission class, in column 26, are examples of this.

The card layout form does not show what information is to be recorded in each field. It only shows where the data are to be punched. Figure 1-8 shows how one card may be punched with data according

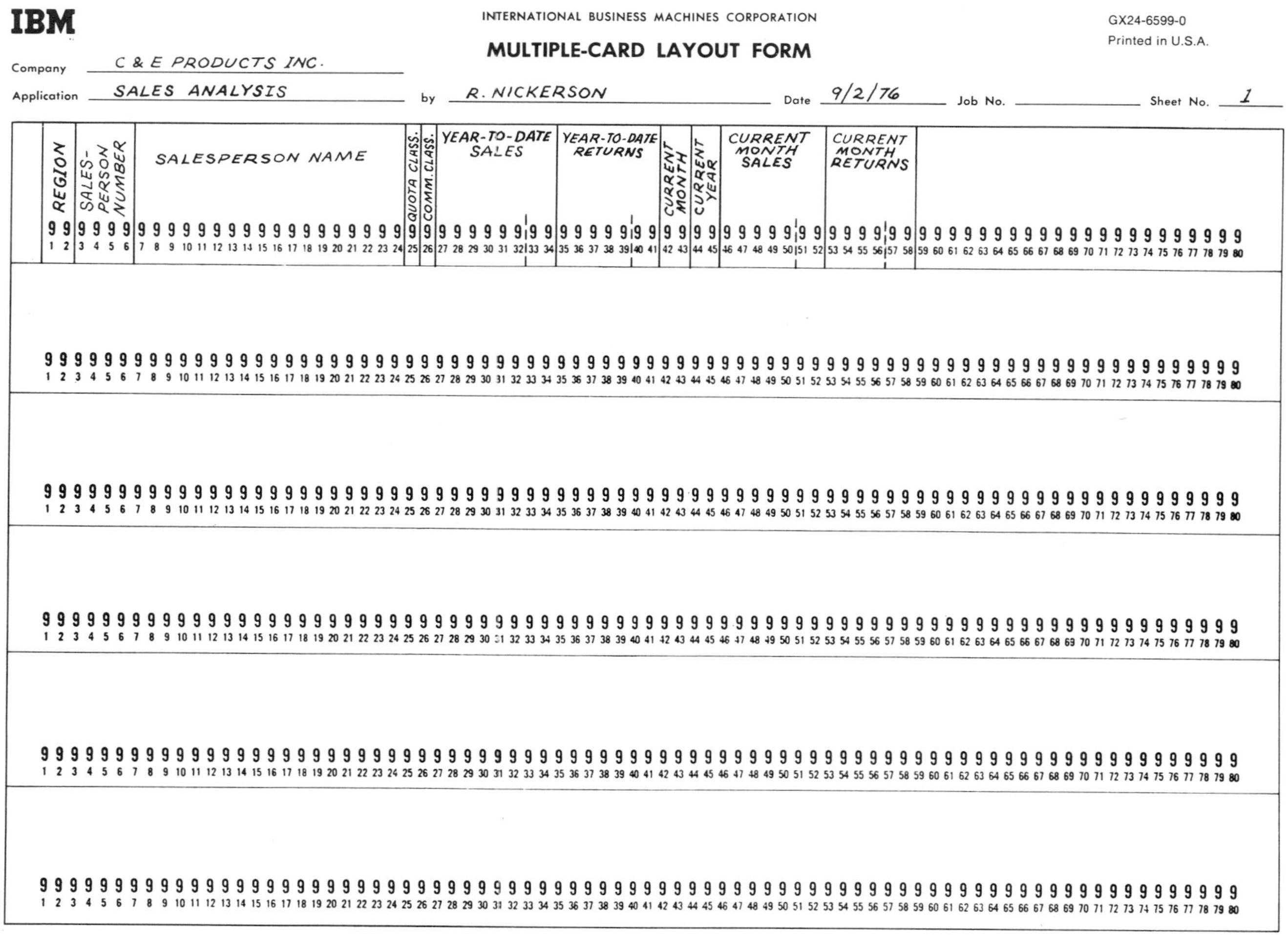

FIGURE 1-9. The Multiple-Card Layout Form

to this layout. In a typical application there are many cards punched with the *same layout but different data.* Thus, for the sales file all cards are punched in the layout shown in Figure 1-9 but each card contains information about a different salesperson.

How the data is punched within a field is often important. Numeric information that is used in calculations is always punched as far to the right within its field as possible. We say that such data is *right-justified.* A decimal point is never punched in a numeric field. The decimal point location is implied on the card layout form by a dashed vertical line between the two columns that are separated by the decimal point. For example, in Figure 1-9 we can see that there is an implied decimal point between columns 50 and 51 of the current-month-sales field. Thus, if 1210835 were punched in this field of a card, the current-month-sales for the salesperson would be $12,108.35. Note that neither a comma nor a dollar sign are punched on the card.

Some computer systems require that numeric fields be completely filled with digits, even if the number being represented is not large enough to fill the field. When this is required, zeroes are used, if necessary, to fill the field to the left of the number. These are called *left zeroes* or *lead zeroes.* For example, if the value to be recorded in the current-month-returns field is $56.50, then the number would be punched as 005650. The first two zeros are the left zeros.

Sometimes a negative amount must be recorded on a punched card. For example, if a customer pays more than the amount of his bill in a billing application, the excess paid is a credit balance and is considered to be a negative number. To record such a number on a punched card, the usual procedure is to punch the last column of the field with both the last digit of the number and a minus sign. In other words, the last column in the field must be punched twice — once with the last digit of the number, and once with the minus sign. (This can be accomplished either by backspacing or by using the multiple-punch key. See Appendix C for details.) For example, if the credit balance were $5.25, then the number would be punched in a five-column field as 00525̄. Since a minus sign is an 11-punch, this way of recording negative amounts is sometimes referred to as using an *11-overpunch.*

As we have seen, numeric information must be punched right-justified in its field. Nonnumeric information is usually punched as far to the left within its field as possible. That is, it is punched *left-justified.* For example, the salesperson name in the card layout shown in Figure 1-9 is punched beginning in column seven. If the name does not fill the entire field, then the extra columns on the right are left blank. If the name is too long for the field, then punching stops at column 24 and the remaining characters in the name are not recorded.

Nonnumeric data is often referred to as *alphanumeric data.* This is because such data may consist of alphabetic and numeric characters and even special characters. The salesperson name is an example of alphanumeric data. Alphanumeric fields may contain entirely numeric characters but then the numbers may not be used in calculations. For example, the salesperson-number field could be considered as an alphanumeric field or a numeric field. However, the current-month-sales field must only be considered a numeric field since it is used in calculations in the program.

Report layout

The printed output from computer processing is often referred to as a *report.* For example, Figure 1–3 shows a report of year-to-date sales information that was produced from processing the data on the sales cards. A report can be thought of as a file of printed information. Like all files, a report consists of a group of related records. Each line on the report is a record of information.

There are several different types of lines that can appear in a report. *Title* and *heading lines* are usually printed at the top of the page and describe the nature of the data to be printed in the report. *Detail lines* appear in the body of the report and provide detailed information about the results of computer processing. Often, one detail line is printed for each input record. *Total lines* usually come at the end of the report. These lines give totals of important figures from the detail lines. Examples of all three of these lines can be seen in Figure 1–3.

In preparing a program to produce a report, the programmer must know where on the page each piece of information is to be printed. The maximum number of lines on a page depends on the computer system and the application. If the report is to be printed on standard paper, the maximum number of lines is usually about 60. Sometimes, however, the output is to be printed on special paper that may be shorter or longer than this. This information must be known by the programmer before he or she starts programming.

Like punched cards, each line is divided into positions in which characters can be recorded. On cards these are called columns; on printed output we refer to these as *print positions.* The maximum number of print positions depends on the computer system. Typically, the maximum is 120, 132, or 144 print positions per line. However, some applications may restrict the print line to fewer print positions.

To describe the layout of printed output we often use a *print chart.* An example of such a form is shown in Figure 1–10. In this illustration, the layout of the year-to-date sales report is shown. Notice

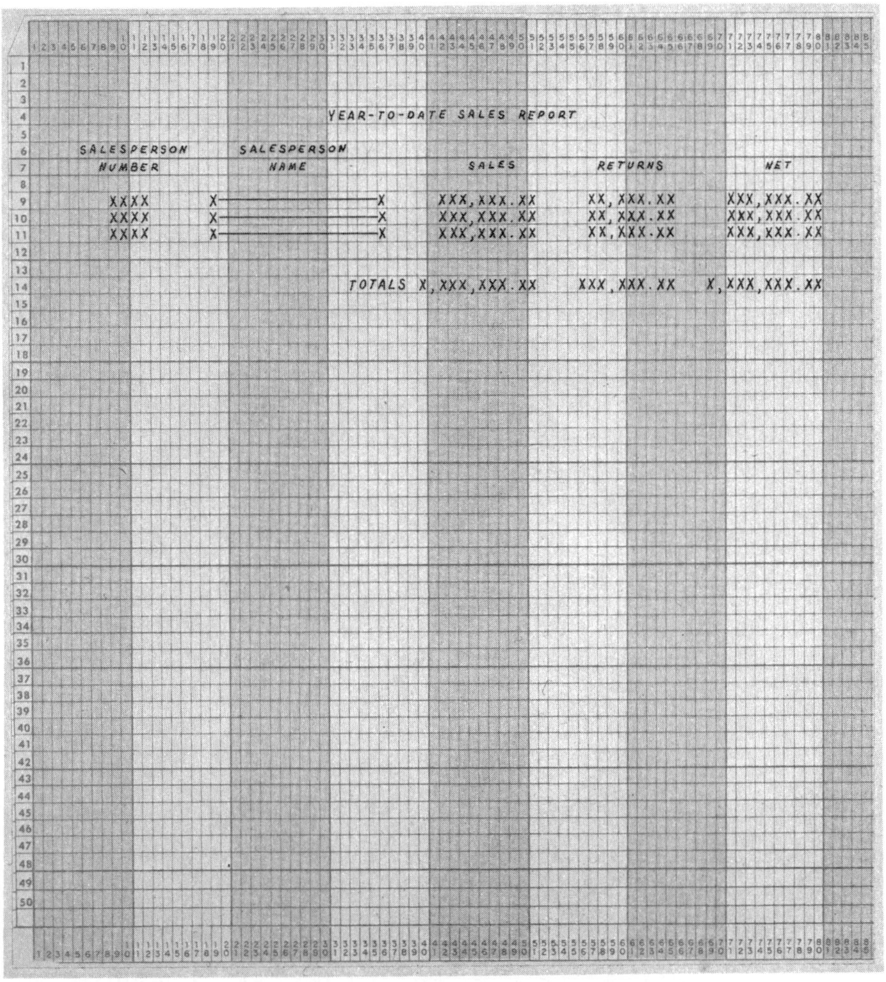

```
                        YEAR-TO-DATE SALES REPORT

   SALESPERSON      SALESPERSON
     NUMBER            NAME                SALES          RETURNS            NET

      XXXX        X-------------X      XXX,XXX.XX      XX,XXX.XX       XXX,XXX.XX
      XXXX        X-------------X      XXX,XXX.XX      XX,XXX.XX       XXX,XXX.XX
      XXXX        X-------------X      XXX,XXX.XX      XX,XXX.XX       XXX,XXX.XX


                                 TOTALS X,XXX,XXX.XX   XXX,XXX.XX   X,XXX,XXX.XX
```

FIGURE 1-10. The Print Chart

that the form is divided into lines and print positions. The print positions are numbered across the top and bottom of the form and the lines are numbered down the left. The line numbers are usually not important, since we are normally concerned only with the vertical spacing of the lines. In other words, we are usually concerned with whether lines are single-spaced, double-spaced, or whatever. However, the print positions are important, since they are the only way of interpreting the horizontal spacing.

All characters to be printed on the final output are shown in the exact print positions where they will be printed. Nonvariable information such as titles and headings is shown exactly as it will appear in the final report. For example, for the report shown in Figure 1-10, the title, YEAR-TO-DATE SALES REPORT, will be printed in print positions 31 through 55. Notice that the headings for the columns require two print lines.

Variable information is indicated by Xs on the print chart. Since we do not know in advance what information will be printed in the number, name, sales, and other fields, we merely indicate the location where the data is to be printed by Xs. For example, the salesperson number is to be printed in print positions 9 through 12. Notice that this corresponds to the length of the field shown on the card layout form. When an input field is to be printed, the output field length should be the same. The salesperson-name field is 18 characters and is printed in print positions 19 through 36. When long fields are shown on a print chart, an X is put in the beginning and ending print positions and a horizontal line is drawn to connect the Xs.

Numeric fields that are normally written with commas and decimal points are shown with these characters in the print chart. Recall that such characters do not appear with the input data. The process of adding these characters is called *editing*; it is done only to improve the readability of the output. On the print chart, we show each editing character in the exact position where it is to be printed. Notice that commas and decimal points each require an entire print position just like other characters.

All detail lines in a report are usually identical. Thus, it is only necessary to show the layout of a detail line once on the print chart. In Figure 1–10 we show several detail lines only to emphasize the fact that these lines are printed in the same way. Notice that the total line is different. It contains both nonvariable and variable data, and the field sizes are different from those of the detail lines.

Vertical spacing is also indicated by the print chart. In the example in Figure 1–10, the detail lines are single-spaced. However, there is a double space between the title line and the column headings and between the column headings and the first detail line. There is a triple space between the last detail line and the total line.

A print chart shows how one page of output is to be printed. If the report requires more than one page, then each page is printed in the same manner.

CHAPTER 2

Introduction to COBOL

In Chapter 1 we introduced some general ideas about computers and programming. Most of these ideas apply to all computer languages. We can now begin to study the COBOL programming language. In this chapter we present an overview of COBOL without going into detail about how to prepare programs. In later chapters we will discuss the specific requirements of COBOL.

2-1. BASIC COBOL CONCEPTS

Figure 2-1 shows a sample COBOL program as it would be prepared by a programmer. This program processes the sales data described in the previous chapter. In a moment we will explain what this program does and how it does it, but for now we are interested only in the COBOL concepts that are illustrated by this program.

Coding

When a programmer prepares a program, he or she first writes down on paper the words and symbols that make up the instructions in the program. This process of writing down the program is called *coding*.

IBM COBOL Coding Form — GX28-1464-5 U/M 050* Printed in U.S.A.

SYSTEM: SALES ANALYSIS	PUNCHING INSTRUCTIONS		PAGE 1 OF 3
PROGRAM: SLSØ1	GRAPHIC: O Ø I 1 Z 2		CARD FORM #
PROGRAMMER: R. NICKERSON	DATE 9/9/76	PUNCH: "oh" "zero" "eye" "one" "zee" "two"	

SEQUENCE (PAGE) (SERIAL) | CONT | A | B | COBOL STATEMENT | IDENTIFICATION

```
01       IDENTIFICATION DIVISION.
02       PROGRAM-ID.  SLSØ1.
03
04       ENVIRONMENT DIVISION.
05       CONFIGURATION SECTION.
06       SOURCE-COMPUTER.  XYZ-1.
07       OBJECT-COMPUTER.  XYZ-1.
08       INPUT-OUTPUT SECTION.
09       FILE-CONTROL.
10           SELECT SALES-PERSON-FILE
11               ASSIGN TO CARD-READER.
12           SELECT REPORT-FILE
13               ASSIGN TO PRINTER.
14
15       DATA DIVISION.
16       FILE SECTION.
17       FD  SALES-PERSON-FILE,
18           LABEL RECORDS ARE OMITTED,
19           RECORD CONTAINS 8Ø CHARACTERS,
20           DATA RECORD IS SALES-PERSON-RECORD.
         Ø1  SALES-PERSON-RECORD.
             Ø2  FILLER                      PICTURE XX.
             Ø2  SP-NUMBER                   PICTURE XXXX.
             Ø2  SP-NAME                     PICTURE X(18).
```

*A standard card form, IBM Electro C61897, is available for punching source statements from this form.
Instructions for using this form are given in any IBM COBOL reference manual.
Address comments concerning this form to IBM Corporation, Programming Publications, 1271 Avenue of the Americas, New York, New York 10020.

*No. of sheets per pad may vary slightly

FIGURE 2-1. Coding for a Sample Program (Part 1)

IBM **COBOL Coding Form** GX28-1464-5 U/M 050* Printed in U.S.A.

SYSTEM		PUNCHING INSTRUCTIONS		PAGE 2 OF 3
PROGRAM		GRAPHIC		CARD FORM # *
PROGRAMMER	DATE	PUNCH		

SEQUENCE (PAGE) (SERIAL) | CONT. | A | B | COBOL STATEMENT | IDENTIFICATION

```
       Ø2  FILLER                          PICTURE X(21).
       Ø2  SP-CURRENT-SALES                PICTURE 9(5)V99.
       Ø2  SP-CURRENT-RETURNS              PICTURE 9(4)V99.
       Ø2  FILLER                          PICTURE X(22).
FD     REPORT-FILE,
       LABEL RECORDS ARE OMITTED,
       RECORD CONTAINS 132 CHARACTERS,
       DATA RECORD IS REPORT-RECORD.
Ø1     REPORT-RECORD.
       Ø2  FILLER                          PICTURE X(1Ø).
       Ø2  RT-NUMBER                       PICTURE XXXX.
       Ø2  FILLER                          PICTURE X(6).
       Ø2  RT-NAME                         PICTURE X(18).
       Ø2  FILLER                          PICTURE X(6).
       Ø2  RT-CURRENT-SALES                PICTURE ZZ,ZZZ.99.
       Ø2  FILLER                          PICTURE X(6).
       Ø2  RT-CURRENT-RETURNS              PICTURE Z,ZZZ.99.
       Ø2  FILLER                          PICTURE X(65).
```

*A standard card form, IBM Electro C61897, is available for punching source statements from this form.
Instructions for using this form are given in any IBM COBOL reference manual.
Address comments concerning this form to IBM Corporation, Programming Publications, 1271 Avenue of the Americas, New York, New York 10020.

*No. of sheets per pad may vary slightly

FIGURE 2-1. (Part 2)

SYSTEM

PROGRAM

PROGRAMMER

PUNCHING INSTRUCTIONS

PAGE 3 OF 3

CARD FORM #

DATE

GRAPHIC

PUNCH

SEQUENCE		CONT	A	B	COBOL STATEMENT
(PAGE)	(SERIAL)				
01					PROCEDURE DIVISION.
02					OPEN-FILES.
03					OPEN INPUT SALES-PERSON-FILE,
04					OUTPUT REPORT-FILE.
05					MAIN-ROUTINE.
06					READ SALES-PERSON-FILE,
07					AT END
08					CLOSE SALES-PERSON-FILE, REPORT-FILE
09					STOP RUN.
10					MOVE SPACES TO REPORT-RECORD.
11					MOVE SP-NUMBER TO RT-NUMBER.
12					MOVE SP-NAME TO RT-NAME.
13					MOVE SP-CURRENT-SALES TO RT-CURRENT-SALES.
14					MOVE SP-CURRENT-RETURNS TO RT-CURRENT-RETURNS.
15					WRITE REPORT-RECORD.
16					GO TO MAIN-ROUTINE.
17					
18					
19					
20					

IDENTIFICATION

*A standard card form, IBM Electro C61897, is available for punching source statements from this form.
Instructions for using this form are given in any IBM COBOL reference manual.
Address comments concerning this form to IBM Corporation, Programming Publications, 1271 Avenue of the Americas, New York, New York 10020.

*No. of sheets per pad may vary slightly.

24

FIGURE 2-1. (Part 3)

The coding is usually done on special sheets of paper called *coding forms*. The program shown in Figure 2-1 is coded on such forms.

Notice that the coding form is divided into a number of lines and that each line has 80 spaces. These spaces correspond to the 80 columns of a punched card. In COBOL coding, the spaces in a line are called columns. As we shall see, each line is punched in a card so that the program can be read by the computer. The characters are punched in the same columns of a card as they are written on the coding form.

When coding a program, it is important to distinguish between easily confused characters. For example the letter O and the number 0 are often indistinguishable when hand written. To separate these and other characters, the sample program in Figure 2-1 uses the conventions shown on the top part of the first form under "punching instructions."

COBOL Program Divisions

All COBOL programs are organized into four *divisions*. These are called the identification division, the environment division, the data division, and the procedure division.

A division consists of the name of the division, followed by all of the lines up to the next division (or to the end of the program in the case of the last division). In the sample program shown in Figure 2-1, the identification division contains only the division name and one line, whereas each of the other divisions has many lines. The divisions must be coded in the order shown in Figure 2-1; that is, the identification division must come first, followed by the environment division, the data division, and, finally, the procedure division.

Each division describes a different aspect of the program. The identification division provides identifying information about the program such as the name of the program. The environment division describes the equipment that is used when the program is executed. This includes the central processing unit and the input/output devices. The data division specifies the characteristics of the files, records, and other data items that are processed in the program. Finally, the procedure division describes the actual procedure that is followed by the computer to process the data when the program is executed.

Within each division are a number of different types of entries. How to form the various entries in a division and what each entry means will be discussed in subsequent chapters.

COBOL Words

To construct the entries within each division we use words and symbols. Words in COBOL are formed in a special way. Each word may consist of up to 30 alphabetic and numeric characters. In addition, hyphens may be used in COBOL words, except that a hyphen cannot appear at the beginning or the end of a word. However, other special characters, including the blank, cannot be used in a word. Thus, for example, SLS01 is a valid word in COBOL. So are SOURCE-COM-PUTER and SP-CURRENT-SALES. Notice that the hyphen is used where we might ordinarily put a space in order to improve the read-ability of the word. Most COBOL words must have at least one alpha-betic character, although some may be entirely numeric.

Some words that are used in a COBOL program have special mean-ings. These are called *reserved words*, because they are reserved for specific purposes. A reserved word cannot be used for any purpose other than its specified use. Examples of reserved words are DIVISION, SOURCE-COMPUTER, and DATA. A complete list of COBOL re-served words is contained in Appendix B. The use of many of these words will be explained in later chapters.

Words that are not reserved are called *user-defined words* because they are made up by the user or programmer. For example, in the identification division, the name of the program is given following the word PROGRAM-ID. Whereas PROGRAM-ID is a reserved word, the name following it is a user-defined word. In the data division, a number of user-defined words are used to identify data. For example, in the sample program the word SP-NAME is used to refer to the salesperson's name field on the input card. Other examples of user-defined words are SP-CURRENT-SALES, REPORT-FILE, and MAIN-ROUTINE.

The Character Set

The basic unit from which all COBOL elements are built is the charac-ter. The group of characters that is available for use in the language is called the *character set*. The character set for ANS COBOL consists of the following 51 characters:

Alphabetic characters (letters):

ABCDEFGHIJKLMNOPQRSTUVWXYZ

Numeric characters (digits):

0123456789

Special characters:
    blank (space)
  + plus sign

-   minus sign or hyphen
*   asterisk
/   slash
=   equal sign
$ dollar sign
,   comma
;   semicolon
.   period or decimal point
"   quotation mark
(left parenthesis
)   right parenthesis
>   greater than symbol
<   less than symbol

Some versions of COBOL do not allow all of these characters or substitute other symbols. These differences are summarized in Appendix A.

As we have seen, characters are used to form words. Words are combined with other characters and other words to form the various entries in the program. These entries are grouped into four divisions. The four divisions comprise a COBOL program.

2-2.   A SAMPLE PROGRAM

We now can begin to understand what the sample program in Figure 2-1 does. The purpose of this program is to process the sales data described at the end of Chapter 1. The program reads a punched card containing sales data and stores the data in the computer's internal storage. It then moves the salesperson number, salesperson name, current sales, and current returns to other parts of internal storage from where these data may be sent to an output device. Finally, it causes these data to be sent to the printer and printed. It repeats this process for each input card, producing one line of output for each card (see Figure 2-6). It stops after the last card has been processed.

The first three divisions of the program are used to specify certain characteristics of the program prior to actual processing. The identification division gives the program an identifying name. In this example the name of the program is SLS01. The environment division specifies what computers are used for processing the program. These are the names following the words SOURCE-COMPUTER and OBJECT-COMPUTER. (The difference between these will be explained in the next chapter.) The environment division also gives a name to each file processed by the program and indicates what type of I/O device is used for the file. In this example, the SALES-PERSON-FILE is the name of the input file from the card reader and the name REPORT-FILE is used for the output file on the printer.

The data division describes each input and output file, record, and field. It gives names to each of these so that they can be referred to during processing. For example, the salesperson number from the input card is given the name SP-NUMBER. The same field in the output record is called RT-NUMBER. Even though these fields contain the same value, they must be given different names, since one is used for input and the other for output.

The last division in the program — the procedure division — describes how the actual processing of the data is to take place. The procedure division is broken up into parts that are called *paragraphs*. Each paragraph is given a name. In this example, the procedure division has two paragraphs named OPEN-FILES and MAIN-ROUTINE. Within each paragraph are one or more *sentences* that contain instructions to the computer about what processing is to take place. Each sentence ends with a period. In the OPEN-FILES paragraph there is one sentence beginning with the word OPEN. (Later we will see what this sentence does.)

In the MAIN-ROUTINE paragraph, the first sentence instructs the computer to read a punched card from the SALES-PERSON-FILE. If there are no more cards then the instructions following the words AT END are executed. This eventually causes the program to terminate with the command STOP RUN. If a data card is read, then the sentences following the READ sentence are executed. The next few sentences cause the input fields from the punched card to be moved to the output fields. For example, the instruction

```
MOVE SP-NUMBER TO RT-NUMBER
```

causes the salesperson number from the input card to be moved (or copied) into the corresponding field in the output record. After all of the data has been moved, the WRITE instruction causes a line to be printed. This line contains the data copied by the previous move instructions. Finally, the last sentence tells the computer to go back to the beginning of the MAIN-ROUTINE paragraph and start the process over again. Thus the instructions in this paragraph are repeated over and over again until all of the input cards have been read and processed.

The instructions within the procedure division are performed in the order in which they are written. Thus, it is important that the sentences be written in a logical order. For example, we could not switch the READ and WRITE instructions, since that would tell the computer to write the output before it has read any input data. Clearly, in this program that makes no sense.

Notice how closely COBOL approximates English. This was one of the objectives in designing the COBOL programming language. In making the language similar to English, not only is it easier to learn and to code but also it is easier to understand COBOL programs after they have been coded.

2-3. RUNNING A COMPUTER PROGRAM

The program coded in Figure 2-1 is a COBOL source program. In order to be processed by a computer it must be converted to a form that the computer can read, combined with special control records, and provided with input data. The actual processing of the program on a computer is called a *run*. This section describes how a COBOL program is run on a computer.

The source program usually is converted to machine-readable form by punching one card for each line on the coding sheet. The program must be punched column for column exactly as it is coded. Any punching errors must be corrected before processing the program with the computer. The cards must be kept in the same order as the coded program. The program punched into cards is often called the *source deck*. Figure 2-2 shows the source deck for the sample program.

In addition to the source deck, the *input data deck* must be punched. Initially, input data that tests the program must be designed and punched into cards. This input data must be punched in the layout prescribed for the program. Figure 2-3 shows several input data cards for the sample program. This program processes any number of input cards, as long as each is punched in the layout shown in Figure 1-9.

Finally, the source deck and the input deck must be combined with special cards called *control records*. These records vary from one type of computer to another and are not part of the COBOL language. Their purpose is to control the processing of the program on a particular computer. Usually there is a group of control records at the beginning, then the source deck, then another group of control records, then the input deck, and then a final group of control records (see Figure 2-4). The entire combination of control records, source deck, and input data deck is called a *job* and can be run on the computer.

The function of control records is linked to the way in which a job is processed. Recall from Section 1-4 that a program goes through two phases — compilation and execution — when processed on a computer. During the first phase, the source program is translated into machine language to produce the object program; in the second phase, the object program is executed. The control records arrange the sequencing of these two phases.

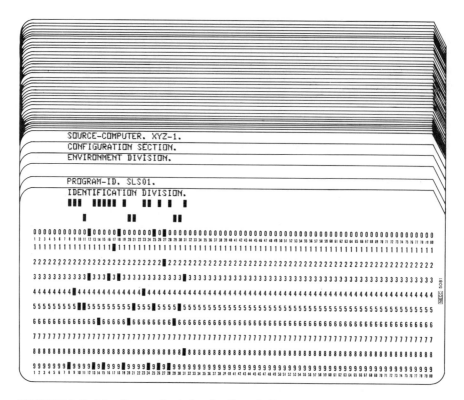

FIGURE 2-2. The Source Deck for the Sample Program

Usually the first group of control records informs the computer that a COBOL source program follows and instructs the computer to get the COBOL compiler program. The compiler program is placed automatically in the computer's internal storage unit. Then the compiler begins reading the source deck. As the compiler does this, it translates the source program into machine language. The compiler program stops processing when it reaches the end of the source program. Now the object program is ready to be processed.

During compilation, the source program is printed by the printer. This printed copy of the program is called the *source program listing*. Figure 2-5 shows the source program listing for the sample program. Notice in the listing that a blank line appears between each division. This is because a blank card was inserted between each division in the source deck (Figure 2-2). Such extra cards have no effect on the processing of the program and may be included anywhere in the source program. Each blank card causes a line to be skipped. Most programmers include extra cards like this so that the source program listing is easier to read.

The next group of control records instructs the computer to place

```
121842COLE ROBERT N      B4292365257525263087614285146385290
031698GUZMAN JOSE        C50006350000000000008760182500018300
121612LOCATELLI FRANK    B50002500000000050008761450000150000
101442ADAMS JUNE R       C80921362501447200087604635210125160
101420EHRHARDT ELISE     A50035002500256000087601390390725000
101375TAYLOR EVERETT     C50120000001000000087600250000125000
011374BENTON ALEX J      B700235013002110008760025000005650
011205HOLT BENTLEY       A701350162001250008760138012028852
071133MARSHALL M S       B72000000000000000087610000000000000
031111FREDERICKS RICHARDC70526000000483500087600000000000000
121083JOHNSON ROBERT     B80512036100837050087612108350056500
111060ROBINSON WILLIAM LA40480000000002500087612350000000000
100912EMERY ELIZABETH G  C40350000000980150087601200350750000
070477SMITH RICHARD A    A30013500000450000087600100000060000
080401REDDING OLIVIA     C61400351621750890876161239923017500
010239HAINES CYNTHIA L   C50750000001200000876260000001000000
090080PARKER JAMES E     B30125001400390000087618200000165000
030016LOCK ANDREW S      B6000025000001550087600357720079850
050005BENNETT ROBERT     C40012500000025500876016003500125000
```

FIGURE 2-3. Input Data for the Sample Program

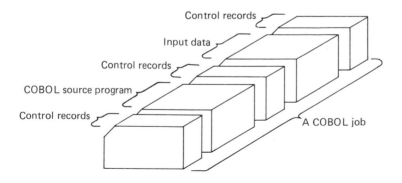

FIGURE 2-4. Deck Set-up for Running a COBOL Program

```
IDENTIFICATION DIVISION.
PROGRAM-ID. SLS01.

ENVIRONMENT DIVISION.
CONFIGURATION SECTION.
SOURCE-COMPUTER. XYZ-1.
OBJECT-COMPUTER. XYZ-1.
INPUT-OUTPUT SECTION.
FILE-CONTROL.
    SELECT SALES-PERSON-FILE
        ASSIGN TO CARD-READER.
    SELECT REPORT-FILE
        ASSIGN TO PRINTER.

DATA DIVISION.
FILE SECTION.
FD  SALES-PERSON-FILE,
    LABEL RECORDS ARE OMITTED,
    RECORD CONTAINS 80 CHARACTERS,
    DATA RECORD IS SALES-PERSON-RECORD.
01  SALES-PERSON-RECORD.
    02  FILLER                      PICTURE XX.
    02  SP-NUMBER                   PICTURE XXXX.
    02  SP-NAME                     PICTURE X(18).
    02  FILLER                      PICTURE X(21).
    02  SP-CURRENT-SALES            PICTURE 9(5)V99.
    02  SP-CURRENT-RETURNS          PICTURE 9(4)V99.
    02  FILLER                      PICTURE X(22).
FD  REPORT-FILE,
    LABEL RECORDS ARE OMITTED,
    RECORD CONTAINS 132 CHARACTERS,
    DATA RECORD IS REPORT-RECORD.
01  REPORT-RECORD.
    02  FILLER                      PICTURE X(10).
    02  RT-NUMBER                   PICTURE XXXX.
    02  FILLER                      PICTURE X(6).
    02  RT-NAME                     PICTURE X(18).
    02  FILLER                      PICTURE X(6).
    02  RT-CURRENT-SALES            PICTURE ZZ,ZZZ.99.
    02  FILLER                      PICTURE X(6).
    02  RT-CURRENT-RETURNS          PICTURE Z,ZZZ.99.
    02  FILLER                      PICTURE X(65).
```

FIGURE 2-5. The Source Program Listing for the Sample Program

```
PROCEDURE DIVISION.
OPEN-FILES.
    OPEN INPUT SALES-PERSON-FILE,
         OUTPUT REPORT-FILE.
MAIN-ROUTINE.
    READ SALES-PERSON-FILE,
        AT END
            CLOSE SALES-PERSON-FILE, REPORT-FILE
            STOP RUN.
    MOVE SPACES TO REPORT-RECORD.
    MOVE SP-NUMBER TO RT-NUMBER.
    MOVE SP-NAME TO RT-NAME.
    MOVE SP-CURRENT-SALES TO RT-CURRENT-SALES.
    MOVE SP-CURRENT-RETURNS TO RT-CURRENT-RETURNS.
    WRITE REPORT-RECORD.
    GO TO MAIN-ROUTINE.
```

FIGURE 2-5. (Continued)

the object program in internal storage and begin execution. During execution, the various instructions in the program are performed. Some of the instructions that are executed cause input data to be read. Hence, the next group of cards in the job must be the input data deck. In addition, some instructions cause results of processing to be printed. This is the actual output from the program. Figure 2-6 shows the output from the sample program.

When execution of this program is completed, the final group of control records tells the computer that the job is finished and instructs the computer to go to the next job.

Control records are vital to the proper running of a job on the computer. Although the actual organization of the control records varies with different computers, their basic functions are the same. They are not related to the COBOL language, but are required if a program is to be run on a computer.

2-4. ERROR DETECTION

In this description of the running of a COBOL program we have assumed that the program contains no errors. In fact, one of the biggest problems that a programmer faces is the detection and correction of errors. More often than not, the program does not complete its run successfully. It is the programmer's responsibility to locate and correct any errors in the program.

0005	BENNETT ROBERT	1,600.35	12.50
0016	LOCK ANDREW S	357.72	79.85
0080	PARKER JAMES E	18,200.00	165.00
0239	HAINES CYNTHIA L	26,000.00	1,000.00
0401	REDDING OLIVIA	16,123.99	2,301.75
0477	SMITH RICHARD A	100.00	60.00
0912	EMERY ELIZABETH G	1,200.35	750.00
1060	ROBINSON WILLIAM L	12,350.00	.00
1083	JOHNSON ROBERT	12,108.35	56.50
1111	FREDERICKS RICHARD	.00	.00
1133	MARSHALL M S	10,000.00	.00
1205	HOLT BENTLEY	1,380.12	288.52
1374	BENTON ALEX J	250.00	56.50
1375	TAYLOR EVERETT	250.00	125.00
1420	EHRHARDT ELISE	1,390.39	725.00
1442	ADAMS JUNE R	4,635.21	125.16
1612	LOCATELLI FRANK	14,500.00	1,500.00
1698	GUZMAN JOSE	1,825.00	183.00
1842	COLE ROBERT N	14,285.14	6,385.29

FIGURE 2-6. The Output from the Sample Program

There are three times that errors may be detected in the processing of the program — during compilation, during execution, and after execution. The computer can detect errors that occur during the first two stages, but the programmer must detect any errors in the third.

Compilation errors are discovered by the computer during the compilation of the program. These are usually errors that the programmer has made in the use of the language; these are called *syntax errors*. For example, COBOL requires a period at the end of each sentence. If the programmer leaves out a period at the end of a sentence, then this is a syntax error. When the compiler program detects any compilation errors, it prints a message that describes the error and where it is located in the program. Even though the compiler has located an error, usually it cannot correct the error and the program is not executed. The programmer must correct any compilation errors that are detected.

If the program has no compilation errors, it is executed by the computer. During execution, other errors may appear. These are called *execution errors*. For example, attempting to divide a number by zero causes an execution error. Detection of such an error causes the computer to print an error code or message and to stop executing the program.

The final type of error is detected only after successful compilation and execution of the program. If the output from the program does not agree with what is expected, there is a *logic error* in the program. For example, in the sample program, if the second MOVE instruction had been incorrectly coded as

```
MOVE SP-NUMBER TO RT-NAME
```

then no compilation or execution error would be detected. However, the final output would be incorrect, since the salesperson number would be printed where the name should be. This error is in the logic of the program. The computer cannot detect such an error, since it cannot understand the logic of the program. It is the programmer's responsibility to check the results of processing and to correct any logic errors that may be found.

Any error in a computer program is called a *bug*. The process of locating and correcting bugs in a program is called *debugging*. Only after a program has been debugged completely can the programmer be reasonably sure that the program is correct.

2-5.   A PREVIEW OF THE PROGRAMMING PROCESS

In the process of preparing a computer program to solve a particular problem the programmer performs a number of tasks. One thing that must be done is to code the program. As we have seen, this involves writing down the instructions in the program. However, before coding can begin, the programmer must understand the problem to be solved and plan the solution procedure.

Understanding the problem involves determining the requirements of the problem and how these requirements can be met. The programmer must know what the program is required to do. This usually involves understanding what output must be produced by the program and its layout and what computations must be performed. The programmer must determine what resources are available to meet these requirements. This includes determining the available input and its format. If a program is going to read punched cards and produce a printed report, the card layout form and print chart must be available.

With an understanding of the problem, the programmer can begin to design a program to solve the problem. This program-designing activity does *not* involve coding the program. Before coding can start, the programmer must think through the solution procedure completely. The programmer sometimes writes down the solution procedure in rough notes in English or draws a diagram that represents the solution graphically.

After the solution to the problem has been planned, the program can be coded. The programmer uses his or her knowledge of the computer language, an understanding of the problem to be solved, and the program design determined previously. With this background, the programmer writes the program to solve the problem.

The next step is to test the program by running it on the computer with test data. The objective is to try to locate errors in the program. Testing the program in this manner will not necessarily find all errors, but it usually will point out any serious problems with the program. The actual process of determining the correctness of a program involves much more than just testing the program on a computer. A program is correct because it makes sense logically. The programmer makes sure of this as he or she plans and codes the program.

Finally, the programming process is completed by bringing together all material that describes the program. This is called *documenting* the program, and the result of this activity is the program's *documentation.* Included in the documentation is the program source listing and the input and output record layouts. The reason for having documentation is so that other programmers will be able to understand how the program functions. Often it is necessary to return to the program after a period of time and to make corrections or changes in the program. With adequate documentation, it is much easier to understand how a program operates.

Throughout most of this book we will be discussing the coding activity of the programming process. However, it must be kept in mind that this is only part of the entire process. In Chapter 8 we will return to the other activities and discuss them in much more detail.

PART TWO

Basic
COBOL Programming

CHAPTER 3

Essential COBOL Elements

In this chapter we begin studying the details of the COBOL language with a description of an essential subset of COBOL. The objective is to discuss just enough COBOL so that simple programs can be prepared. We describe each division in turn and use the sample program from the last chapter to illustrate the concepts.

3-1. THE IDENTIFICATION DIVISION

The identification division is the simplest part of any COBOL program. Its purpose is to specify a name for the program and to give other identifying information.

Each division in a COBOL program begins with the name of the division followed by the word DIVISION and a period. Thus the identification division begins with:

```
IDENTIFICATION DIVISION.
```

Within the identification division are a number of *paragraphs*. (Recall from the last chapter that the procedure division is also divided into paragraphs.) Each paragraph begins with the name of the paragraph followed by a period. Notice that the word "paragraph" does

not appear with the paragraph name. The only paragraph that is required in the identification division has the name

```
PROGRAM-ID.
```

The name of this paragraph is a reserved word and must be coded
exactly as shown. (Other paragraphs that may be used in the identification division will be discussed in Chapter 8.)

The only thing that may appear in the PROGRAM-ID paragraph
is a single entry that gives the name of the program. In general, an
entry is a description of some characteristic of the program. An entry
always ends with a period. Some entries are single words and some
consist of several words. The entry in the PROGRAM-ID paragraph
is a single user-defined word that the programmer selects as a name
for his or her program. In the sample program this entry is SLS01.

Recall that a word may contain up to 30 alphabetic and numeric
characters, with hyphens inserted for readability. Although any user-
defined word may be used for a program name, most computer systems
only examine the first five to eight characters to distinguish between
programs. (The specific requirements for different computers are
described in Appendix A.) Thus the programmer should be sure that
the first few characters of any program name are unique.

Figure 3-1 shows two forms of the identification division for
the sample program. In the first form (Figure 3-1 (a)) the program
name appears on the same line as the paragraph name. When this is
done, there must be at least one space after the period following
the paragraph name. In general, there must always be at least one
space after any period that comes at the end of some part of the
program. More spaces may be used and often are included to make
the program more readable.

```
IDENTIFICATION DIVISION.
PROGRAM-ID. SLS01.
```

(a) Common form

```
IDENTIFICATION DIVISION.
PROGRAM-ID.
   SLS01.
```

(b) Alternate form

FIGURE 3-1. The Identification Division for the Sample Program

An alternative way of coding the identification division is shown in Figure 3-1 (b). In this example, the program name appears on the next line following the paragraph header. The indentation helps make the program more readable. (It is also required by the coding rules of COBOL. These will be discussed in Section 3-5.)

These examples point out the fact that there is a lot of flexibility in the way in which a COBOL program may be coded. Although the specific examples in the following sections show one particular form, it is important to remember that other forms, within the rules of COBOL, are possible.

3-2. THE ENVIRONMENT DIVISION

The environment division indicates what computer equipment is used when the program is run. In a sense, the environment division is the link between the computer and the program. The program needs to know what CPU is used to compile and execute the program and what input/output devices are used during execution. Figure 3-2 shows the environment division for the sample program.

The environment division is divided into two *sections*. Sections contain paragraphs which in turn are composed of entries. (There are no sections in the identification division, only paragraphs.) A section always begins with the name of the section followed by the word SECTION and a period. The two sections in the environment division are the CONFIGURATION section and the INPUT-OUTPUT section. The names of these sections are reserved words and must be coded exactly.

The CONFIGURATION section specifies the central computer "configuration" that is used when the program is compiled and executed. There are two paragraphs in this section — the SOURCE-

```
ENVIRONMENT DIVISION.
CONFIGURATION SECTION.
SOURCE-COMPUTER. XYZ-1.
OBJECT-COMPUTER. XYZ-1.
INPUT-OUTPUT SECTION.
FILE-CONTROL.
     SELECT SALES-PERSON-FILE
         ASSIGN TO CARD-READER.
     SELECT REPORT-FILE
         ASSIGN TO PRINTER.
```

FIGURE 3-2. The Environment Division for the Sample Program

COMPUTER paragraph and the OBJECT-COMPUTER paragraph. The SOURCE-COMPUTER paragraph contains an entry that gives the name of the computer that is used to compile the program. This is the computer that accepts the source program. The OBJECT-COM-PUTER paragraph gives the name of the computer that is used to execute the object program. Recall that the object program is the machine-language equivalent of the source program that results from the compilation process. The reason that both the source computer and object computer must be specified is because in some cases these are different. Sometimes one computer is used to compile the program and another is used for execution. However, in most situations the source computer and the object computer are the same and thus identical entries appear in both paragraphs.

The computer names that are used in the SOURCE-COMPUTER and OBJECT-COMPUTER paragraphs are COBOL words that are specified by the computer manufacturer. Usually they take the form of the company name or initials followed by the computer model number. In the sample program we use the name XYZ-1 for the source computer and object computer. This might mean XYZ Company, computer model 1. Appendix A describes the names that must be used with several common computers. Finally, the computer name that is used, like all entries in a COBOL program, must be followed by a period.

The second section that appears in the environment division is the INPUT-OUTPUT section. One purpose of this section is to specify the input/output devices that are used by the program. Although there are several paragraphs that can appear in the INPUT-OUTPUT section, only one is necessary in the sample program. This is the FILE-CONTROL paragraph.

Within the FILE-CONTROL paragraph is one entry for each file that is used by the program. Recall that a file is a group of related records. The records may be groups of punched cards, lines of print, or some form of magnetic record such as is stored on magnetic tape or disk. For the sample program there are two files — an input file of punched cards containing sales data and an output file of printed information.

Each file in a COBOL program must be given a unique name. The name is a user-defined word and must follow the rules of COBOL words. It is a good idea to make up file names that are related to the type of information in the file. This way it is easier to remember what the file names stand for when coding the program. It is also a good idea to include the suffix -FILE in all file names. This is so that the pro-grammer can distinguish file names from names for other things in the program. (We will see later that names are also used for records and fields.) In the sample program we have used the name SALES-

PERSON-FILE for the card input file and the name REPORT-FILE for the printed output.

There must be one SELECT entry in the FILE-CONTROL paragraph for each file used in the program. This entry links the file name with the input or output device that is used for the file. The SELECT entry consists of two *clauses*. When an entry is more than a few words in length it is divided into clauses; each clause describes some characteristic of the entry. The SELECT entry is composed of the SELECT clause and the ASSIGN clause. The SELECT clause gives the name of the file following the word SELECT. The ASSIGN clause gives the name of the input or output device used for that file following the words ASSIGN TO. Thus, for the card input file we have the following entry:

```
SELECT SALES-PERSON-FILE
    ASSIGN TO CARD-READER.
```

The meaning of this entry is that the SALES-PERSON-FILE uses the CARD-READER device for input.

The name in the ASSIGN clause depends on the particular input and output devices available with the computer. The computer manufacturer specifies the exact name that must be used for each I/O device. Some of the names that are used with common computers are mentioned in Appendix A. We will use device names such as CARD-READER and PRINTER throughout this book.

Figure 3-2 shows the SELECT entries for the sample program. Since there are two files, there must be two SELECT entries. If more files were used by the program, then more SELECT entries would be needed. The examples in the next few chapters deal solely with programs that use card input and printed output. In Part III we will look at programs that have more than two input/output files.

In the sample program, the SELECT clause is coded on one line and the ASSIGN clause on the next. It is possible to put both clauses on the same line. However, by splitting the SELECT entry between two lines, it is easier to make changes should an error be found or the program requirements be changed. Finally, notice that the period comes at the end of the entire entry, even though it is split between two lines.

3-3. THE DATA DIVISION

The purpose of the data division is to describe the logical arrangement of the data that is processed by the program. A program normally reads data stored on input records, processes the data according to some procedure, and produces results that form output records. Some-times, during the processing, intermediate data that does not appear in the output is produced. All data — input, output, and intermediate — must be specified in the data division.

Figure 3-3 shows the data division for the sample program. Nor-mally, the data division is divided into two sections called the FILE section and the WORKING-STORAGE section. The FILE section is used to describe input and output data (files) and the WORKING-STORAGE section is used to describe intermediate or "working" data. In the sample program, only the FILE section appears, since no intermediate results are produced by the program. The WORKING-STORAGE section will be described and illustrated in Chapter 4.

Sections in the data division do not contain paragraphs as do sections in the environment division. Rather, sections in the data division are composed only of entries. In the FILE section there must

```
DATA DIVISION.
FILE SECTION.
FD   SALES-PERSON-FILE,
     LABEL RECORDS ARE OMITTED,
     RECORD CONTAINS 80 CHARACTERS,
     DATA RECORD IS SALES-PERSON-RECORD.
01   SALES-PERSON-RECORD.
     02   FILLER                      PICTURE XX.
     02   SP-NUMBER                   PICTURE XXXX.
     02   SP-NAME                     PICTURE X(18).
     02   FILLER                      PICTURE X(21).
     02   SP-CURRENT-SALES            PICTURE 9(5)V99.
     02   SP-CURRENT-RETURNS          PICTURE 9(4)V99.
     02   FILLER                      PICTURE X(22).
FD   REPORT-FILE,
     LABEL RECORDS ARE OMITTED,
     RECORD CONTAINS 132 CHARACTERS,
     DATA RECORD IS REPORT-RECORD.
01   REPORT-RECORD.
     02   FILLER                      PICTURE X(10).
     02   RT-NUMBER                   PICTURE XXXX.
     02   FILLER                      PICTURE X(6).
     02   RT-NAME                     PICTURE X(18).
     02   FILLER                      PICTURE X(6).
     02   RT-CURRENT-SALES            PICTURE ZZ,ZZZ.99.
     02   FILLER                      PICTURE X(6).
     02   RT-CURRENT-RETURNS          PICTURE Z,ZZZ.99.
     02   FILLER                      PICTURE X(65).
```

FIGURE 3-3. The Data Division for the Sample Program

be one *file description* (FD) *entry* for each file that the program processes. This entry consists of the letters FD followed by the name of the file and several clauses. Recall that in the environment division each file is given a name in the SELECT entry. For each file there must be a SELECT entry in the environment division and an FD entry with the same file name in the data division. Thus, in the sample program, we have two FD entries, one for the SALES-PERSON-FILE and one for the REPORT-FILE.

Following the file name in an FD entry are three important clauses. The first is:

LABEL RECORDS ARE OMITTED

This clause says that special descriptive records called *label records* are not used with the file. Label records are used with magnetic tape and disk files to help identify such files. When they are used, special processing must be performed by the computer. This will be explained more fully in the chapter dealing with tape and disk processing. However, label records are never used with card and printer files. The computer must know that they are not included so that the special label record processing is not performed by the computer. Hence, this clause is required for all card and printer files.

The next clause is called the RECORD CONTAINS clause. Recall that a file is composed of a group of records. Each record can contain a certain number of characters. For example, a punched card contains up to 80 characters. The purpose of the RECORD CONTAINS clause is to specify the maximum number of characters in the records in the file. Thus the clause

RECORD CONTAINS 80 CHARACTERS

indicates that each record in this file contains 80 characters. For a printed file, the maximum number of characters depends on the length of the printed line. We assume that the printer used for the sample program has 132 print positions. Hence, the appropriate RECORD CONTAINS clause for the printer file is:

RECORD CONTAINS 132 CHARACTERS

The final clause in the FD entry gives the name of the record within the file. Every record processed by a program must have a name. This is a user-defined word and must follow the rules for COBOL words. It is usually best to make up names for records that relate to the file name. This way it is easier to keep track of the records and to what file each record belongs. One good practice is to use the same name as the file except with the suffix -RECORD. We have done this in the sample program. For example, the name of the record in the SALES-PERSON-FILE is SALES-PERSON-RECORD.

The record name appears in the last clause in the FD entry. This clause consists of the words DATA RECORD IS followed by the record name. Thus for the SALES-PERSON-FILE this clause is:

```
DATA RECORD IS SALES-PERSON-RECORD
```

A similar clause appears in the FD entry for the REPORT-FILE.

In the sample program (Figure 3-3), each clause in the FD entry is coded on a separate line. This is not required, but is good practice since it makes the program easier to read and easier to change if errors are found. Commas may be used to separate clauses, as in the sample program, or they may be left out. As we will see, commas may be used in a number of places to improve the readability of the program. The order of the clauses in the FD entry is not important, but the order shown in the sample program is commonly used. Finally, notice that a period appears at the end of the entire FD entry, not at the end of each clause. A period is always used in COBOL at the end of every entry.

Following each FD entry in the data division is a group of *data description entries.* The purposes of these entries is to describe the data that is contained in each record of the file. Each data description entry begins with a number called a *level number.* These numbers are two digits, such as 01, 02, 05, 15, 22, and so forth. We will have much more to say about level numbers in Chapter 6, but for now we will only use the numbers 01 and 02.

The first entry following the FD entry always has level number 01 and consists of the record name followed by a period. This record name must be the same name that appears in the DATA RECORD IS clause of the previous FD entry. Thus, the 01 entry following the FD entry for the SALES-PERSON-FILE must be

```
01  SALES-PERSON-RECORD.
```

Next come a series of 02 entries that describe the fields in the record. There must be one 02 entry for each field that is processed by the program. All of the 02 entries taken together describe the record that is named in the preceeding 01 entry.

Now we can see the relationship between the various entries in the data division. The entries specify various "levels" of description of the data. The highest level is the file, and it is specified by the FD entry. Within each file is a record that is specified by an 01 entry. The record is composed of fields, each described by an 02 entry. The entire structure of FD, 01, and 02 entries must be repeated for each file that is processed by the program.

Each field of an input or output record that is used in a program must be given a name. The name that is selected is a user-defined word and must follow the rules for COBOL words. For example, the salesperson-number field in the input record of the sample program is given the name SP-NUMBER.

It is a good practice to relate the name of the field to the record to which the field belongs. One way of doing this is to begin the names of all fields in a record with characters that form an abbreviation of the record name. For example, in the sample program we have used the prefix SP- for each field in the SALES-PERSON-RECORD and the prefix RT- for each field in the REPORT-RECORD. Notice that we could have used SALES-PERSON- as a prefix for the field names in the record, but the names would be very long; the abbreviated form is often just as clear. The body of the field name, following the prefix, should be related to the type of data in the field. Thus we use SP-NUMBER for the number field in the salesperson record and SP-NAME for the name field in this record.

Each field should be given a unique name. The computer keeps track of the fields in a record by their names. If two fields have the same name, the computer cannot determine which field is being identified when the name is used. By following the approach suggested in the previous paragraph, field names can be created that are unique and easily understood. For example, we know that SP-NUMBER identifies the number field in the salesperson record. For the corresponding field in the report record we use the name RT-NUMBER. Although these names identify fields that contain the same data they are unique names. Still, it is easy to remember which name refers to the number field in which record.

Each 02 entry must contain either a data name or the reserved word FILLER. This word is used when we do not want to give a name to a field or group of fields. Even though a record contains many fields, it is only necessary to name those fields that are used in the program. The areas between these named fields are called *fillers* and are identified by the word FILLER in the 02 entry.

The 02 entries must be listed in the same order as the fields and fillers in the record. Figure 3-4 shows the card layout form for the salesperson record. The 02 entries for this record in the sample program appear in the same order as the fields in the card layout. For example, the first field is not used in this program. Hence, the first entry is a filler. The next field contains the salesperson number and is identified by the SP-NUMBER entry. Following this is the salesperson-name field, which also requires an entry in the program. The next field needed by the program is the current-month-sales field. Between this field and the salesperson-name field are a number of fields that are not used. These can all be grouped together and identified by one FILLER entry. Following the current month sales is the current month returns which is also used by the program and thus requires an entry. The remaining columns of the card are not used

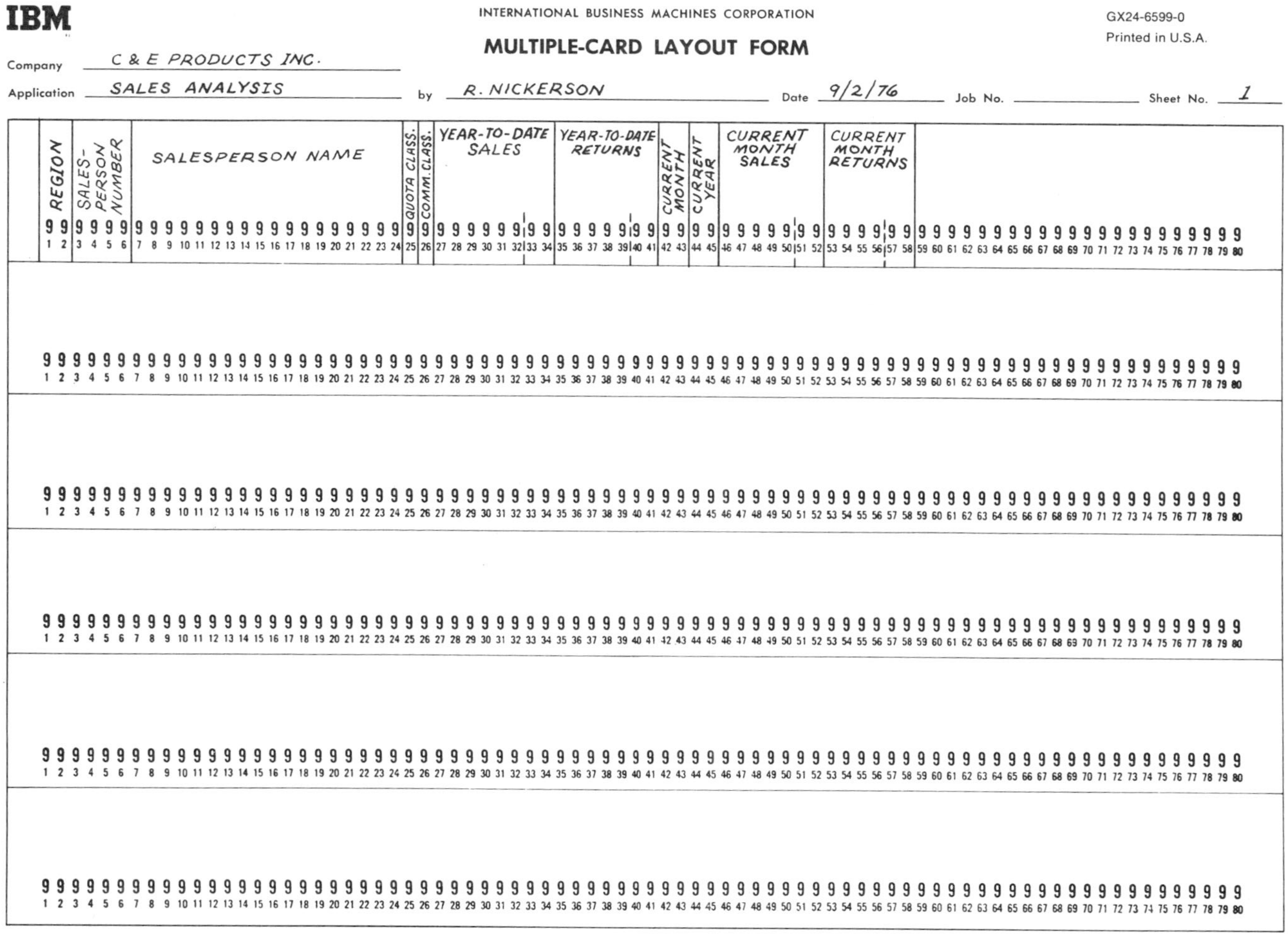

INTERNATIONAL BUSINESS MACHINES CORPORATION

MULTIPLE-CARD LAYOUT FORM

GX24-6599-0
Printed in U.S.A.

Company ___C & E PRODUCTS INC.___

Application ___SALES ANALYSIS___   by ___R. NICKERSON___   Date ___9/2/76___   Job No. _____   Sheet No. ___1___

REGION	SALES-PERSON NUMBER	SALESPERSON NAME	QUOTA CLASS	COMM. CLASS	YEAR-TO-DATE SALES	YEAR-TO-DATE RETURNS	CURRENT MONTH	CURRENT YEAR	CURRENT MONTH SALES	CURRENT MONTH RETURNS

FIGURE 3–4. The Card Layout for the Sample Program

and are thus identified as a FILLER. Notice that there must be one 02 entry with a data name for each field that is used in the program and one 02 entry with the word FILLER for each group of characters that are not used.

To describe the type of data in each field and its length a PICTURE clause is used in each 02 entry. This clause consists of the reserved word PICTURE followed by a group of symbols that describe the layout of the field. This group of symbols is called the *picture* of the field. If a field is a filler or contains alphanumeric data, a series of Xs is used in the picture. (Recall that alphanumeric data may consist of alphabetic, numeric, and special characters.) There must be one X for each character position in the field. For example, the first filler occupies two card columns. Hence its picture is XX. Similarly, the salesperson-number field requires four columns. Its picture is XXXX. When a long series of Xs needs to be coded, an abbreviated form may be used in which one X is written followed by the number of times it should be repeated. This number is enclosed in parentheses and is called a *repetition factor*. For example, the salesperson name field occupies 18 columns. We could code its picture as eighteen Xs. However, by using a repetition factor we can write X(18). Similarly, the filler following this field is 21 columns; hence its picture is X(21).

When we have a numeric field, we use the symbol 9 instead of X. The symbol 9 in a picture means that the field is numeric; the symbol X means that it is alphanumeric. For example, the salesperson-number field could have been specified by the picture 9999 instead of XXXX since it contains all numeric data. The reason that Xs are used instead of 9s is because the field is not edited or used in arithmetic calculations. (We will discuss editing shortly.) Whenever a numeric field is used in calculations or is edited it *must* be described using 9s. Otherwise, the symbol X may be used in its picture. If the field contains any nonnumeric characters, Xs must be used.

When a decimal point is implied in the card layout by a dashed vertical line, the symbol V is used in the picture in the corresponding position. For example, the current-month-sales field consists of seven digits, with two to the right of the decimal point. Thus, its picture is 99999V99. The V does not indicate a card column, only the location of an implied decimal point. Notice in the sample program that this picture is shortened by using a repetition factor for the first five 9s. That is, it is coded 9(5)V99.

The PICTURE clauses must account for all character positions in the record. Since a punched card has 80 columns, the picture clauses for the card layout must identify exactly 80 characters. We can easily check this by counting the number of Xs and 9s where the repetition factors are interpreted as indicating repeated symbols. However, the Vs must not be counted. If the total number of Xs and 9s does not equal the number of columns in the card then an error has occurred and the program must be corrected.

Another source of error is in not using the correct number of columns for a field. For example, if the salesperson-name field had been given the incorrect picture X(17) instead of X(18) then all fields following it would be shifted to the left by one column. The effect would be that the computer would read data from the wrong columns for these fields. Thus, great care must be taken to make sure that the pictures match the fields precisely.

Figure 3-5 shows a print chart with the layout of the printed report that is produced by the sample program. Only one line is shown since all lines in the report are printed in an identical format. The data description entries following the FD entry for the REPORT-FILE in Figure 3-3 specify for the computer how this report is to appear. Notice that the 02 entries are listed in the same order as the fields and fillers in the report line. The first part of the line contains no data so it is specified as a filler. Then the field containing the salesperson number is printed. In the output record, this field is given the name RT-NUMBER. It is specified in the second 02 entry. Following this is another filler and then the RT-NAME field entry. Then comes another filler, the RT-CURRENT-SALES field, another filler, and the RT-CURRENT-RETURNS field. Finally there is a filler for the remainder of the line that follows the last data field. Thus, the fields and fillers of a printed line must be specified in the same manner as the fields and fillers of a punched card. There must be one 02 entry for each field and each filler and the entries must be in the same order in which the data is to be printed in the output line.

The picture clauses for a printed line use Xs and 9s for alphanumeric and numeric fields just as is done with punched cards. For example, the first filler in the output record is ten print positions in length, and thus its picture is X(10). Similarly, the picture for the RT-NUMBER field is XXXX. When 9s are used for a numeric field, the data is printed exactly as it is stored in the computer's internal

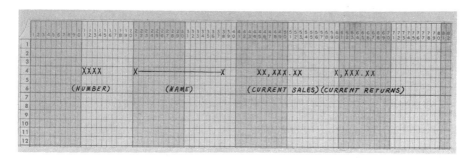

FIGURE 3-5. The Report Layout for the Sample Program

storage. For example, if a five character field contains 18302 in the computer's internal storage and 9(5) is the field's picture, then the output is printed as 18302. If the number to be printed is smaller than the field size, then the left part of the output field is filled with zeros. For example, if the number to be printed in the five column numeric field were actually 302, then the output would appear as 00302. (If the number to be printed were larger than the field size then it could not be printed. This is an error that must be carefully avoided since it often is not detected automatically by the computer.)

Notice in the previous example that if the number 302 had represented three dollars and two cents, no decimal point would be printed. In order to print decimal points and commas and to keep left zeros from printing, special editing characters are used in output pictures. *Editing* is the process of modifying output in order to make it easier to read.

To cause a decimal point to be printed in an output field, a decimal point is put in the field's picture in the exact position in which it is to be printed. For example, in the five column numeric field described previously we could have used 999.99 for the picture of the field. Then if the data were 18302, where the last two digits are to the right of the decimal point, the output would be printed as 183.02. Notice that the decimal point takes a separate print position and thus this field occupies a total of six print positions.

With this same picture, the value 302 would be printed as 003.02. In order to eliminate the left zeros in the field we use the symbol Z instead of 9 in each position in which we wish to delete a left zero. This process of deleting left zeros is called *zero suppression*. A Z is placed in each position of the field's picture in which zero suppression is to take place. For example, if we had used the picture ZZZ.99 and the data had been 302, then the result would be printed as 3.02. Notice that we do not use the picture ZZZ.ZZ. We do not wish to suppress left zeros that may appear to the right of the decimal point. For example, if we had used this picture and the data were 2 (representing two cents) then the output would be just the digit 2 rather than .02. Thus, we use Zs up to and including the last position in the field in which we wish to suppress lead zeros. Notice that we could have used the picture ZZ9.99. In this case two cents would print as 0.02, since any zero just to the left of the decimal point is not to be suppressed. Finally, the use of zero suppression does not eliminate zeros that appear within the number. Thus, with a picture of ZZZ.99 the value 01000 would print as 10.00. The single left zero is suppressed but the other zeros are printed.

For longer fields, commas may be printed by including the comma in the picture. For example, in the sample program we have used the picture ZZ,ZZZ.99 for the RT-CURRENT-SALES field. When this value is printed, any left zeros are suppressed, a decimal point is inserted, and a comma is printed. For example, the number 0184325 would be printed as 1,843.25. Notice that if a comma is not necessary because the number is too short, it is suppressed along with the left zeros. For example, the number 0010000 would be printed as 100.00. However, whether or not the comma is printed, a full print position is required for it in the final output record.

There are many different output forms that can be produced by different combinations of editing characters. Figure 3-6 shows some additional examples using zero suppression, decimal points, and commas. Other editing characters will be described in later chapters. Finally, notice that editing is included only in output pictures of printed reports. Editing characters never would be used to describe a punched card input record. Input data is always unedited.

When coding the pictures for an output record, all print positions must be accounted for. In the FD entry, we indicate the number of print positions in the record by the RECORD CONTAINS clause. In the sample program this is 132 characters. We can check to see that all positions have been accounted for by counting the number of Xs, 9s, Zs, decimal points, and commas, taking into account any repetition factors. The total must be equal to the number of print positions in a line.

In coding the data description entries, certain forms help to make the entries easier to read. Usually all 02 entries are indented the same amount below their corresponding 01 entry. This helps to emphasize that the 02 entries comprise the record named in the preceeding 01 entry. It is also a good idea to align all PICTURE clauses. This way it is easier to read and locate errors.

The PICTURE clause is sometimes coded with the words PICTURE IS followed by the field's picture. The word IS in this phrase is optional and is only included to improve readability. Most programmers, however, leave it out, since what is meant is clear without it. In addition, the word PICTURE can be abbreviated as PIC if desired. Optional words and abbreviations appear in a number of places in COBOL. In general, abbreviations should not be used and optional words should not be left out unless what is meant is entirely clear. The use of PIC instead of PICTURE IS is one place where the common practice is to use the shorter form.

Finally, it is important to remember that each data description entry in the program must end with a period. In an 02 entry this period follows the PICTURE clause. However, it is not part of the field's picture (as is the decimal point used in editing), but is required to indicate the end of the clause.

Data*	Picture	Output	Picture	Output
183̬02	999.99	183.02	ZZZ.99	183.02
001̬00	999.99	001.00	ZZZ.99	1.00
000̬05	999.99	000.05	ZZZ.99	.05
000̬00	999.99	000.00	ZZZ.99	.00
000̬00	ZZ9.99	0.00	ZZZ.ZZ	
246̬	999.99	246.00	ZZZ.99	246.00
1035	9999	1035	ZZZZ	1035
0020	9999	0020	ZZZZ	20
0000	9999	0000	ZZZZ	
0000	ZZZ9	0	ZZ99	00
1035	9,999	1,035	Z,ZZZ	1,035
0020	9,999	0,020	Z,ZZZ	20
5306̬15	ZZZZ.99	5306.15	Z,ZZZ.99	5,306.15
007̬2̬50	ZZZZ.99	72.50	Z,ZZZ.99	72.50

*The symbol ∧ indicates the location of the implied decimal point.

FIGURE 3-6. Examples of Editing

3-4. THE PROCEDURE DIVISION

As we know, all COBOL programs have four divisions. The first three — the identification, environment, and data divisions — specify various aspects of the program but do not describe any of the processing that is to take place. The actual instructions that specify what processing steps are to take place during the execution of the program are included in the procedure division. It is only through instructions in the procedure division that the programmer can communicate to the computer the operations that are to be performed.

Figure 3-7 shows the procedure division of the sample program. In general, a procedure division can be composed of sections, which in turn are made up of paragraphs. However, sections in the procedure division usually are used only in very large programs; their use will be explained and illustrated in a later chapter.

The procedure division for the sample program has no sections, but is divided into two paragraphs named OPEN-FILES and MAIN-ROUTINE. Paragraphs in the procedure division are given names that are user-defined words. In the first three divisions, all paragraph names are reserved words. However, in the procedure division, it is the programmer's responsibility to make up the paragraph names.

The programmer usually groups instructions in the procedure division into paragraphs according to the functions performed by the instructions. The name for the paragraph should relate to the function of the instructions in the paragraph. For example, in the sample program, the paragraph name OPEN-FILES indicates that the purpose of the instructions in this paragraph is to open the files. (We will explain in a moment what this means.) Similarly, the paragraph name MAIN-ROUTINE indicates that this paragraph contains the main part of the program. Thus, the programmer should select meaningful paragraph names that relate to the type of processing performed in the paragraph.

The procedure division may have as many paragraphs as the programmer wishes. We could have a separate paragraph for each instruction, but this rarely is done. The programmer usually includes paragraph names for segments of instructions so that the logical steps in the processing can be easily followed. Too many paragraph names makes

```
PROCEDURE DIVISION.
OPEN-FILES.
    OPEN INPUT SALES-PERSON-FILE,
        OUTPUT REPORT-FILE.
MAIN-ROUTINE.
    READ SALES-PERSON-FILE,
        AT END
            CLOSE SALES-PERSON-FILE, REPORT-FILE
            STOP RUN.
    MOVE SPACES TO REPORT-RECORD.
    MOVE SP-NUMBER TO RT-NUMBER.
    MOVE SP-NAME TO RT-NAME.
    MOVE SP-CURRENT-SALES TO RT-CURRENT-SALES.
    MOVE SP-CURRENT-RETURNS TO RT-CURRENT-RETURNS.
    WRITE REPORT-RECORD.
    GO TO MAIN-ROUTINE.
```

FIGURE 3-7. The Procedure Division for the Sample Program

the program just as hard to follow as too few. Finally, as we shall see, paragraph names serve other purposes than just dividing the procedure division into groups of instructions.

Within each paragraph are one or more *sentences*. A sentence describes an operation or a series of operations that the computer is to perform. Each sentence ends with a period. (Unlike the other divisions, there are no entries in the procedure division.) Some sentences are short enough to be coded on one line and some extend over several lines. Each sentence is composed of one or more *statements*. A statement describes some operation that the computer is to perform. As we will see, many statements contain *phrases* that describe a part of the operation specified by the statement.

In the sample program, the first paragraph contains one sentence. Within this sentence is one statement called the OPEN statement. The purpose of this statement is to instruct the computer to make the files ready for processing. This is called *opening* the file. Each file must be opened before the file can be processed by the computer. Basically, when a file is opened, the computer checks to be sure that the appropriate device for the file (specified in the SELECT entry of the environment division) is operating. As we will see later, if the file were stored on magnetic tape or disk other processing would take place when the file is opened. A file need be opened only once, but it must be opened before any data can be read from the file or written to the file.

The OPEN statement consists of the reserved word OPEN, followed by the word INPUT if the file contains input data or OUTPUT if the file is used for output data. The name of the file comes after the word INPUT or OUTPUT. For example, to open the two files in the sample program we could use the following statements:

```
OPEN INPUT SALES-PERSON-FILE.
OPEN OUTPUT REPORT-FILE.
```

Notice that the file names are the same as those used in the SELECT entry. Each file must be opened as either an input file or an output file but not both.

In the above example, each statement is followed by a period, so each is a sentence. Another approach is to put a period only at the end of the second statement. In this case the sentence would be composed of two statements. A third way of coding these instructions is to use one OPEN statement for both files. This is shown in Figure 3-7. In this case, the word OPEN appears once at the beginning of the statement, followed by one phrase for each file, consisting of the word INPUT or OUTPUT and the file name. To complete the sentence, a period appears at the end of the last phrase. Notice also that a comma is used to separate the phrases. Commas such as these are optional and are used only to make the program easier to read. In general, commas may be used to separate phrases and statements within a sentence. However, each sentence must always be terminated with a period.

The sentences in the procedure division are executed in the order in which they are written. Thus the first thing that the computer does during execution of the sample program is to open the files. It then proceeds to the MAIN-ROUTINE paragraph and the READ statement. The purpose of this statement is to cause the computer to read a record from an input file. Data must be read before it can be processed. The name of the file from which the record is to be read comes after the reserved word READ. This file name must have appeared previously in an INPUT phrase of an OPEN statement. Following the file name in the READ statement is the AT END phrase. (For the moment we need not be concerned with the purpose of this phrase.)

When a READ statement is executed, the data on a record in the input file is read by the input device and transferred to the computer's internal storage. A computer's internal storage is composed of a large number of *storage locations*. Usually each storage location can store one character. When a punched card containing 80 characters is read, each character is stored in a separate location; and thus 80 storage locations are required for the input data.

One way of thinking of a computer's internal storage is in terms of a large number of boxes similar to post office boxes. Figure 3-8 illustrates this idea; each box in this figure represents a storage location. In this example there are 12 storage locations, but in a typical computer there are thousands and even hundreds of thousands of storage locations.

The computer keeps track of the storage locations by giving each location a unique number called an *address*. The address of each storage location in Figure 3-8 appears in the upper left-hand corner of each

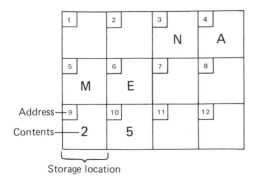

FIGURE 3-8. Internal Storage

box. In a similar manner, post office boxes have addresses to distinguish them. To locate a particular post office box, we search through the boxes until the one with the desired address is located. Similarly, the computer locates a particular storage location by means of its address.

The *contents* of a storage location is what is stored in the location. For example, in Figure 3-8, the contents of storage location 10 is the digit 5. The contents of locations 3 through 6 is the word NAME. Some storage locations in Figure 3-8 have nothing in them. In fact, these empty storage locations are interpreted as blanks or spaces by the computer.

We must not confuse a storage address with the contents of the storage location. A storage location contains data that can change from time to time. However, the address of each location is fixed. The computer uses the address to find the storage location. Once the location is found, the computer can put data in the location or retrieve data from the location. If it puts data in a storage location, the data that was there previously is destroyed; when it retrieves data from a location, the data is merely copied out of the location and thus the original data is not destroyed. For example, in Figure 3-8, if the computer is told to retrieve the data from storage location 10, it would get the digit 5. If it is told to retrieve the data from locations 3 through 6, it would get the word NAME. In either case, the original data in internal storage would be unchanged. However, if the computer were told to store the word COMPUTER in locations 1 through 8, any data in these locations would be destroyed and replaced by the new data. The result would be as shown in Figure 3-9.

In COBOL, we do not use addresses to refer to storage locations. Instead, we use names for fields, and the computer keeps track of the addresses of the storage locations where the data in each field is stored. This is one of the purposes of the data division. In addition to specifying the layout of an input or output record, each set of

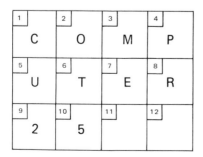

FIGURE 3-9. Internal Storage

data description entries for a record causes the computer to reserve an area in internal storage for the data in the record. If the record is 80 characters in length, then 80 storage locations are reserved; if it is 132 characters, then 132 locations are set aside in internal storage for the record. Each field occupies a particular section of the area for the record. Each time the field name is used in the program, the computer goes to the same locations in internal storage. It can retrieve the data from the storage locations or store new data in the locations.

When a READ statement is executed, a new record is read and the data is stored in the same locations as the previous record, destroying the data from this record. Reading progresses through the records in the input file, one record at a time. It is not possible to go backwards and reread a previous record. Therefore, before going on to a new record, all processing with the data in the current record must be completed.

In the sample program, the only processing involves printing some of the data from the input record. Before this data can be printed, it must be moved to the area in internal storage where the output record is stored. This is accomplished by a series of MOVE statements. Each move statement consists of the reserved word MOVE followed by a field name, the word TO, and another field name. The effect is to cause the data in the storage locations for the first field name to be moved to the storage locations specified by the second field name. Actually, this process involves copying the data, since the original data is not destroyed. For example, the statement

    MOVE SP-NUMBER TO RT-NUMBER.

causes the number field from the salesperson record to be moved to the number field in the report record. The first field named in the MOVE statement is called the *sending field* and the second field is called the *receiving field*.

Before the individual fields can be moved, the entire area reserved for the output record must be blanked out. Recall that between each field in the output record is a filler. These fillers refer to storage locations between the areas reserved for the named data fields in internal storage. These storage locations may contain miscellaneous data left over from some other program. If they are not cleared out before the record is written, the extraneous data will be printed along with the desired data.

The easiest way to clear a record in the computer's internal storage is by moving spaces or blanks to the entire area. The entire record can be referred to by using the record name as the receiving field in the MOVE statement. To blank out the area reserved for the record, we use the word SPACES as the sending field. For example, in the sample program we blank out all 132 storage locations reserved for the output record by the statement:

```
MOVE SPACES TO REPORT-RECORD.
```

After the output record has been cleared out, the data for each individual output field can be moved in. This requires a separate statement for each field. Since there are four output fields in the report line, four MOVE statements are needed to move the data from the input record to the output record. The order of the statements does not matter as long as they all come after the statement that blanks out the output record and before any instruction to write the record.

Notice that each MOVE statement is terminated with a period and hence is a sentence. This is not essential in this instance; we could have made one sentence with all five MOVE statements by putting a period only after the last statement. However, in most situations such as this, each statement is made into a separate sentence. Also, notice that each statement appears on a separate line. This is not required but is a good idea since it makes the program easier to read and easier to correct if an error occurs.

In order to produce output, the WRITE statement is used. This statement causes the data from a record in the computer's internal storage to be transferred to an output device. The WRITE statement consists of the reserved word WRITE followed by the name of the record to be written. Notice that this is different from the READ statement, in which a file name is used. We always READ a *file* and WRITE a *record* in COBOL. In the sample program the WRITE statement is

```
WRITE REPORT-RECORD.
```

This instruction is executed after all of the move operations have been performed. As the result of this instruction, one line of print is produced by the printer.

The basic logic of the sample program can be summarized as follows:

1. Open the input and output files.
2. Read an input record into internal storage.
3. Blank out the output record's area in internal storage.
4. Move the appropriate input fields to their corresponding output fields.
5. Write an output record from internal storage.

With only these instructions, the computer would process only one input record and produce one output line. There is no instruction so far to cause the computer to repeat the operation for another input record.

One of the real advantages of computers is their ability to do the same set of operations over and over again. However, to get the computer to do this we must include a specific instruction that causes the processing to be repeated. To do this we add the following to the above list:

6. Go back to instruction 2.

This instruction says go back to the second instruction and continue from that point. This causes the computer to read another card and print another line. Then the sixth instruction is executed again and the process is repeated for a third card. This repetition continues until there is no more data to be processed.

A sequence of instructions in a program that is repeatedly executed is called a *loop*. The process of repeatedly executing the instructions in a loop is called *looping*. The ability to loop is one of the most powerful aspects of computer processing.

Notice in this program logic that we did not instruct the computer to go back to the first instruction. If we had, the computer would open the files again. In this type of processing the files should be opened only once.

In COBOL, looping is effected by the use of the GO TO statement. This statement consists of the words GO TO followed by a paragraph name. The effect is to cause the computer to go to the first instruction in the paragraph named and continue from that point. In the sample program this statement is:

```
GO TO MAIN-ROUTINE.
```

MAIN-ROUTINE is the name of the paragraph that contains the READ statement. The computer goes to the beginning of this paragraph and continues execution of the program.

As we have said, the sample program continues to loop as long as there is input data to be read. But what happens when the card reader runs out of data cards? The computer must be told what to do when this occurs. This is the purpose of the AT END phrase in the READ statement. At the end of the input data there is usually a special control record that indicates that no more data is available. When this record is read, the computer executes the statements following the words AT END instead of going on to the statements following the READ statement. For every previous record, these statements are bypassed; it is only at the end of processing that they are executed.

At the end of processing, we must instruct the computer to close the files and stop execution. Recall that before a file can be used for input or output it must be opened with an OPEN statement. The CLOSE statement is used to instruct the computer that no more processing of the file is to take place. All files must be closed at the end of processing. The CLOSE statement consists of the reserved word CLOSE, followed by the name of the file or files to be closed. We can use a separate CLOSE statement for each file or include all file names in one CLOSE statement. In the sample program, both files are closed with one statement as follows:

```
CLOSE SALES-PERSON-FILE, REPORT-FILE
```

The comma separating the file names is not essential but helps improve the readability of the statement.

After the files are closed, the computer can be instructed to stop execution of the program. This is accomplished with the statement:

```
STOP RUN
```

This statement tells the computer to stop running this program and to go on to the next program. Once this statement has been executed, the computer will no longer execute any statements in this program.

The complete READ statement in the sample program is as follows:

```
READ SALES-PERSON-FILE,
    AT END
        CLOSE SALES-PERSON-FILE, REPORT-FILE
        STOP RUN.
```

To summarize, the effect of this statement is to cause the computer to read the next record in the SALES-PERSON-FILE. If the record read is *not* the control record at the end of the file, then the computer goes on to the next sentence. That is, the computer continues execution with the next statement following the period at the end of the READ statement. If the record read is the control record at the end of the file then the computer executes the statements in the AT END phrase. First, it closes the SALES-PERSON-FILE and the REPORT-FILE and then it stops the run.

It is important to recognize that a period must appear after the STOP RUN statement and not earlier. The period is used to tell the computer what statements are included in the AT END phrase. If it were left out, then the computer would think that the next statement (which is a MOVE statement in the sample program) is also in the AT END phrase. If a period appears after the CLOSE statement, then the STOP RUN statement would not be included in the AT END phrase. We must include all statements (and no more) that we wish to be executed after the last record in the file has been read between the reserved words AT END and the period.

Notice also that the commas serve no purpose except to make the sentence easier to read. In addition, putting the various parts of the sentence on separate lines and indenting serves the purpose of improving readability. A good rule is to put each statement on a separate line and each phrase within a statement on separate lines. In addition, phrases and statements that are part of a long sentence should be indented. Thus, in the sample program, the AT END phrase is indented below the first part of the READ statement. The CLOSE and STOP RUN statements are indented below the words AT END. With this approach, it is very clear what parts of the sentence are related and in what way. Finally, notice that all of the sentences within a paragraph are indented below the paragraph name. This makes it clear which sentences belong to which paragraph. (In addition, we will see later that certain indentation is required by the rules of COBOL.)

In the sample program we have included the CLOSE and STOP RUN statements within the READ statement. Another approach is to put these statements in a separate paragraph that is only executed at the end of processing. This approach is shown in Figure 3-10. Notice that this program contains three paragraphs. The first two are practically the same as those in the original version of the sample program (Figure 3-7). However, a third paragraph named END-OF-

```
PROCEDURE DIVISION.
OPEN-FILES.
     OPEN INPUT SALES-PERSON-FILE,
         OUTPUT REPORT-FILE.
MAIN-ROUTINE.
     READ SALES-PERSON-FILE,
         AT END GO TO END-OF-JOB-ROUTINE.
     MOVE SPACES TO REPORT-RECORD.
     MOVE SP-NUMBER TO RT-NUMBER.
     MOVE SP-NAME TO RT-NAME.
     MOVE SP-CURRENT-SALES TO RT-CURRENT-SALES.
     MOVE SP-CURRENT-RETURNS TO RT-CURRENT-RETURNS.
     WRITE REPORT-RECORD.
     GO TO MAIN-ROUTINE.
END-OF-JOB-ROUTINE.
     CLOSE SALES-PERSON-FILE, REPORT-FILE.
     STOP RUN.
```

FIGURE 3-10. An Alternate Form of the Procedure Division for the Sample Program

JOB-ROUTINE has been added which contains the CLOSE and STOP RUN statements. Notice that each of these is now a separate sentence, terminated with a period, since they are no longer part of the AT END phrase.

In order to execute the instructions in the END-OF-JOB-ROUTINE at the end of processing, the AT END phrase has been modified to include a GO TO statement. This statement causes the computer to go to the END-OF-JOB-ROUTINE when the control record following the last record in the file is read. Thus, the program ends as before by closing the files and stopping the run.

This program illustrates the fact that the GO TO statement can be used to go forward or backward in a program. In general, the statements are executed in the sequence in which they are coded, one after the other. In addition, the program automatically goes from one paragraph to the next. This sequential execution of instructions continues unless it is broken by an instruction such as a GO TO statement. Such a process of breaking the normal sequence of execution of the program at a point and continuing elsewhere is called *branching* or *transfer of control*. In general, it is possible to branch to any other point in a program that has a paragraph name by using a GO TO statement.

In the sample program in Figure 3-10, the GO TO statement at the end of the MAIN-ROUTINE paragraph is used to transfer control back to the beginning of the paragraph. Thus, this GO TO statement creates a loop that is executed once for each input card. The GO TO statement in the AT END phrase is used to branch out of the MAIN-ROUTINE paragraph to the END-Of-JOB-ROUTINE paragraph when the final control record is read. Thus, this program uses two GO TO statements, one to branch forward in the program and one to branch backward.

Comparing Figures 3-7 and 3-10 we see that both programs accomplish the same result, only in slightly different ways. Usually there are many ways of coding a program to solve a specific problem. It is the programmer's responsibility to figure out how the problem can be solved and to code the program to do it. Understanding the problem and designing the solution are often the most difficult parts of the programmer's job. The programmer must think through the problem until he or she thoroughly understands what steps are necessary to solve it. Then the programmer can begin to write the COBOL program. Even then, there are often several ways in which the program can be written.

Besides producing a correct program, the most important thing that the programmer must do when coding a program is to make the program easy to read. A program is read many times by the original programmer and by other programmers as well. This is because the program usually has errors in it that must be corrected and because programs often need to be modified at some time in the future. To make any changes in the program, someone has to read over the instructions and try to understand the program. Thus, it is important that the program be easily readable.

In general, programs that have a lot of branches in them are difficult to read. This is because the programmer must jump around the program listing every time that a branch is indicated. It is best if the programmer can read the instructions in the sequence in which they are written without branching. Thus, programs with a lot of GO TO statements are hard to follow. For example, the procedure division for the sample program in Figure 3-7 is easier to read than the one in Figure 3-10 because it has fewer branches. Following guidelines such as those mentioned in this section generally makes programs easier to read.

3-5. THE CODING FORMAT

In Chapter 2 we saw how COBOL programs are usually written, or coded, on special forms called coding forms. Figure 2-1 shows the sample program coded on such a form. When a program is coded, it must follow certain rules regarding the format of the various parts of the program. The purpose of the coding form is to help the programmer arrange the program correctly. This section describes the coding format for COBOL.

As we know, a line on the coding form is divided into 80 spaces called columns. These correspond to the 80 columns of a punched card. Each line is punched in a card exactly as it is coded on the form. At this point we are not going to be concerned with the first seven columns or columns 73 through 80. Although important, these columns need not be used for the types of programs that can be coded using the elements of COBOL described so far. We will explain their use later.

All parts of a COBOL program that have been discussed in this chapter appear in columns 8 through 72. Nothing can begin before column 8 or extend beyond column 72. These columns are divided into two areas known as area A and area B. Area A consists of columns 8, 9, 10, and 11. Area B contains columns 12 through 72. The COBOL coding format requires that certain elements must begin in area A, others must begin in area B, and some may begin in either area. When we say that an element must begin in an area we mean that the first character of the element must be in any one of the columns of that area. Of course if an element begins in area A it may extend into area B.

Division names, section names, and paragraph names must all begin in area A. The FD in a file description entry and the 01 level number must also begin in area A. The 02 level number may begin in either area A or area B although the usual practice is to put it in area B. Names and clauses within an FD, 01, or 02 entry must begin in area B. Sentences in the procedure division and entries in the identification and environment divisions must begin in area B. If an entry, sentence, phrase, or clause is too long for a line (that is, if it goes beyond column 72), it must be continued onto the next line. The continued part must begin in area B.

Other than these rules, COBOL is unrestricted in its coding format. For example, within an area we may indent as much as we want. Although there must be at least one space between parts of a sentence or entry, we may use extra spaces if we want. We can continue any part of a sentence or entry onto the next line. (However, for readability it is best to put each phrase or clause on a separate line.) Finally, we can use blank lines between other lines to separate parts of the program.

```
IDENTIFICATION DIVISION.
  Paragraphs
    Entries


ENVIRONMENT DIVISION.
  Sections
    Paragraphs
      Entries
        Clauses


DATA DIVISION.
  Sections
    Entries
      Clauses


PROCEDURE DIVISION.
  Sections
    Paragraphs
      Sentences
        Statements
          Phrases
```

FIGURE 3-11. The Grammatical Structure of COBOL Programs

The only punctuation that is required is a period after any entry, sentence, or paragraph name, and after the word SECTION or DIVISION. After any period of this sort, there must be at least one space, although extra spaces are allowed. Commas are optional between clauses, phrases, and sentences. A semicolon may be used instead of a comma. (The semicolon is not allowed in all versions of COBOL. See Appendix A for punctuation differences.)

3-6. SUMMARY OF THE STRUCTURE OF COBOL

As we have seen, a COBOL program is composed of elements that often resemble English. We refer to these elements by names that are borrowed from English grammar such as phrase, clause, sentence, and paragraph. This overall grammatical structure of a COBOL program is summarized in Figure 3-11.

CHAPTER 4

Basic Operations

With the COBOL elements described in Chapter 3 we can write programs that read, move, and write data. Although some programs are of this type, most programs involve processing operations such as performing arithmetic calculations and making logical decisions. This chapter discusses the basic arithmetic and logical instructions that are used in COBOL. Since these instructions describe the manipulation of data during the execution of the program, they are coded by statements in the procedure division.

4-1. ARITHMETIC OPERATIONS

Arithmetic operations involve calculations such as addition, subtraction, multiplication, and division. Each calculation that is to be performed must be coded in a separate statement. If the operation is addition, the ADD statement is used. For subtraction, the SUBTRACT statement is used. Similarly, the MULTIPLY and DIVIDE statements are used for the operations of multiplication and division.

In an arithmetic instruction we must tell the computer what data is to be used in the calculation and what to do with the result. The ADD statement consists of the reserved word ADD followed by the names of the fields that contain the data to be added, then the word

GIVING, and finally the name of the field that receives the result of the addition. For example, the statement

```
ADD A-FIELD, B-FIELD GIVING C-FIELD.
```

instructs the computer to add the current contents of the fields named A-FIELD and B-FIELD and to store the result in the field name C-FIELD. For example, if A-FIELD contains the value 15.60 and B-FIELD is 24.30, then, after execution of this instruction, C-FIELD will be equal to 39.90. The calculation does not destroy the contents of A-FIELD or B-FIELD, but it does destroy the previous value of C-FIELD and replaces it with the newly calculated sum. Notice in this example that a comma separates the names of the first two fields. This is optional and is only included to improve readability.

The names of the fields that contain the data to be added must have pictures that identify them as numeric data. That is, their pictures must contain only 9s and perhaps a V. Their pictures cannot contain the symbol X or any editing characters (Z, period, or comma). The field named after the word GIVING may be either a numeric field with no editing or a numeric edited field. However, if the field is edited, it cannot be used in any further calculations.

In this example only two values are added. However, it is possible with one statement to add any number of values. For example, the following statement adds the values of four fields and stores their sum in a fifth field:

```
ADD S-FIELD, T-FIELD, U-FIELD, V-FIELD GIVING W-FIELD.
```

The SUBTRACT instruction consists of the reserved word SUBTRACT followed by the name of a field, the word FROM, another field name, the word GIVING, and a final field name. For example, consider the following statement:

```
SUBTRACT A-DATA FROM B-DATA GIVING C-DATA.
```

In this example the value of the first field, A-DATA, is subtracted from the value of the second field, B-DATA, and the result is stored in the third field, C-DATA. Notice that the word FROM must be included. In effect we are telling the computer to perform the following calculation:

```
  B-DATA
- A-DATA
  ------
  C-DATA
```

The MULTIPLY instruction has a form illustrated by the following statement:

```
MULTIPLY S-AMOUNT BY T-AMOUNT GIVING U-AMOUNT.
```

The effect is that the values of the first two fields, which are separated by the word BY, are multiplied and the result is stored in the third field, following the word GIVING. That is, the computer performs the calculation:

```
  S-AMOUNT
x T-AMOUNT
  U-AMOUNT
```

The DIVIDE instruction has two basic forms, depending on how the programmer wishes to state the operation. In the first form, the computer is instructed to DIVIDE the first field INTO the second field GIVING the third field. For example, the statement

```
DIVIDE A-FIELD INTO B-FIELD GIVING C-FIELD.
```

results in the calculation:

```
                C-FIELD
A-FIELD )B-FIELD
```

An alternative form of the DIVIDE instruction tells the computer to divide the first field BY the second. For example, the following statement is equivalent to the previous example

```
DIVIDE B-FIELD BY A-FIELD GIVING C-FIELD.
```

As an example of the use of these arithmetic statements in a program, consider the calculation of an employee's pay shown in Figure 4-1. In this example, the number of hours worked on each day of the week are stored in five separate fields. (The prefix IN- identifies these as input fields.) These values must be added to get the total number of hours worked during the week. (As we will see, the prefix WK- means "working" and identifies a field that contains an intermediate result.)

```
ADD IN-MON-HOURS, IN-TUES-HOURS, IN-WED-HOURS,
    IN-THURS-HOURS, IN-FRI-HOURS
    GIVING WK-TOTAL-HOURS.
MULTIPLY WK-TOTAL-HOURS BY WK-PAY-RATE
    GIVING WK-GROSS-PAY.
MULTIPLY WK-GROSS-PAY BY WK-TAX-RATE
    GIVING WK-WITHHOLDING-TAX.
SUBTRACT WK-WITHHOLDING-TAX FROM WK-GROSS-PAY
    GIVING WK-NET-PAY.
```

FIGURE 4-1. Payroll Calculation

The total hours can then be multiplied by the pay rate to get the gross pay for the week. This value must be multiplied by the tax rate to get the amount of the withholding tax. Finally, the withholding tax is subtracted from the gross pay to give the employee's net or take-home pay.

Notice that the statements in this sequence must be coded in the order shown. This is because at each step in the computation a value calculated in the previous step is used. The computer always executes statements in the order in which they are coded. If the programmer does not code the statements in a logical sequence, errors could occur. The programmer must understand how the calculation is to take place and must code the program appropriately.

Each statement in Figure 4-1 is a separate sentence terminated with a period. In this example, all statements require more than one line to code. This often happens with arithmetic statements, since they are usually too long to fit on one line. In continuing statements such as these it is best to indent the continued part.

Each of the arithmetic statements described in this section has another form that leaves off the GIVING part of the statement. For example, the SUBTRACT instruction may be coded:

```
SUBTRACT A-DATA FROM B-DATA.
```

The effect of this instruction is to subtract the value of A-DATA from the value of B-DATA and to store the result in B-DATA. Thus the value of the field named B-DATA is first used in the calculation and then replaced by the result of the calculation. For example, if A-DATA is 25 and B-DATA equals 35, then the result of the subtraction is 10. This value is stored in the field named B-DATA, destroying its previous value. Thus, after execution of this statement, B-DATA is equal to 10.

When this form of the arithmetic statement is used, all fields must have numeric pictures without editing. This is because the values from all fields are used in the calculation, and only unedited numeric data may be used in such operations. In general, all fields in any arithmetic statement must be numeric and unedited except for the field named in the GIVING part, which may have an edited or unedited numeric picture.

The alternative form of the ADD instruction requires that the word TO be inserted before the last field name. For example, the following statement adds the value of A-FIELD to the value of B-FIELD and stores the result in B-FIELD:

```
ADD A-FIELD TO B-FIELD.
```

We could also add the values of several fields with this form, as in the following example:

```
ADD S-FIELD, T-FIELD, U-FIELD TO V-FIELD.
```

The MULTIPLY instruction without the GIVING part performs the indicated multiplication and replaces the second field with the result. For example, the statement

```
MULTIPLY S-AMOUNT BY T-AMOUNT.
```

replaces T-AMOUNT with the product of S-AMOUNT and the previous value of T-AMOUNT.

When the GIVING part is not used with the DIVIDE instruction, the first field must be divided INTO the second. That is, the form of the DIVIDE instruction using the word BY cannot be used without GIVING. For example, the statement

```
DIVIDE A-FIELD INTO B-FIELD.
```

causes the value of A-FIELD to be divided into the current value of B-FIELD and the result to be stored in B-FIELD, replacing the current value of that field.

The DIVIDE instruction has another form when the GIVING part is used. This form specifies a name for a field that receives the remainder from the division operation. Without this field, the remainder is lost after the division operation. For example, assume that we wish to calculate the number of dozen in a given number of eggs and to find the number remaining after the number of dozens have been taken out. To do this we would divide the number of eggs by twelve. The quotient would be the number of dozen; the remainder would be the number of extra eggs. In COBOL we can code this operation as follows:

```
DIVIDE NUMBER-EGGS BY TWELVE
    GIVING NUMBER-DOZEN REMAINDER NUMBER-REMAINING.
```

The REMAINDER part of this statement specifies the name of the field that is to receive the remainder from the division operation. As a numeric example, assume that NUMBER-EGGS is 226. Then after the instruction is executed, NUMBER-DOZEN is 18 and NUMBER-REMAINING is 10.

Not all versions of COBOL allow the REMAINDER part of the DIVIDE statement (see Appendix A). When it is not allowed, the remainder must be calculated as follows:

```
DIVIDE NUMBER-EGGS BY TWELVE
    GIVING NUMBER-DOZEN.
MULTIPLY NUMBER-DOZEN BY TWELVE
    GIVING NUMBER-AMOUNT.
```

```
SUBTRACT NUMBER-AMOUNT FROM NUMBER-EGGS
     GIVING NUMBER-REMAINING.
```

Although more statements are required, the result is exactly the same as before.

As we can see, there are several different forms for each arithmetic statement. The various forms discussed in this section are summarized in Figure 4-2.

4-2. CONSTANT AND VARIABLE DATA

As we know, a field name refers to a group of storage locations. The data that is contained in such a group of locations can change from time to time. For example, a READ statement may cause new data to be read in and stored in the locations identified by a field name. Simi-

```
ADD _____ , _____ GIVING _____

ADD _____ TO _____


SUBTRACT _____ FROM _____ GIVING _____

SUBTRACT _____ FROM _____


MULTIPLY _____ BY _____ GIVING _____

MULTIPLY _____ BY _____


DIVIDE _____ INTO _____ GIVING _____

DIVIDE _____ BY _____ GIVING _____

DIVIDE _____ INTO _____

DIVIDE _____ INTO _____ GIVING _____ REMAINDER _____

DIVIDE _____ BY _____ GIVING _____ REMAINDER _____
```

FIGURE 4-2. Summary of Arithmetic Statement Forms

larly, using a field name as a receiving field in a MOVE statement or after the word GIVING in an ADD statement causes the data to be changed. Data that can be altered during processing by operations such as these are often called *variable* data. Whenever the field name of a variable value is used in a statement (such as the sending field of a MOVE statement) the current value assigned to that name is retrieved from internal storage.

Another type of data used in programs is called *constant* data because it remains unchanged during processing. One form of constant data is simply a number such as 150 or 7.25. Such numbers used in a COBOL program are called *numeric literals* because they "literally" specify numeric values. A numeric literal may contain any group of digits plus an optional decimal point and perhaps a plus or minus sign. It may not contain a comma. For example, the following are valid numeric literals in COBOL:

```
.075    -3.63    +1050    43.00    -76385    12
```

A numeric literal can have up to 18 digits in it. This allows for very large numbers if needed. (A numeric input or output field is also limited to 18 or fewer digits.)

A numeric literal may be used in an arithmetic statement in any place where a field name is allowed except as the name that receives the result of the calculation. For example, if we wish to add 100 to the value of A-FIELD and store the result in B-FIELD we could use the following statement:

```
ADD 100, A-FIELD GIVING B-FIELD.
```

We could not, however, have used a numeric literal in place of B-FIELD.

Numeric literals can also be used in the MOVE statement to assign values to field names. For example, the following statement stores the value 250 in the field named C-FIELD:

```
MOVE 250 TO C-FIELD.
```

The receiving field in such a MOVE statement must have a numeric picture (with or without editing). Note, however, that we could not use a numeric literal as the receiving field.

Another form of constant in COBOL is known as a *figurative constant*. This type of constant consists of a reserved word that "figuratively" represents the data value. For example, in Chapter 3 we used the word SPACES in a MOVE statement to blank out an output record. This word is a figurative constant and refers to a series of spaces or blanks. We could also use the word SPACE to refer to a single blank character. (Actually, SPACE and SPACES are synonymous and may be used interchangeably.)

Another figurative constant that is sometimes used in arithmetic processing is ZERO, which also may be written ZEROS or ZEROES. This constant refers to the numeric value 0. For example, if we wished to assign the value zero to X-FIELD we could use a MOVE statement as follows:

```
MOVE ZERO TO X-FIELD.
```

X-FIELD in this example would normally have a numeric picture (either edited or unedited) although it may be alphanumeric.

4-3. WORKING STORAGE

In a COBOL program *all* data names used in the procedure division must be specified in the data division. Many names that are used are associated with input or output records in the FILE section. However, often data names are needed that do not identify input or output fields. For example, in the payroll calculation in Figure 4-1 we needed several names to hold intermediate results in the calculations. We used the name WK-TOTAL-HOURS for the result of the calculation of the total hours worked during the week. This was not the name of an input field. This name was also used in the calculation of WK-GROSS-PAY. Because the name was used in a calculation it could not have an edited picture. Thus it would not normally be an output field.

In COBOL we need a way of specifying fields that are not used either for input or output but rather for intermediate values during calculations. The WORKING-STORAGE section of the data division is used for this purpose. Figure 4-3 illustrates the WORKING-STORAGE section needed for the payroll calculation. This section comes after the FILE section in the data division. Fields such as those needed in the payroll calculation are given the level number 77. These fields do not belong to a record and sometimes are called *independent items*. The level number 77 must begin in area A but the field name begins in area B.

```
WORKING-STORAGE SECTION.
77  WK-TOTAL-HOURS        PIC 99V9.
77  WK-GROSS-PAY          PIC 999V99.
77  WK-WITHHOLDING-TAX    PIC 999V99.
77  WK-NET-PAY            PIC 999V99.
77  WK-PAY-RATE           PIC 9V99     VALUE 3.50.
77  WK-TAX-RATE           PIC V99      VALUE .12.
```

FIGURE 4-3. The WORKING-STORAGE Section for the Payroll Calculation

Notice that the pictures of each independent item in this example are numeric but not edited. As we have seen, in the payroll calculation these pictures must not be edited since the data names are used in calculations.

Two of the entries in Figure 4-3 have an additional clause after the picture. This is called the VALUE clause and is used to give an initial value to a data name. If a name is not assigned a value in a program, then the name refers to whatever happens to be in the storage locations assigned to the name. This could be some data left over from another program or just about anything. (We sometimes call such unknown data "garbage.") If we use a data name that refers to such unspecified data then the results would be unknown. We can assign a value to a data name through an input operation, by using the name for the result of a calculation or move operation, or by a VALUE clause.

The VALUE clause consists of the word VALUE followed by the actual value to be assigned to the data name. This value is often a numeric literal, as illustrated in Figure 4-3. Thus, the name WK-PAY-RATE is given the initial value 3.50 and WK-TAX-RATE is assigned .12 (for 12 percent). We can also use a figurative constant in the VALUE clause. For example, if we wish to assign an initial value of zero to a name we could include the clause:

```
VALUE ZERO
```

Notice that the VALUE clause is part of the 77 entry. Thus, the period that terminates the entry comes after the VALUE clause and not after the PICTURE clause.

VALUE clauses may *not* appear in the FILE section. (There is one exception to this rule which will be explained in a later chapter.) Therefore, any field that must receive an initial value through a VALUE clause must be specified in the WORKING-STORAGE section.

It is a good practice to use the prefix WK- or WS- (for "working" or "working storage") for field names that are specified in the WORK-ING-STORAGE section. We have used similar prefixes for the names of fields that are part of input or output records. This way the programmer can easily identify where in the data division the name is described and to what type of field it refers.

4-4. LOGICAL OPERATIONS

In many programs it is necessary to perform different sequences of instructions based on some condition. For example, in calculating payroll, the pay rate may depend on whether or not the employee works overtime. If the employee works more than 40 hours in a week, the payrate for all overtime hours is often one and one-half times the regular rate. In calculating the payroll for such a situation we must perform different calculations depending on whether or not the hours worked are greater than 40.

In the COBOL procedure division the IF statement is used to make such logical decisions. In its simplest form, the IF statement consists of the word IF followed by a *relation condition*, and then a COBOL statement. A relation condition is an expression of how two values may be related. For example, the relation condition

```
WK-TOTAL-HOURS IS GREATER THAN 40.0
```

expresses a relationship between the total-hours field and the numeric literal 40.0. In general, a relation condition consists of a field name or literal followed by a *relational operator* and then another field name or literal. The simplest relational operators are:

```
IS GREATER THAN
IS LESS THAN
IS EQUAL TO
```

On each side of a relational operator we must have a field name or a literal.

In a simple IF statement, the relation condition is tested to see if it is true or false. That is, the computer evaluates the comparison indicated by the relational operator and determines whether or not it is correct. If the condition is *true*, then the computer executes the *statement* following the condition before going on. If the condition is *false*, then the computer skips this *statement* and goes on to the next *sentence* in sequence.

As an example, consider this sentence:

```
IF X-AMOUNT IS EQUAL TO Y-AMOUNT
    MOVE A-FIELD TO B-FIELD.
```

The relation condition instructs the computer to compare the values of X-AMOUNT and Y-AMOUNT and determine if they are equal. If the values are equal, then the MOVE statement is executed and then the computer goes on to the next sentence. If they are not equal then the MOVE statement is not executed and the computer goes directly to the next sentence. Notice that, whether or not the MOVE statement is executed, the computer goes on to the next sentence.

The IF statement in this example is terminated by a period. This makes it a sentence. This period is necessary so that the computer knows where the next sentence begins and, thus, what to do if the condition is false. It is possible to have many statements following the condition, with a period only at the end of the last statement. In this case, the computer executes all of the statements up to the period if the condition is true but bypasses all of these statements if the condition is false. For example, consider the sentence:

```
IF 25.5 IS LESS THAN Z-AMOUNT
    ADD A-DATA, B-DATA GIVING C-DATA
    SUBTRACT C-DATA FROM D-DATA.
```

In this case the relation condition determines whether the value 25.5 is less than the value of the field named Z-AMOUNT. If it is, then the ADD and SUBTRACT statements are executed. Notice that both of these statements are executed if the condition is true because the period comes after the second statement. If the condition is false, both statements are skipped and the computer goes directly to the next sentence.

We can see now one of the reasons why it is important to distinguish between *sentences* and *statements*. A sentence is always terminated with a period and is composed of one or more statements. We call the IF statement a *statement* because it does not always form a separate sentence. (For example, in a later chapter we will see that there may be an IF statement within another IF statement.) In the simple examples that we have shown so far we have formed a sentence out of an IF statement by putting a period at the end. Within the sentence are other statements such as MOVE and ADD statements. These statements are executed only if the relation condition is true.

Figure 4-4 shows the payroll calculation modified to calculate

```
ADD IN-MON-HOURS, IN-TUES-HOURS, IN-WED-HOURS,
    IN-THURS-HOURS, IN-FRI-HOURS
    GIVING WK-TOTAL-HOURS.
MULTIPLY WK-TOTAL-HOURS BY WK-PAY-RATE
    GIVING WK-GROSS-PAY.
IF WK-TOTAL-HOURS IS GREATER THAN 40
    MULTIPLY WK-PAY-RATE BY .5 GIVING WK-OVERTIME-RATE
    SUBTRACT 40 FROM WK-TOTAL-HOURS GIVING WK-OVERTIME-HOURS
    MULTIPLY WK-OVERTIME-HOURS BY WK-OVERTIME-RATE
        GIVING WK-OVERTIME-PAY
    ADD WK-OVERTIME-PAY TO WK-GROSS-PAY.
MULTIPLY WK-GROSS-PAY BY WK-TAX-RATE
    GIVING WK-WITHHOLDING-TAX.
SUBTRACT WK-WITHHOLDING-TAX FROM WK-GROSS-PAY
    GIVING WK-NET-PAY.
```

FIGURE 4-4. Payroll Calculation with Overtime

overtime pay. In this example, the total hours are calculated first, followed by the calculation of the gross pay at the regular pay rate. Then, if the employee has worked more than 40 hours during the week, the extra pay for overtime is calculated and added to the gross pay. The extra pay is one-half times the regular pay rate times the number of hours over 40 worked during the week. Finally, the withholding tax and net pay are calculated as before.

We can see from this example the type of processing that can be accomplished using the IF statement. By proper use of this statement the programmer can accomplish very complex processing tasks in the program. However, the programmer must understand the logic necessary to accomplish the processing. The program must be planned completely and the IF statement used carefully to be sure that logic errors do not appear.

Notice in the IF statement in Figure 4-4 and in the other examples that the statements following the condition are indented. As we have seen, indentation helps to set off parts of the program to make it easier to read and understand. It is a good practice to indent all statements after the condition in an IF statement. This way it is very clear what statements are executed if the condition is true.

In the form of the IF statement described so far, the next sentence is executed whether or not the condition is true. In some situations it is desirable to execute the next group of statements only if the condition is false. In this case, the IF statement can be modified to include an ELSE phrase. When this phrase is used, no period terminates the statements after the condition. Rather, the word ELSE appears, followed by one or more additional statements and then a period. The effect is that the statements after the condition but before the word ELSE are executed if the condition is true, while the statements after ELSE, up to the final period, are executed if the condition is false. In either case, after executing the appropriate statements, the computer goes on to the next sentence in sequence.

For example, consider this sentence:

```
IF X-AMOUNT IS EQUAL TO 75
    MOVE A-FIELD TO B-FIELD
    ADD 100 TO Y-AMOUNT
ELSE
    MOVE A-FIELD TO C-FIELD
    SUBTRACT 100 FROM Y-FIELD.
```

If the value of the field named X-AMOUNT is 75, then the first MOVE statement and the ADD statement are executed. If X-AMOUNT is not equal to 75, then the second MOVE statement and the SUBTRACT statement are executed. Notice that a period comes at the end of the entire sentence, not after the ADD statement. After executing either the first group of statements or the second group, the computer continues on to the next sentence in sequence.

When using a complex IF statement with an ELSE phrase, style becomes especially important. For example, we could have coded the previous sentence as:

```
IF X-AMOUNT IS EQUAL TO 75 MOVE A-FIELD TO B-FIELD
ADD 100 TO Y-AMOUNT ELSE MOVE A-FIELD TO C-FIELD
SUBTRACT 100 FROM Y-FIELD.
```

Although the effect would be the same, it is much more difficult for the programmer to understand what is meant. In general, each statement within the IF statement should be put on a separate line and indented. The word ELSE should be written on a separate line and should begin in the same column as the word IF.

Sometimes it is necessary to test a condition and, if it is true, to continue to the next sentence in sequence; but if it is false, some other statements are to be executed first. One way of accomplishing this is to use the statement

```
NEXT SENTENCE
```

after the relation condition. For example, consider this sentence:

```
IF S-DATA IS EQUAL TO T-DATA
    NEXT SENTENCE
ELSE
    MOVE A-FIELD TO B-FIELD.
```

In this example, the NEXT SENTENCE statement causes the computer to go on to the next sentence if the condition is true. However, if the condition is false, the statement following the word ELSE is executed before going on.

Practically any COBOL statement can be used within an IF statement (even another IF statement, although this is an advanced topic covered in a later chapter). One statement that sometimes appears is the GO TO statement. When this statement is executed from within an IF statement, the computer branches to the paragraph indicated and continues from that point. For example, consider the sentence:

```
IF Z-AMOUNT IS LESS THAN 50
    GO TO ERROR-ROUTINE.
```

If the condition indicated in the IF statement is true, then the GO TO statement is executed; the computer does *not* go on to the next sentence in sequence. However, if the condition is false, the GO TO statement is bypassed and the next sentence in sequence is executed.

As we have said before, the use of GO TO statements can make the program difficult to understand. The fact that within the IF statement there can appear a number of other statements makes it possible to avoid using the GO TO statement in many situations. However, there are circumstances where a GO TO statement is useful. For example, when it is necessary to branch out of a loop because some extraordinary condition has occurred an IF statement containing a GO TO is usually best. However, whenever a GO TO statement is used like this the statement should direct the computer to branch *down* the program (that is, toward the end). This way it is not necessary to jump back to some previous point and the program is easier to follow.

So far we have used only three simple relational operators. Each of these can be modified to include the word NOT. Then we have the following operators:

```
IS NOT GREATER THAN
IS NOT LESS THAN
IS NOT EQUAL TO
```

For example, the following sentence causes an ADD statement to be executed if the value of S-DATA is *not* equal to 100:

```
IF S-DATA IS NOT EQUAL TO 100
    ADD 1 TO S-DATA.
```

Some versions of COBOL allow mathematical symbols to be substituted for the words in the relational operators. For example, the symbol > may be used instead of IS GREATER THAN. The word NOT may also be used with these symbols. Thus NOT > is the same as IS NOT GREATER THAN. The other symbols are < for IS LESS THAN and = for IS EQUAL TO. Not all versions of COBOL allow these symbols. See Appendix A for details.

4-5. OPERATIONS WITH NONNUMERIC DATA

All of the examples that we have shown so far use relational operators to compare numeric data. However, these operators can also be used to compare nonnumeric (alphanumeric) data. For example, assume that there are two alphanumeric fields named A-FIELD and B-FIELD. We can test to see if they contain the same data by using an IF statement such as the following:

```
IF A-FIELD IS EQUAL TO B-FIELD
    MOVE C-DATA TO D-DATA.
```

The condition in this statement is true if both fields contain identical data. Otherwise the condition is false.

When two nonnumeric values are compared to determine if one is greater than or less than the other, the comparison is based on the *collating sequence* of characters. The collating sequence gives the ordering of the characters used by the computer. For the alphabetic characters, the collating sequence is just the standard alphabetic ordering. The letter A is considered less than the letter B; the letter C is greater than the letters A or B. We can compare words in this way to determine their alphabetic ordering. Thus, the name JEAN is considered less than JOHN but greater than JACK. The collating sequence for nonalphabetic characters depends on the computer being used (see Appendix A).

Sometimes the value of a field needs to be compared with a constant value. For numeric data, a numeric literal is used in the relation test. For nonnumeric comparisons a *nonnumeric literal* is used. The difference is that a nonnumeric literal is enclosed in apostrophes and may contain any group of characters. For example, 'JEAN' is a nonnumeric literal. Actually, ANS COBOL requires nonnumeric literals to be enclosed in quotation marks (e.g., "JEAN"). However, most computers use the apostrophe or single quotation mark instead. We will use it throughout this book.

As an example of the use of a nonnumeric literal consider the sentence:

```
IF IN-NAME-FIELD IS EQUAL TO 'JEAN'
    MOVE IN-NAME-FIELD TO OUT-NAME-FIELD.
```

In this example, the MOVE statement is executed only if IN-NAME-FIELD contains the value JEAN. This field must have an alphanumeric picture, since it contains nonnumeric data.

As we shall see, being able to compare fields with nonnumeric literals is very useful. Nonnumeric literals can also be used in the VALUE clause in the data division. When this is done, the field named in the entry is assigned an initial value equal to the literal. For example, consider the entry:

```
77  WK-NAME-FIELD     PIC XXXX      VALUE 'JACK'.
```

In this example, the field named WK-NAME-FIELD is assigned an initial value consisting of the characters JACK. Notice that the picture of this field indicates it is alphanumeric. This is necessary since it has a nonnumeric value.

Nonnumeric literals can also be used in the MOVE statement instead of a sending field name. For example, we could use the statement

```
MOVE 'MARY' TO OUT-NAME-FIELD
```

to change the value of the field. In the following chapter we will see an example of the use of nonnumeric literals in a COBOL program.

4-6. AN ILLUSTRATIVE PROGRAM

Figure 4-5 shows a COBOL program that uses many of the features discussed in this chapter. This program processes the sales data described in Chapter 1. The fields needed for this program are the salesperson number, salesperson name, current sales, and current returns. The program calculates the net current sales by subtracting the current returns from the current sales. It then calculates the sales commission as a percentage of the net current sales. The output consists of one line for each salesperson, giving the salesperson number and name, the net current sales, and the commission. A sample of the output from the program is shown in Figure 4-6.

Notice that the identification division for the program in Figure 4-5 is the same as the identification division for the sample program in Chapter 3 except for the program name. Also, the environment divisions in these programs are identical. For most programs of this type, these two divisions are fairly standard.

The first part of the data division describing the input record for the program given in Figure 4-5 is the same as the sample program in Chapter 3. The same input fields are used for both programs. Notice, however, that we use the abbreviation PIC for PICTURE in this program. The output record description is different because the output to be printed by this program is not the same as before. Finally, in the data division we need a WORKING-STORAGE section, since intermediate results are produced by this program. Working fields are needed for the net current sales and the commission.

The procedure division consists of four paragraphs. The first is used to open the input and output files. Recall that this must be done before any data can be read or written. The second paragraph contains the READ statement, with the AT END phrase to describe the processing that is to take place after the last record has been read. The third paragraph describes the processing necessary to calculate the commission. First the net current sales is calculated by subtracting the current returns from the current sales. Then the commission calculation is performed based on the net current sales. If the net current sales is less than $5000, then the commission is 7.5 percent of the net current sales plus $100. However, if the net current sales is $5000 or more, then the commission is 10 percent of net current

```
IDENTIFICATION DIVISION.
PROGRAM-ID. SLS02.

ENVIRONMENT DIVISION.
CONFIGURATION SECTION.
SOURCE-COMPUTER. XYZ-1.
OBJECT-COMPUTER. XYZ-1.
INPUT-OUTPUT SECTION.
FILE-CONTROL.
    SELECT SALES-PERSON-FILE
        ASSIGN TO CARD-READER.
    SELECT REPORT-FILE
        ASSIGN TO PRINTER.

DATA DIVISION.
FILE SECTION.
FD  SALES-PERSON-FILE,
    LABEL RECORDS ARE OMITTED,
    RECORD CONTAINS 80 CHARACTERS,
    DATA RECORD IS SALES-PERSON-RECORD.
01  SALES-PERSON-RECORD.
    02  FILLER                  PIC XX.
    02  SP-NUMBER               PIC XXXX.
    02  SP-NAME                 PIC X(18).
    02  FILLER                  PIC X(21).
    02  SP-CURRENT-SALES        PIC 9(5)V99.
    02  SP-CURRENT-RETURNS      PIC 9(4)V99.
    02  FILLER                  PIC X(22).
FD  REPORT-FILE,
    LABEL RECORDS ARE OMITTED,
    RECORD CONTAINS 132 CHARACTERS,
    DATA RECORD IS REPORT-RECORD.
01  REPORT-RECORD.
    02  FILLER                  PIC X(10).
    02  RT-NUMBER               PIC XXXX.
    02  FILLER                  PIC X(6).
    02  RT-NAME                 PIC X(18).
    02  FILLER                  PIC X(6).
    02  RT-NET-CURRENT-SALES    PIC ZZ,ZZZ.99. -
    02  FILLER                  PIC X(6).
    02  RT-COMMISSION           PIC Z,ZZZ.99.
    02  FILLER                  PIC X(65).
WORKING-STORAGE SECTION.
77  WK-NET-CURRENT-SALES        PIC 9(5)V99.
77  WK-COMMISSION               PIC 9(4)V99.
```

FIGURE 4-5. An Illustrative Program (Part 1 of 2)

```
PROCEDURE DIVISION.
OPEN-FILES.
    OPEN INPUT SALES-PERSON-FILE,
        OUTPUT REPORT-FILE.
READ-INPUT.
    READ SALES-PERSON-FILE,
        AT END
            CLOSE SALES-PERSON-FILE, REPORT-FILE
            STOP RUN.
CALCULATE-COMMISSION.
    SUBTRACT SP-CURRENT-RETURNS FROM SP-CURRENT-SALES
        GIVING WK-NET-CURRENT-SALES.
    IF WK-NET-CURRENT-SALES IS LESS THAN 5000.00
        MULTIPLY WK-NET-CURRENT-SALES BY .075
            GIVING WK-COMMISSION
        ADD 100.00 TO WK-COMMISSION
    ELSE
        MULTIPLY WK-NET-CURRENT-SALES BY .10
            GIVING WK-COMMISSION
        ADD 150.00 TO WK-COMMISSION.
WRITE-OUTPUT.
    MOVE SPACES TO REPORT-RECORD.
    MOVE SP-NUMBER TO RT-NUMBER.
    MOVE SP-NAME TO RT-NAME.
    MOVE WK-NET-CURRENT-SALES TO RT-NET-CURRENT-SALES.
    MOVE WK-COMMISSION TO RT-COMMISSION.
    WRITE REPORT-RECORD.
    GO TO READ-INPUT.
```

FIGURE 4-5. (Part 2 of 2)

sales plus $150. Notice that the percentage must be expressed as fractions (.075 and .10) and that in either case the multiplication must take place before the addition. Finally, after the commission is calculated, the fourth paragraph is executed, causing the appropriate data to be moved to the output fields and the output record to be written. The last statement in the program causes the computer to branch back to the READ-INPUT paragraph and start the processing over again.

4-7. PROGRAM FLOWCHARTS

A tool that is often used to help develop a computer program is the *program flowchart*. A flowchart is a diagram of the logic in a com-

0005	BENNETT ROBERT	1,587.85	219.08
0016	LOCK ANDREW S	277.87	120.84
0080	PARKER JAMES E	18,035.00	1,953.50
0239	HAINES CYNTHIA L	25,000.00	2,650.00
0401	REDDING OLIVIA	13,822.24	1,532.22
0477	SMITH RICHARD A	40.00	103.00
0912	EMERY ELIZABETH G	450.35	133.77
1060	ROBINSON WILLIAM L	-12,350.00	1,385.00
1083	JOHNSON ROBERT	12,051.85	1,355.18
1111	FREDERICKS RICHARD	.00	100.00
1133	MARSHALL M S	10,000.00	1,150.00
1205	HOLT BENTLEY	1,091.60	181.87
1374	BENTON ALEX J	193.50	114.51
1375	TAYLOR EVERETT	125.00	109.37
1420	EHRHARDT ELISE	665.39	149.90
1442	ADAMS JUNE R	4,510.05	438.25
1612	LOCATELLI FRANK	13,000.00	1,450.00
1698	GUZMAN JOSE	1,642.00	223.15
1842	COLE ROBERT N	7,899.85	939.98

FIGURE 4-6. Output from the Illustrative Program

puter program. The flowchart is drawn by using special symbols; each symbol represents a basic step in the program's logic. Within each symbol is written a phrase that describes the activity at that step. The symbols are connected by lines that show the sequence in which the steps are to take place. For a COBOL program we draw a flowchart of the logic in the procedure division.

In a flowchart, the shape of the symbol indicates the type of activity that is to take place. Figure 4-7 shows the standard flowchart symbols that are approved by the American National Standards Institute. The *process symbol* is used to represent any general processing activity, such as arithmetic calculations and data manipulation, but not input/output or decision making. For these latter two activities the *input/output symbol* and *decision symbol* shown in the figure are used. The *terminal point symbol* is used to show the beginning and end of a program. The *connector symbol* is used to connect parts of a flowchart. *Flowlines* show the direction of the flow of logic in the flowchart. The normal direction is from top to bottom and left to right. Arrowheads on the lines are optional if the normal flow is assumed but are required if the direction of flow is other than normal. Finally, the *annotation symbol* is used for additional comments or descriptions. It may be open on either the right or left. The dashed line extends to the symbol that requires comment.

Figure 4-8 shows a flowchart of the sample program discussed in Chapters 2 and 3. This program reads a sales record; moves the sales-

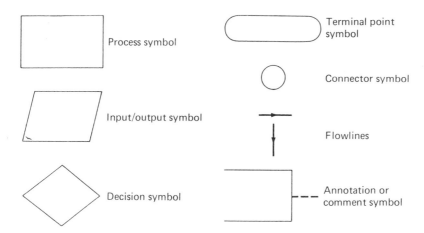

FIGURE 4-7. ANS Program Flowchart Symbols

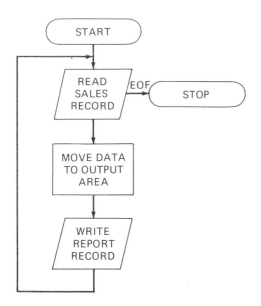

FIGURE 4-8. Flowchart for the First Sample Program

person name, number, current sales, and current returns to the output record; and prints a line. It repeats these steps for each input record and stops after the last record is read. The procedure division for the program is shown in Figure 3-7.

The flowchart for the program follows the same logical steps as the program's logic. Within each symbol is written a general description of the activity that takes place. The flowchart symbols do not necessarily correspond directly to individual instructions in the program.

Sometimes one symbol represents several instructions. For example, the process symbol in Figure 4-8 corresponds to five MOVE statements in the actual program.

The appropriate symbol is used for each type of activity in the program logic. The beginning and end of the logic flow are represented by the terminal point symbol. The READ and WRITE activities are represented with the input/output symbol. The process symbol is used for data movement. Flowlines connect the symbols in the flowchart. By following the flowlines beginning at the START symbol, the logic of the program can be understood. Notice that out of the side of the flowchart symbol for the input operation is a flowline labeled "EOF." This shows what is to happen when the "End-Of-File" condition is reached; that is, what happens after the last record in the file is read. To depict a loop in a flowchart, a flowline is drawn from the end of the loop to the beginning. In Figure 4-8 the loop is shown by the flowline that leaves the flowchart symbol for the output operation and enters the flowchart above the input symbol. This line is equivalent to a GO TO statement in COBOL. Notice that arrowheads are used on the flowlines to show the direction of the logical flow.

Figure 4-9 shows the flowchart for the sample program discussed in Section 4-6 (see Figure 4-5). Among other things, this flowchart shows how the decision symbol is used. This symbol shows the point where the net current sales is tested to see if it is less than $5000.00. Whenever a decision symbol is used, two or more flowlines must leave the symbol. These lines represent the possible answers to the question asked in the decision symbol. These flowlines must be labeled with the possible answers. Thus, the decision symbol shows alternate processing paths based on a logical decision.

The flowchart in Figure 4-9 also shows the use of the connector symbol. This symbol is used when it is necessary but inconvenient to connect distant parts of a flowchart with a flowline or when it is necessary to continue a flowchart onto another page. When the connector symbol is used, it appears once where the flow logic leaves one part of the chart and again where the logic enters the other part. Within each set of connectors is placed an identifying letter or number. In Figure 4-9, the letter A identifies the pair of connectors. If another set of connector symbols is needed for another part of the flowchart, a different letter or symbol such as B is used.

Finally, Figure 4-9 shows how the annotation symbol is used. In this example, it provides additional explanation of the MOVE operation. The symbol does not appear in the normal flow of logic, but rather, off to the side of another symbol. The dashed line connects the annotation symbol to the symbol that requires additional explanation.

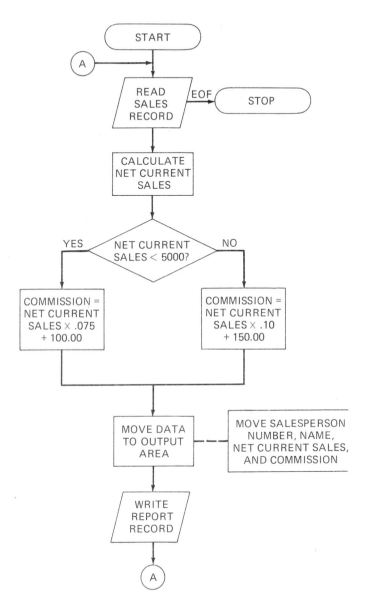

FIGURE 4-9. Flowchart for the Second Sample Program

In these flowcharts we have not shown the steps required to open and close the files. Often these steps are left out of the flowchart, so that only the fundamental logic of the program is displayed. Some programmers, however, prefer to include these operations in the flowchart.

When a flowchart is used to develop a program, the programmer first prepares rough sketches of the flowchart. Several rough flowcharts may be prepared so that different procedures can be compared. After a procedure is selected for the program, a final flowchart is drawn. Then when the program is coded, the programmer need only follow the flowlines and code the program instructions for each activity in the flowchart.

CHAPTER 5

Program Structure

The way in which the instructions in a program are organized is called the *structure* of the program. When a programmer codes a COBOL procedure division he or she builds a structure of COBOL statements. If the structure is well built, the program is correct, easy to understand, and easily modified. On the other hand, a poorly structured program may have errors that are difficult to detect, may be hard to read, and may be troublesome to change.

The purpose of this chapter is to discuss ways in which well-structured COBOL programs are coded. In the first section we look at program structure in general. In the second section we describe some COBOL statements that may be used to code a well-structured program. These statements are illustrated in a sample program in the third section. Finally, in the last section we look at more COBOL statements used in structuring programs.

5-1. BASIC PROGRAM STRUCTURE

There are three basic structures of statements in a program. These are sequence structures, decision structures, and loop structures. In a *sequence structure*, the statements are executed in the order in which they are written, one after the other. For example, a series of MOVE statements used to move data to an output record is a sequence structure. A *decision structure* is used to select which of two other structures is to be executed next. In COBOL, the IF statement may be used to create a decision structure. If the condition is true, then one set of statements is executed; otherwise, another set is executed. In a *loop structure*, a series of statements is executed repetitively. So far we have used a GO TO statement at the end of a series of statements to branch to the beginning and thus create a loop structure. We will discuss other ways of creating loop structures later.

Figure 5-1 summarizes the three basic program structures in flowchart form. Figure 5-1(a) shows a sequence structure in which one step is performed after another. In Figure 5-1(b), a decision structure is shown in which one of two alternate process steps is executed based on a decision. One of the process steps may be left out of the flowchart if necessary. In a loop structure (Figure 5-1(c)), a decision is needed to determine when the loop should be stopped. If required, the process step above or below the decision may be left out of the flowchart.

Within a structure we can embed any other structures that we need. For example, within a loop we may have a sequence of statements, decision structures, and even other loops. Within a decision structure we can have sequences, loops, and other decisions. In terms of the flowchart forms shown in Figure 5-1, this means that we can substitute any structure for any process step (rectangle) within a structure. For example, in Figure 5-2 we see a number of embedded program structures. A complete program is a sequence of basic structures and embedded structures.

There are other structures that can appear in a program. However, these three basic structures may be used to construct any program. In fact, some computer scientists have proven that any program can be written using just these three structures.*

Another idea associated with program structure is that a program may be broken into groups of related instructions called *modules* or *procedures*. A module is a series of statements that performs one function related to the overall purpose of the program. For example, in a simple program that reads a record, performs some calculations on the data from that record, and writes some output, there are three basic functions being performed. They are read, calculate, and write. We can organize such a program into three modules — a read module, a calculation module, and a write module.

*C. Bohm and G. Jacopini, "Flow Diagrams, Turing Machines and Languages with Only Two Formation Rules," *Communications of the ACM* 9, no. 5 (May 1966): 366-71. In proving their result, Bohm and Jacopini used a different loop structure than the one shown in Figure 5-1(c). However, it can be shown that the general loop structure used in the text can be constructed from the Bohm and Jacopini structures.

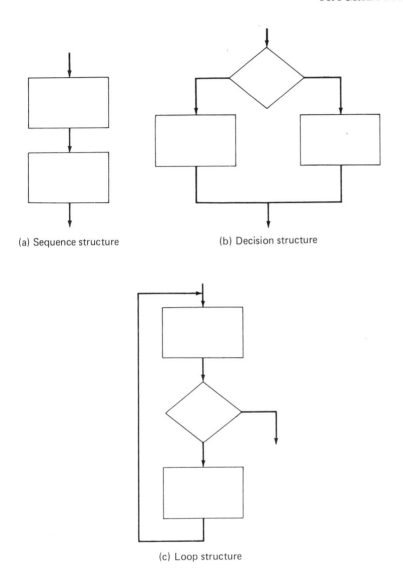

(a) Sequence structure   (b) Decision structure

(c) Loop structure

FIGURE 5-1. Basic Program Structures

The sample program in Chapter 4 (Figure 4-5) is organized in roughly this manner. The three paragraphs named READ-INPUT, CALCULATE-COMMISSION, and WRITE-OUTPUT represent the three basic modules of this program. More complex programs may have many more modules, and each module may be more than one paragraph in length. However, in any program organized in this fashion, each module should perform only one function.

Any module should have only one point at which the program may enter the module. That is, it should not be possible to branch

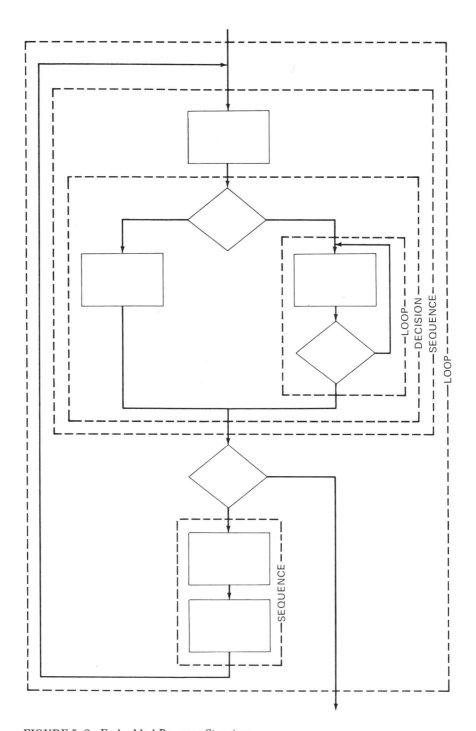

FIGURE 5-2. Embedded Program Structures

into the module at different points. Similarly, there should be only one point at which the program can leave the module and go on. This is called the exit point. The reason for having only one entry and one exit point is that this makes it easier to understand how the module performs its function.

Within a module, the basic sequence, decision, and loop structures described previously are used. These structures are combined to form the overall organization of the module.

When modular programming is used, the modules are not usually organized so that the program goes naturally from one module to the next as in the sample program in Chapter 4. Normally, a special module is coded that controls the execution of the other modules. This special module is sometimes called a *control module*, while the original modules are called *processing modules*. Within the control module are statements that cause the processing modules to be performed. In effect, such a statement causes the computer to branch to a module, execute the statements in the module, and then branch back to the control module at the point where it left off. In the next section we will discuss the COBOL statements that do this. But for now let us just assume that such statements exist and see how a control module would be organized.

Assume that we have broken a program down into three processing modules — read, calculate, and write. We wish to write a control module that causes these processing modules to be performed once for each input record. Then the control module has the following structure:

Repeat the following until the last record has been read:
    Perform the read module
    Perform the calculate module
    Perform the write module

Notice that the control module consists of a loop with a simple sequence of statements to perform each processing module in turn.

The reason for using control modules is that it helps us understand and organize the program. We can think of the program in terms of *levels*. At the highest level is the control module. If we look at just this level then we can understand the basic organization of the program. In fact, we don't have to even look at the processing modules to get an idea of how the program functions. At a level below the control module are the processing modules. If we want to know the details of the particular processing activities, then we can look at the processing modules.

When we are designing a program we also think in terms of levels. First we design the overall logic and code the control module. Then we concentrate on the details of each processing module. This modular design strategy helps us organize our thoughts so that we don't have to concentrate on too much detail at any one time.

A good way to see the levels and modules in a program is with a *module hierarchy diagram*. Such a diagram for the simple example that we have been using is shown in Figure 5-3. In a module hierarchy diagram, each module is represented by a box with the name of the module written inside. The boxes are organized in rows, with the highest level modules at the top and lower level modules farther down the diagram. The lines show how the modules are logically connected. In Figure 5-3, the control module is at the highest level and all processing modules are at the next level. The lines indicate that the control module causes the other modules to be performed. No lines connect the processing modules since they are not performed by each other. Notice that there must be one module at the top with no lines leading into it. This module is the main control module and is the only module that is not performed by some other module.

Figure 5-4 shows an example of a module hierarchy diagram for a more complex program. In this example the main control module performs four modules — an input module, a control module for process 1, a control module for process 2, and an output module. Notice that two of these lower level modules are used to control other processing modules. The control module for process 1 performs modules for processes A, B, and C. The control module for process 2 performs modules for processes B and D. Notice that the module for process B is used in two places. This shows one of the advantages of using modular programming; modules may be used at several places without rewriting them. However, a module must not be reused lower in the hierarchy on the same path as it appeared higher in the diagram. For example, in Figure 5-5, module B is used below itself. This is incorrect, since it implies that module B uses module B which in turn uses module B and so forth. In other words, this could go on without stopping.

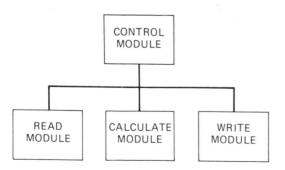

FIGURE 5-3. A Simple Module Hierarchy Diagram

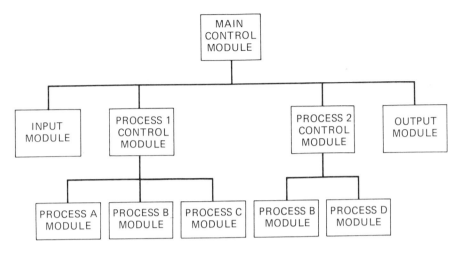

FIGURE 5-4. A Complex Module Hierarchy Diagram

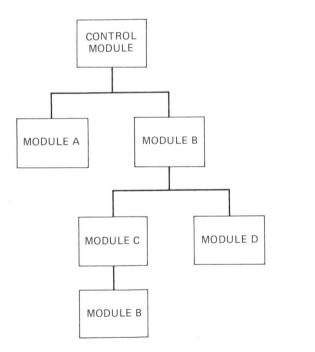

FIGURE 5-5. An Incorrect Module Hierarchy

Module hierarchy diagrams are very useful for planning and understanding a program. Sometimes these diagrams are called "trees"
because they resemble family trees. In the next section we will see
how modular programming is accomplished in COBOL.

5-2. THE PERFORM STATEMENT

Modules are formed in a COBOL program from a paragraph or a sequence of paragraphs. In order to execute the statements in a module from a control module, the PERFORM statement is used.

In the simplest case, one paragraph is used for a module. The module is identified by the name of the paragraph. The PERFORM statement necessary to execute the module consists of the reserved word PERFORM followed by the paragraph name. For example, assume that we have a paragraph named READ-INPUT. In the control module this paragraph would be performed by the statement:

```
PERFORM READ-INPUT.
```

In effect the PERFORM statement causes the computer to branch to the READ-INPUT paragraph. The statements in this paragraph are executed in the normal manner. When the last statement in the READ-INPUT paragraph is reached, the computer automatically branches back to the control module and continues with the next statement following the PERFORM statement. This sequence is illustrated in Figure 5-6.

Notice that the PERFORM statement has the *effect* of putting two GO TO statements in the program. The first GO TO statement causes the computer to branch to the paragraph; the second causes the computer to branch back to where it left off. However, all of

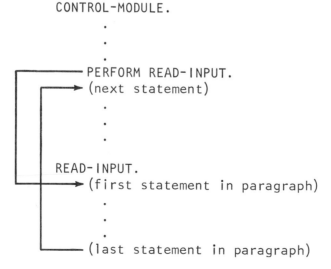

FIGURE 5-6. The Execution of the PERFORM Statement

this is handled automatically by the PERFORM statement; the programmer does *not* actually use GO TO statements.

Because of the way the PERFORM statement functions, a paragraph may be performed at several different points in a program. For example, after performing the READ-INPUT paragraph once, as in Figure 5-4, we may perform it again several steps farther on in the program. No matter where the PERFORM statement appears, the computer always comes back to that point after completing the execution of the indicated paragraph.

Usually a module consists of more than one paragraph. When this is the case we use another form of the PERFORM in which the first and last paragraphs in the module are named. The effect is to perform all paragraphs, beginning with the first paragraph in the module through the last paragraph in the module. For example, assume that a calculation module contained several paragraphs where the first paragraph is named CALCULATIONS-BEGIN and the last is called CALCULATIONS-END. In order to perform this module we use the statement:

```
PERFORM CALCULATIONS-BEGIN
    THRU CALCULATIONS-END.
```

The name of the first paragraph in the module comes after the word PERFORM. Following this is the word THRU (for "through") and then the name of the last paragraph in the module. When this PERFORM statement is executed, the computer branches to the first statement in the CALCULATIONS-BEGIN paragraph. Then the statements in this and the following paragraphs are executed. Finally, when the last statement in the paragraph named CALCULATIONS-END is reached, the computer branches back to the point in the control module where it left off. This is illustrated in Figure 5-7. Notice in this illustration that any paragraphs between the first and last in the module are executed along with the first and last paragraphs.

Within a module we can have any COBOL statements that are needed, including other PERFORM statements. We may have sequence, decision, and loop structures in various combinations to accomplish the necessary processing. Sometimes it is necessary to branch within the module. For example, we may have to use a GO TO statement to create a loop within the module or to branch to another part of the module if a particular condition exists. However, the program should *never* branch out of the module to another module. Besides being confusing, this practice may result in data being lost. The reason for this is that when a module is performed, certain control information available at the time is saved. This information must be saved so that it won't accidentally be destroyed during the execution of the

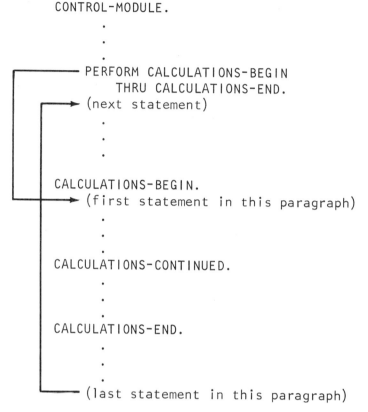

```
CONTROL-MODULE.
          .
          .
          .
      PERFORM CALCULATIONS-BEGIN
          THRU CALCULATIONS-END.
     (next statement)
          .
          .
          .

CALCULATIONS-BEGIN.
     (first statement in this paragraph)
          .
          .
          .

CALCULATIONS-CONTINUED.
          .
          .
          .

CALCULATIONS-END.
          .
          .
          .
     (last statement in this paragraph)
```

FIGURE 5-7. The Execution of the PERFORM Statement for Multiple Paragraphs

module. When the computer returns to the control module in the normal manner, this information is replaced and the processing continues normally. However, if the computer does not return to the control module normally (as, for example, when a GO TO statement is used to branch out of a module), this information is not replaced and, as a result, processing could be affected. The only way to guarantee that this critical information is restored is to execute the statements in the module up through the last statement. Only after the last statement is executed is the information replaced.

This restriction that we must go through the last statement in a module in order to guarantee proper processing can sometimes create problems. For example, during the execution of a module, a condition may occur that indicates that the program should not continue, but rather, should branch back to the control module. In order to guarantee proper processing we must branch instead to the last statement in the module. However, under such conditions we usually don't want to execute this last statement either.

In order to overcome this problem, we provide a "dummy" statement at the end of the module. This statement has no effect on processing but only serves as a point to branch to in a module so that we can exit from the module in the normal manner. The statement used for this purpose is simply the word EXIT. When used, this statement must appear as the only sentence in a paragraph. This paragraph would normally be the last paragraph in a module and would be named as the last paragraph in the PERFORM statement.

These ideas are illustrated in Figure 5-8. In this case, a module to compute some value consists of three paragraphs. The first, named COMPUTE-VALUE-BEGIN, does some form of calculation. The last paragraph, named COMPUTE-VALUE-END, consists only of the EXIT statement. In the paragraph named CV-CHECK, the value is checked to see if it is equal to zero. If it is, then the computer branches to the COMPUTE-VALUE-END paragraph and thus returns to the control module. If the condition in the IF statement is not true, some more processing is done before reaching the last paragraph in the module.

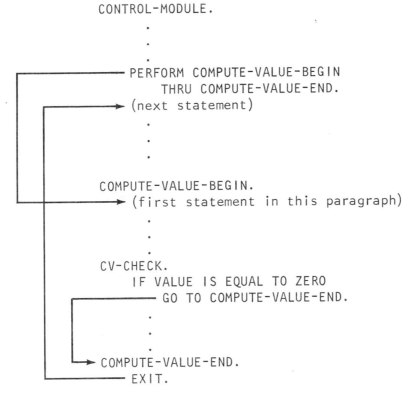

FIGURE 5-8. Performing a Module Containing an EXIT Statement

Even though an EXIT statement is not needed in a module, it is a good idea to have one. There are several reasons for this. For one, having a final paragraph with an EXIT statement clearly establishes the exit point in the module. As we said before, every module should have only one entry point and one exit point. The entry point is clearly marked by the first paragraph in the module. With an EXIT statement, the exit point is also clearly marked.

Another important reason for always using an EXIT statement is that it makes it easier to modify the program if necessary. For example, if we need to add another paragraph to the COMPUTE-VALUE module in Figure 5-8, we merely have to insert it before the COMPUTE-VALUE-END paragraph. It is not necessary to modify any other statements in the module or to modify the PERFORM statement in the control module.

The names used for the paragraphs in a module should represent the function of the module. Recall that each module should perform one function related to the overall purpose of the program. The module should have a name that identifies this function. For example, the module illustrated in Figure 5-8 has the name COMPUTE-VALUE.

To distinguish the paragraphs within a module, suffixes should be used. The first paragraph should have the suffix -BEGIN, while the last should have the suffix -END. This way it is very clear where the beginning and end of the module are located. The PERFORM statement is always of the form

```
PERFORM module-name-BEGIN
    THRU module-name-END.
```

The end paragraph, of course, always should contain just the EXIT statement.

Within a module, the paragraph names should use prefixes that relate to the name of the module. For example, in Figure 5-8 we use the prefix CV- for the paragraph in the COMPUTE-VALUE module. (Recall that we used this same idea for fields within records in the data division.)

When the conventions described here are followed, it is easy to understand the modular structure of the program. These ideas are illustrated in a complete program in the next section.

5-3. AN ILLUSTRATIVE PROGRAM

The sample program in Chapter 4 (Figure 4-5) may be rewritten in a modular fashion. This program calculates sales commissions and involves three processing functions — reading input, calculating commissions, and writing output. If we break the program up into three processing modules along these lines then we get the module hierarchy diagram shown in Figure 5-9. The READ-INPUT module reads an input record containing sales data. The CALCULATE-COMMISSION module uses the sales data to determine the salesperson's commission. Finally, the WRITE-OUTPUT module blanks out the output record, moves data to the output fields, and writes a single output line.

The control module performs the three processing modules in sequence in a loop. Each module is performed once for each input record. The control module also opens and closes the files and stops execution at the end of the run.

Figure 5-10 shows the procedure division for this version of the program. The control module and the three processing modules can be seen clearly in this listing of the program. Blank cards are used to separate the modules and to make the listing easier to read. The name of the first paragraph of each module, including the control module, uses the suffix -BEGIN. Similarly, the name of the last paragraph of each module has the suffix -END. Using this convention for all modules, including the control module, makes it easy to locate the beginning and end of each module.

The last paragraph of each processing module contains an EXIT statement. In the main control module, the last paragraph consists of a STOP RUN statement. By being consistent in these structural characteristics of the modules, the program is not only easier to understand but also easier to modify.

The statements necessary to perform the processing modules are all contained in the paragraph named MC-PROCESS-LOOP in the control module. (The prefix MC- in this paragraph's name is used to identify it as belonging to the MAIN-CONTROL module.) Each PERFORM statement names the first and last paragraphs in a module,

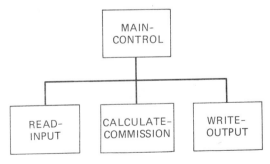

FIGURE 5-9. The Module Hierarchy Diagram for the Commission Calculating Program

```
PROCEDURE DIVISION.

MAIN-CONTROL-BEGIN.
    OPEN INPUT SALES-PERSON-FILE,
        OUTPUT REPORT-FILE.
MC-PROCESS-LOOP.
    PERFORM READ-INPUT-BEGIN
        THRU READ-INPUT-END.
    IF WK-EOF-FLAG IS EQUAL TO 'Y'
        CLOSE SALES-PERSON-FILE, REPORT-FILE
        GO TO MAIN-CONTROL-END.
    PERFORM CALCULATE-COMMISSION-BEGIN
        THRU CALCULATE-COMMISSION-END.
    PERFORM WRITE-OUTPUT-BEGIN
        THRU WRITE-OUTPUT-END.
    GO TO MC-PROCESS-LOOP.
MAIN-CONTROL-END.
    STOP RUN.


READ-INPUT-BEGIN.
    READ SALES-PERSON-FILE,
        AT END MOVE 'Y' TO WK-EOF-FLAG.
READ-INPUT-END.
    EXIT.


CALCULATE-COMMISSION-BEGIN.
    SUBTRACT SP-CURRENT-RETURNS FROM SP-CURRENT-SALES
        GIVING WK-NET-CURRENT-SALES.
    IF WK-NET-CURRENT-SALES IS LESS THAN 5000.00
        MULTIPLY WK-NET-CURRENT-SALES BY .075
            GIVING WK-COMMISSION
        ADD 100.00 TO WK-COMMISSION
    ELSE
        MULTIPLY WK-NET-CURRENT-SALES BY .10
            GIVING WK-COMMISSION
        ADD 150.00 TO WK-COMMISSION.
CALCULATE-COMMISSION-END.
    EXIT.


WRITE-OUTPUT-BEGIN.
    MOVE SPACES TO REPORT-RECORD.
    MOVE SP-NUMBER TO RT-NUMBER.
    MOVE SP-NAME TO RT-NAME.
    MOVE WK-NET-CURRENT-SALES TO RT-NET-CURRENT-SALES.
    MOVE WK-COMMISSION TO RT-COMMISSION.
    WRITE REPORT-RECORD.
WRITE-OUTPUT-END.
    EXIT.
```

FIGURE 5-10. The Procedure Division for the Modular Commission Calculating
Program

thus causing the computer to execute an entire processing module before returning to the control module. At the end of the MC-PROC-ESS-LOOP paragraph, a GO TO statement causes the computer to branch back to the beginning of the paragraph. Thus this paragraph is a loop that is repeated once for each input record.

In order to stop execution of the process loop in the control module after the last card has been read, a special field called a *flag* is used. A flag is a field that can take on different values depending on conditions that occur during processing. When the condition associated with the flag occurs, the flag is *set* to a special value. The flag then can be *tested* in other parts of the program to see if the condition has occurred. In a way, this field is used to "flag" a condition when it occurs. (Because of their function, flags are sometimes called *switches* or *signals*.)

In this program, a flag is needed to signal that the end of the input file has been reached. The field that is used as the end-of-file flag is called WK-EOF-FLAG and is defined in the WORKING-STORAGE section by a 77-level entry as follows:

```
77  WK-EOF-FLAG        PIC X       VALUE 'N'.
```

This field is a single alphanumeric character with an initial value of N. The N stands for "no," indicating that the condition that the flag is supposed to signal does not exist.

In the READ-INPUT module, the flag is "set," or "turned on," in the AT END phrase of the READ statement (see Figure 5–10). When the control record at the end of the input file is read, the MOVE statement in the AT END phrase is executed. This moves the value Y to the end-of-file flag, indicating that "yes," the end of the input file has been reached.

Within the control module, an IF statement tests to see if the flag's value is Y after each performance of the READ-INPUT module. Normally, the flag has the value N and processing continues sequentially through the statements in the loop. However, when the IF statement detects that the flag has been set to the value of Y, the statements within the IF statement are executed. These cause the computer to close the files and branch to the last paragraph in the control module. Since this paragraph contains the STOP RUN statement, execution of the program is terminated.

This program illustrates the basic ideas behind modular programming. Normally, such a short program is not written in this modular fashion, but rather, is coded in the manner illustrated in Chapter 4. However, most programs are not as brief as this one, and the modular approach becomes very useful. Very long programs have many modules with several levels in the module hierarchy. In subsequent chapters we will illustrate more complex modular programs.

5-4. LOOP CONTROL WITH THE PERFORM STATEMENT

So far, the only way that we have been able to create loop structures in a COBOL program is with a GO TO statement. Although this is a commonly used approach to looping, it is not always the best. The problem with using a GO TO statement for loops is that a person reading the program does not know that a group of statements is part of a loop until the GO TO statement at the end is reached. Ideally, when each structure in a program is read, it should be very clear whether the structure is a loop, a decision, or a sequence. But with the GO TO statement as the only loop control mechanism, what appears to be a sequence structure may turn out to be a loop.

In COBOL, loops also can be controlled by using special forms of the PERFORM statement. Often such loop structures are easier to understand than those created by a GO TO statement. In this section we examine one of these special forms of the PERFORM statement. We then discuss under what conditions it is best to use a GO TO statement or a PERFORM statement for loop control.

When using a PERFORM statement for looping, the statements that are included in the loop are coded as a separate module. However, no GO TO statement is used for loop control in the module. Instead, a special PERFORM statement is used that causes the computer to repeat the module over and over again as if it were a loop. In effect, the PERFORM statement tells the computer to repeatedly perform the module until a particular condition occurs. This repetition is completed before going on to the next statement in sequence following the PERFORM statement.

The condition that indicates when the repetition of the module should stop is included as an extra phrase at the end of the PERFORM statement. The condition follows the word UNTIL and may be any conditional expression of the type used in the IF statement. As an example, consider the following statement:

```
PERFORM MODULE-A-BEGIN
    THRU MODULE-A-END
    UNTIL X-AMOUNT IS GREATER THAN 10.
```

This statement instructs the computer to repeat MODULE-A until X-AMOUNT is greater than 10. If the condition is true before performing MODULE-A the first time, then the module is not performed at all and the computer goes on to the next statement in sequence. If the condition is not true, then the module is performed and the condition is checked again. This is repeated until the condition becomes true, at which time the computer continues on to the next statement.

We can use this form of the PERFORM statement to control the processing loop in the example in the previous section. The procedure division listing for this version of the program is shown in Figure 5-11. In this form of the program, all of the PERFORM statements for the processing modules are put in a special control module called PROCESS-LOOP. This module performs the READ-INPUT, CALCULATE-COMMISSION, and WRITE-OUTPUT modules in turn. A test of the end-of-file flag is made after each performance of the READ-INPUT module so that the other modules can be bypassed after the last input card has been read.

In the MAIN-CONTROL module, the computer is instructed to perform the PROCESS-LOOP module repeatedly until the end-of-file flag is equal to Y. First the files are opened, then the PROCESS-LOOP module is executed repeatedly until all input data have been read and processed, then the files are closed and execution is stopped.

This version of the program adds another level to the module hierarchy. This is shown in the diagram in Figure 5-12. With this example we can see the advantages and disadvantages of using the PERFORM statement for loop control. The main advantage is that all uses of the GO TO statement for loop control can be eliminated. This makes all loop structures readily apparent when reading through the program. The main disadvantage is that it may make the structure more difficult to understand than if a GO TO statement is used. The reason for this is that when the PERFORM statement is used for loop control, more levels in the module hierarchy are needed, and sometimes these new levels contain only a few PERFORM statements. This means that the programmer must read through many short modules before he or she can understand the detailed processing of the program. In other words, the program may be so highly modular that the programmer spends more time trying to understand the modular structure than would be necessary if the program contained a few more GO TO statements.

What we can conclude from this is that there must be some balance between the modularity of the program and the use of GO TO statements for looping. Probably the best approach is that if there are only a few statements in the loop, so that the entire processing sequence can be understood at a glance, a GO TO statement should be used for the loop. However, if there are many statements in the loop, then the loop should be modularized and a PERFORM statement used to control it. There is no definite cut-off as to the number that represents an easily comprehendable group of statements. However, a maximum of five to nine statements in a GO TO–controlled loop is reasonable.

```
PROCEDURE DIVISION.

MAIN-CONTROL-BEGIN.
    OPEN INPUT SALES-PERSON-FILE,
        OUTPUT REPORT-FILE.
    PERFORM PROCESS-LOOP-BEGIN
        THRU PROCESS-LOOP-END
        UNTIL WK-EOF-FLAG IS EQUAL TO 'Y'.
    CLOSE SALES-PERSON-FILE, REPORT-FILE.
MAIN-CONTROL-END.
    STOP RUN.

PROCESS-LOOP-BEGIN.
    PERFORM READ-INPUT-BEGIN
        THRU READ-INPUT-END.
    IF WK-EOF-FLAG IS EQUAL TO 'Y'
        GO TO PROCESS-LOOP-END.
    PERFORM CALCULATE-COMMISSION-BEGIN
        THRU CALCULATE-COMMISSION-END.
    PERFORM WRITE-OUTPUT-BEGIN
        THRU WRITE-OUTPUT-END.
PROCESS-LOOP-END.
    EXIT.

READ-INPUT-BEGIN.
    READ SALES-PERSON-FILE,
        AT END MOVE 'Y' TO WK-EOF-FLAG.
READ-INPUT-END.
    EXIT.

CALCULATE-COMMISSION-BEGIN.
    SUBTRACT SP-CURRENT-RETURNS FROM SP-CURRENT-SALES
        GIVING WK-NET-CURRENT-SALES.
    IF WK-NET-CURRENT-SALES IS LESS THAN 5000.00
        MULTIPLY WK-NET-CURRENT-SALES BY .075
            GIVING WK-COMMISSION
        ADD 100.00 TO WK-COMMISSION
    ELSE
        MULTIPLY WK-NET-CURRENT-SALES BY .10
            GIVING WK-COMMISSION
        ADD 150.00 TO WK-COMMISSION.
CALCULATE-COMMISSION-END.
    EXIT.

WRITE-OUTPUT-BEGIN.
    MOVE SPACES TO REPORT-RECORD.
    MOVE SP-NUMBER TO RT-NUMBER.
    MOVE SP-NAME TO RT-NAME.
    MOVE WK-NET-CURRENT-SALES TO RT-NET-CURRENT-SALES.
    MOVE WK-COMMISSION TO RT-COMMISSION.
    WRITE REPORT-RECORD.
WRITE-OUTPUT-END.
    EXIT.
```

FIGURE 5-11. The Procedure Division for the Modular Commission Calculating Program with Loop Control Using a PERFORM Statement

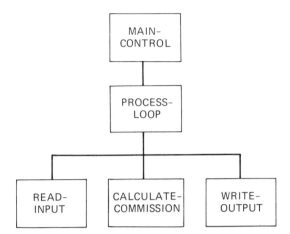

FIGURE 5-12. The Module Hierarchy Diagram for the Modified Commission
Calculating Program

5-5. MODULAR FLOWCHARTS

In Chapter 4 we discussed the program flowchart as a tool for representing the logic in a computer program. For programs that are *not*
designed in a modular fashion, one flowchart is drawn for the entire
procedure division of the program. However, when a modular design
is used, a separate flowchart is prepared for each module. The module
hierarchy diagram does not show the sequence in which the modules
are executed; it only shows how the modules are interconnected.
A *set* of flowcharts is needed for a modular program to depict the
logical flow from one module to another and within each module.

Figure 5-13 shows a set of flowcharts for the first modular program
discussed in this chapter (see Figures 5-9 and 5-10). The main control
module (Figure 5-13 (a)) performs three processing modules in sequence within a loop. Processing is stopped when the end-of-file flag
is equal to Y. To show that a module is to be performed at a point
in the flow logic, a *striped symbol* is used in Figure 5-13 (a). This is
formed by drawing a horizontal line near the top of the appropriate
symbol and writing the name of the module to be performed above
the line. Below the line may be written other explanations of the
processing of the module.

A striped symbol indicates that a module is to be performed at
that point in the logical flow. For each striped symbol there must
be a flowchart for the module that is to be performed. Figures 5-13
(b), 5-13 (c), and 5-13 (d) show the flowcharts of the processing
modules for the sample program. The terminal point symbol at the
beginning of each module's flowchart contains the name of the module.
For the exit point, a terminal symbol is used with the word EXIT or

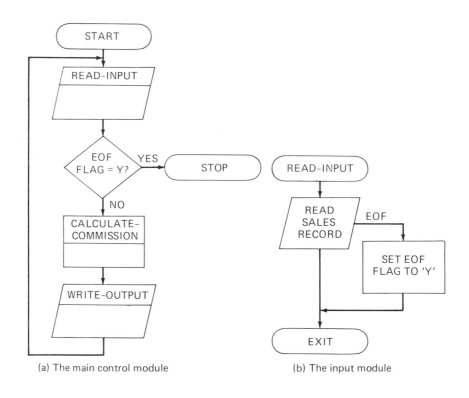

(a) The main control module

(b) The input module

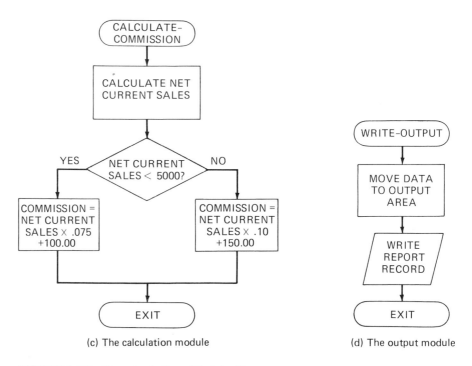

(c) The calculation module

(d) The output module

FIGURE 5-13. Flowcharts for a Modular Program

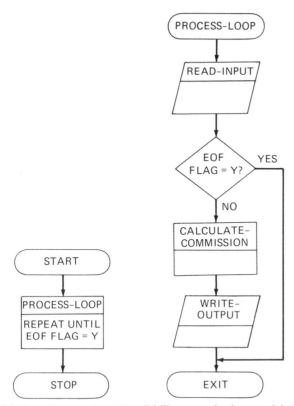

(a) The main control module   (b) The processing loop module

FIGURE 5-14. Flowcharts for the Modified Modular Program

RETURN. Between the entry and exit points standard flowchart symbols are used to display the module's logic.

In the second sample program in this chapter, the main control module is modified so that the processing loop is performed in a separate module (see Figures 5-11 and 5-12). Figure 5-14 shows the flowcharts for the main control and processing loop modules of this program. The processing modules are the same as in Figures 5-13 (b), 5-13 (c), and 5-13 (d). Notice that in Figure 5-14 (a) the main control module consists of only one operation. This involves repeatedly performing the processing loop module until the end-of-file flag is equal to Y.

When a programmer develops a modular program, he or she first determines what functions need to be performed by the program. Each function becomes a module in the program. A module hierarchy diagram is drawn to show the relationship between the modules. Next a program flowchart is prepared for each module in the program. The flowcharts show the processing logic within the modules. The programmer can then code each module directly from the flowchart.

CHAPTER 6

Data Structure

In Chapter 1 we discussed how data are organized into files, records, and fields. In Chapter 3 we saw how this organization was represented in a COBOL program's data division. In this chapter we expand these ideas and describe the general structure of the data processed in a COBOL program.

6-1. DATA ORGANIZATION

A unit of data that is processed in a COBOL program is called a *data item*, or simply an *item*. In Chapter 4 we used this term for fields defined in the WORKING-STORAGE section. These were called *independent items* and given the level number 77. A field that is defined as part of a record in the FILE section is also called an item. In fact, a record itself is considered to be an item.

In COBOL there are two general types of data items — group items and elementary items. A *group item* is one that is composed of other items; that is, a group item is subdivided into smaller items. For example, a record is a group item because it is made up of fields which, as we have said, are items. An *elementary item* is one that is *not* further subdivided. The fields within a record are examples of elementary items. An independent item is also a type of elementary item.

Only an elementary item may have a PICTURE clause in its description. A group item can never have a PICTURE clause associated with it. In fact, this is the way elementary items are distinguished from group items; the former always have PICTURE clauses while the latter never do.

Within a group item there must be one or more elementary items. A group item is described by the pictures of the elementary items that are contained in it. Within a group item there also may be other group items. That is, a large group item may be composed of smaller group items. These smaller group items may in turn be made up of even smaller group items or perhaps of elementary items. Eventually, of course, the smallest items in the group must be elementary items.

This organization of data into group items and elementary items implies that data can be structured in levels. At the highest level is the most all-inclusive group item. Below this are the smaller group items. These items are further broken down into other group or elementary items. At the lowest level are the elementary items of the structure. This organization is very much like the hierarchical structure of modules discussed in Chapter 5.

As an example of this hierarchical data structure, consider the sales data with the layout shown in Figure 6-1. This is the same layout as we have used before (Figure 1-9) except that some fields have been joined together to form group items. For example, the first 24 columns are a group item containing the salesperson's identification data. Within this item is another group item, containing the salesperson's code data and an elementary item for the salesperson's name. The salesperson's code group is further broken down into two elementary items — one for the salesperson's region and one for the person's number.

Notice that when group items appear in a record description they

IBM

INTERNATIONAL BUSINESS MACHINES CORPORATION

MULTIPLE-CARD LAYOUT FORM

GX24-6599-0
Printed in U.S.A.

Company __C & E PRODUCTS INC.__

Application __SALES ANALYSIS__ by __R. NICKERSON__ Date __10/14/76__ Job No. _____ Sheet No. __1__

SALESPERSON ID			CLS.	YEAR-TO-DATE		DATE	CURRENT MONTH		
CODE		NAME		SALES	RETURNS		SALES	RETURNS	
REGION	NUMBER		QUOTA COMM			MONTH YEAR			

FIGURE 6-1. The Record Layout for the Sales Data

must be composed of adjacent fields. Thus we can form a group item out of the year-to-date sales and returns fields and another out of the current month's sales and returns. However, we could not form a group item from the year-to-date sales and the current month's sales since these fields are not adjacent to each other.

Another way of representing the hierarchical structure of data is with a "tree" similar to the module hierarchy diagram of Chapter 5. Figure 6-2 shows this representation of the sales data. At the top of the diagram is the most all-inclusive item, the salesperson record. At the next level are the five group items of which the record is composed. These group items are further broken down into other group items or elementary items. The elementary items are never subdivided further and always lie at the end of a "path" down the "tree."

This diagram corresponds exactly with the record layout shown in Figure 6-1. Each group or elementary item is shown in its proper position in the data structure. Although the data hierarchy diagram does not contain information about field size and data types, it does help us to see the structure of the data to be processed in the program.

The data hierarchy diagram is also related to the way in which a record is specified in the COBOL program's data division. When the record description is coded in the program, each level in the hierarchy is given a different *level number*. For simplicity, we have only used level numbers 01 and 02 so far. However, a level number may be any number from 01 to 49. Records, at the top of the data hierarchy, are always given level number 01. In Figure 6-2 we show this to the left of the diagram. Each subsequent level is given a higher level number. The numbers always must be increasing as we go down the "tree," but we can skip numbers in the progression if we wish. In Figure 6-2 we indicate that all items of the second level are given level number 05. All items at the third level have level number 10. Finally, fourth level items are assigned level number 15.

In this example we have used the progression 01-05-10-15 to identify the levels in the data hierarchy. We could have used any other increasing progression such as 01-02-03-04. However, it is common practice to skip some numbers in the sequence. This way, if the requirements of the program change in the future, other levels may be inserted in the hierarchy without having to change the existing level numbers. For example, we could use level number 03 to form new group items in the hierarchy.

After the level numbers have been assigned, we can code the description of the item for the data division. Figure 6-3 shows the complete coding for the salesperson's record. Each item is given the level number corresponding to its level in the data hierarchy (Figure 6-2). The items are described in the order in which they appear in the record layout. Each group item is completely specified down to its elementary

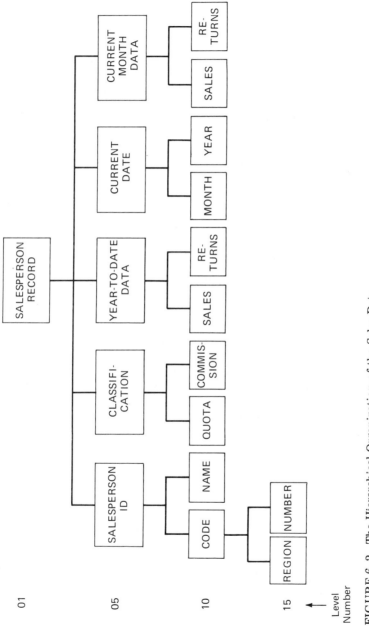

FIGURE 6-2. The Hierarchical Organization of the Sales Data

113

```
01   SALES-PERSON-RECORD.
     05   SP-SALES-PERSON-ID.
          10   SP-CODE.
                   15   SP-REGION          PIC XX.
                   15   SP-NUMBER          PIC XXXX.
          10   SP-NAME                      PIC X(18).
     05   SP-CLASSIFICATION.
          10   SP-QUOTA-CLASS              PIC X.
          10   SP-COMM-CLASS               PIC 9.
     05   SP-Y-T-D-DATA.
          10   SP-Y-T-D-SALES              PIC 9(6)V99.
          10   SP-Y-T-D-RETURNS            PIC 9(5)V99.
     05   SP-CURRENT-DATE.
          10   SP-CURRENT-MONTH            PIC 99.
          10   SP-CURRENT-YEAR             PIC 99.
     05   SP-CURRENT-MONTH-DATA.
          10   SP-CURRENT-SALES            PIC 9(5)V99.
          10   SP-CURRENT-RETURNS          PIC 9(4)V99.
     05   FILLER                           PIC X(22).
```

FIGURE 6-3. The Record Description for the Sales Data

items before going on to the next group item. As a matter of style, each level is indented to show its relationship to the other levels. A PICTURE clause must be included for each elementary item. The FILLER at the end of the description is necessary to account for all 80 columns of the card. It is an elementary item, but is logically at the same level as the second-level group items.

The concept of a hierarchial data structure is one of the basic ideas of COBOL. In the next few sections we will see how this idea relates to the way in which data is processed in the program.

6-2. DATA TYPES

Each data item specified in a COBOL program refers to one of several types of data. The data type associated with an item depends on the item's picture and on whether it is a group item or an elementary item. Although there are a number of data types, we are concerned only with the three most common ones. These are alphanumeric, numeric, and edited-numeric data.

As we saw in Chapter 1, alphanumeric data consists of any set of characters available to the computer. An alphanumeric item may contain any combination of alphabetic, numeric, or special characters. Numeric data consist only of numeric characters. Usually such data are processed by arithmetic or logical instructions in the program. Edited-numeric data consist of numeric characters, possibly with some editing characters such as commas and periods. Such data normally appear only in printed output records.

If an item is an *elementary item*, then the characters in its PICTURE clause determine its data type. Alphanumeric items must have pictures consisting of the character X (with perhaps a repetition factor). If the item is numeric then it may have 9s and Vs in its picture. A numeric-edited item may have 9s, Zs, decimal points, and commas in its PICTURE clause. (There are several other characters that may appear in the pictures of elementary items associated with each of these data types. Some of these will be explained in a later chapter.)

If an item is a *group item*, then it is considered to be alphanumeric. This is true no matter what pictures are specified for the elementary items in the group. For example, in Figure 6-3 the group item named SP-Y-T-D-DATA contains two elementary items, each with numeric pictures. If either of the two elementary items is used, it is considered numeric data. However, if the items are taken together as a group item then the data are considered alphanumeric. In effect, the picture of a group item consists of a number of Xs. The number is equal to the total count of character positions in the elementary items in the group. The picture of the SP-Y-T-D-DATA group item is in effect X(15).

When a VALUE clause is used for an item in the WORKING-STORAGE section, the literal in the clause must correspond with the item's data type. If the item is alphanumeric (including group items), then a nonnumeric literal must be used in any VALUE clause. (Recall that a nonnumeric literal consists of a series of characters enclosed in quotation marks.) Alternatively, the figurative constants ZEROS and SPACES may be used. For a numeric item, only numeric literals or the figurative constant ZEROS may be used in the VALUE clause. (A numeric literal may contain only numeric characters and perhaps a period and a plus or minus sign. It is not enclosed in quotation marks.) Normally, VALUE clauses are not used with edited-numeric items.

6-3. PROCESSING DIFFERENT TYPES OF DATA

The data type associated with an item often affects the processing that can be performed on the item. Some statements in COBOL cannot be executed using data of certain types. Other statements have different effects depending on what type of data is being processed. In this section we discuss some of the rules regarding data types and data processing statements.

In Chapter 4 we mentioned some of the restrictions on the type of data that can be processed by an arithmetic statement. Only numeric data items may be used in such a calculation. For example, in the statement

```
ADD A-FIELD TO B-FIELD
```

both A-FIELD and B-FIELD must be numeric. However, if the GIV-ING phrase is used, then the item named in the phrase may be either numeric or numeric-edited, provided the item is not used in another calculation. For example, in the statement

```
ADD A-FIELD, B-FIELD GIVING C-FIELD
```

the item named C-FIELD may be numeric or numeric-edited. If it is edited, it cannot be used in another calculation except as the item that receives the result. If a literal is used in an arithmetic statement, it also must be numeric. However, a literal never can be used in place of a data name for the result of the calculation. Group items may never be used in arithmetic statements because they always are considered alphanumeric.

In the relation condition of an IF statement, the items being compared should be of the same type. In other words, only numeric items should be compared with other numeric items and similarly for alphanumeric and numeric-edited items. (There are exceptions to this rule, but they are complex and generally should be avoided.) If a literal is compared with an item, the literal should be numeric if the item is numeric and nonnumeric if the item is alphanumeric or numeric-edited. A group item may be used in a relation condition, but it may be compared only with an alphanumeric item or another group item.

The most complex requirements regarding data types involve the MOVE statement. The data type of the sending and receiving items need not be the same. However, not all combinations are permissible. The rules are summarized in Figure 6-4.

A group item may be used as a sending or receiving item in a MOVE statement. This is one of the main reasons for specifying group items. Large groups of data may be moved with one instruction, while the elementary items in the group may be processed individually. We have used this principle in previous sample program to clear output records. For example, the statement

```
MOVE SPACES TO REPORT-RECORD
```

moves blanks into each position of the group item named REPORT-RECORD. Since a group item always is considered to be alphanumeric, the rules related to alphanumeric items in Figure 6-4 apply to group items.

Sending Item	Receiving Item		
	Alphanumeric	Numeric	Numeric-edited
Alphanumeric	Yes	No[1]	No[1]
Numeric	Yes[2]	Yes	Yes
Numeric-edited	Yes	No	No
ZEROS	Yes	Yes	Yes
SPACES	Yes	No	No
Numeric literal	Yes[2]	Yes	Yes
Non-numeric literal	Yes	No[1]	No[1]

Notes:
1. There are certain complex situations where these moves are permissible. However, they should be avoided.
2. These moves are permissible only if the numeric value is an integer (i.e. a whole number).

FIGURE 6-4. Permissible Moves

With the MOVE statement it also is important to understand how the lengths of the sending and receiving items affect the move. We first consider the case where the receiving item is alphanumeric. If the sending and receiving items in the MOVE statement are the same length, then the sending item is copied exactly into the receiving item. This is illustrated in Figure 6-5(a). If the sending item is *shorter* than the receiving item then the data are copied left-justified into the receiving item and the extra positions on the right are filled with blanks. Figure 6-5(b) illustrates this situation. If the sending item is *longer* than the receiving item then the data are copied from the left part of the sending item until the receiving item is filled. Additional characters in the sending item are not moved. We say that these characters are *truncated*. Figure 6-5(c) shows an example of this.

For the case where the receiving item is numeric, the data are moved so that the decimal points in the sending and receiving items

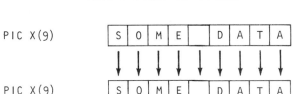

(a)   Sending and receiving items are the same length

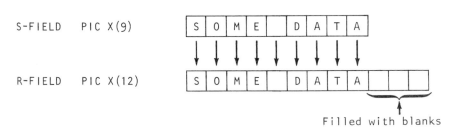

(b)   Sending item is shorter than receiving item

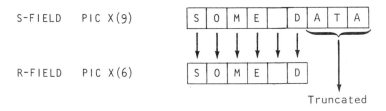

(c)   Sending item is longer than receiving item

FIGURE 6-5. The Effect of Item Length on the Move Operation with an Alpha-
         numeric Receiving Item

are aligned. If there are not enough positions to the right or left of
the decimal point in the receiving item, then the extra characters in
the sending item are truncated. If there are extra positions in the
receiving item to the right or left of the decimal point, they are filled
with zeros. When a decimal point position is not explicitly given for
the item, it is assumed to be immediately following the rightmost
character. The data then are moved according to these rules. A number
of examples of numeric moves are shown in Figure 6-6. If the receiving item is numeric-edited, then the move takes place in the same
manner as described for numeric items, except that the receiving item
is edited appropriately.

    We can see from this discussion that the rules for the MOVE state-
ment can be very complex when the lengths of the sending and receiving items are different. In general, it is best to avoid these

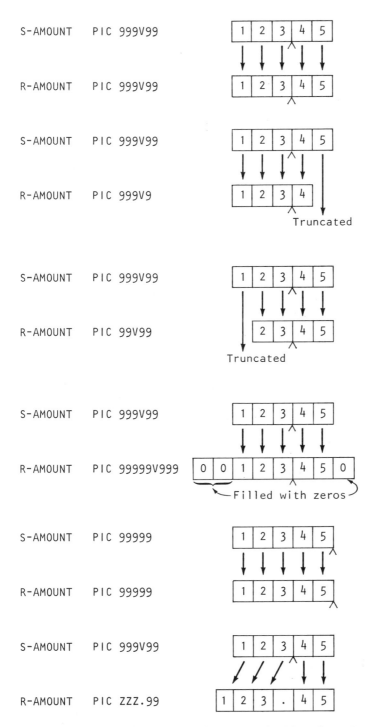

FIGURE 6-6. The Effect of Item Length on the Move Operation with a Numeric Receiving Item

complexities. If the sending and receiving items are alphanumeric, then they should be the same length. If they are numeric, then the number of places to the left and right of the decimal point should correspond. If the receiving item is numeric-edited, then the number of places allowed for numeric characters should be the same as the sending item.

6-4. PROCESSING INPUT AND OUTPUT RECORDS IN WORKING STORAGE

So far we have always given the description of the input and output records for a program in the FILE section of the data division. It also is possible to describe these records in the WORKING-STORAGE section. Figure 6-7 shows how this would be done for the last sample program in Chapter 5. With this approach, the complete descriptions of the input and output records appear in the WORKING-STORAGE section and not in the FILE section. In the FILE section, an 01-level entry must be included for the input or output record for each file. This entry must have an alphanumeric picture that gives the total length of the input or output record. The name of this record must be different from the name for the record used in the WORKING-STORAGE section. The name used in the FILE section must be the same as the name given in the DATA RECORD clause of the FD entry. All of these requirements are illustrated in Figure 6-7.

When this approach is used, input data is first read into the record specified in the FILE section and then moved to the record given in the WORKING-STORAGE section. For example, we can code these operations by the statements:

```
READ SALES-PERSON-FILE,
    AT END . . .
MOVE SALES-PERSON-DATA TO SALES-PERSON-RECORD.
```

For output we must do exactly the opposite of this. That is, first we move the data from the WORKING-STORAGE section to the FILE section. Then the output record is written. The following statements can be used for this:

```
MOVE REPORT-RECORD TO REPORT-DATA.
WRITE REPORT-DATA.
```

There are several advantages to this approach. One of the main advantages is that the VALUE clause may be used to give initial values to output fields described in the WORKING-STORAGE section. (Recall that the VALUE clause cannot be used in the FILE section.)

```
DATA DIVISION.
FILE SECTION.
FD  SALES-PERSON-FILE,
    LABEL RECORDS ARE OMITTED,
    RECORD CONTAINS 80 CHARACTERS,
    DATA RECORD IS SALES-PERSON-DATA.
01  SALES-PERSON-DATA            PIC X(80).
FD  REPORT-FILE,
    LABEL RECORDS ARE OMITTED,
    RECORD CONTAINS 132 CHARACTERS,
    DATA RECORD IS REPORT-DATA.
01  REPORT-DATA                  PIC X(132).
WORKING-STORAGE SECTION.
77  WK-NET-CURRENT-SALES         PIC 9(5)V99.
77  WK-COMMISSION                PIC 9(4)V99.
77  WK-EOF-FLAG                  PIC X          VALUE 'N'.
01  SALES-PERSON-RECORD.
    02  FILLER                   PIC XX.
    02  SP-NUMBER                PIC XXXX.
    02  SP-NAME                  PIC X(18).
    02  FILLER                   PIC X(21).
    02  SP-CURRENT-SALES         PIC 9(5)V99.
    02  SP-CURRENT-RETURNS       PIC 9(4)V99.
    02  FILLER                   PIC X(22).
01  REPORT-RECORD.
    02  FILLER                   PIC X(10)      VALUE SPACES.
    02  RT-NUMBER                PIC XXXX.
    02  FILLER                   PIC X(6)       VALUE SPACES.
    02  RT-NAME                  PIC X(18).
    02  FILLER                   PIC X(6)       VALUE SPACES.
    02  RT-NET-CURRENT-SALES     PIC ZZ,ZZZ.99.
    02  FILLER                   PIC X(6)       VALUE SPACES.
    02  RT-COMMISSION            PIC Z,ZZZ.99.
    02  FILLER                   PIC X(65)      VALUE SPACES.
```

FIGURE 6-7. The Data Division with Input and Output Records Described in
            Working Storage

In the next chapter we will see how this can be used for specifying
headings and other descriptive output. We also can use this to blank
out the intermediate fields in an output record. This is done by adding
the clause

```
VALUE SPACES
```

to the description of each FILLER in the output record. Figure 6-7
shows an example of this for the REPORT-RECORD. Since these
fields are initialized to blanks, it is not necessary to move SPACES
to REPORT-RECORD in the procedure division. This is one less thing
for the programmer to worry about and saves some processing time.

Another advantage of describing input and output records in WORKING-STORAGE is that it makes it easier to process multiple records. Often within an input file there are several different types of records. In the examples that we have been using so far this has not been the case; each input record contained the same type of data. However, this is not always the case. For example, we can design the sales data so that there are two input records for each salesperson. The first contains master data such as the salesperson's identification data and the year-to-date figures. The second record has the current sales data. In this situation we describe two input records in the WORK-ING-STORAGE section and use two READ/MOVE combinations to read all of the data for a salesperson. This is illustrated in Figure 6-8.

For output there are similar situations. Often there are several different types of output records. For example, there may be heading lines, detail lines, and total lines, all with different layouts. All of these are described in WORKING-STORAGE. Each is moved to the FILE section just before it is to be printed.

Because of these advantages of describing input and output records in the WORKING-STORAGE section, special forms of the READ and WRITE statements are included in COBOL to facilitate this type of processing. A single statement may be used to read an input record and move it to WORKING-STORAGE. This statement is a READ statement with the addition of the word INTO followed by the name of the record in WORKING-STORAGE. For example, the READ/-MOVE combinations in Figure 6-8 may be replaced by the following:

```
READ SALES-PERSON-FILE INTO SALES-PERSON-MASTER-RECORD,
    AT END . . .
READ SALES-PERSON-FILE INTO SALES-PERSON-CURRENT-RECORD,
    AT END . . .
```

The effect of these statements is exactly the same as the combinations used in Figure 6-8. In other words, the READ/INTO statement is equivalent to a READ statement followed by a MOVE statement.

To write a record described in WORKING-STORAGE, the WRITE/-FROM statement is used. This statement is the same as a WRITE statement with the addition of the word FROM and the name of the output record in WORKING-STORAGE. For example, the RE-PORT-RECORD described in Figure 6-7 may be written using the statement:

```
WRITE REPORT-DATA FROM REPORT-RECORD.
```

In effect, the WRITE/FROM statement is equivalent to a MOVE statement followed by a WRITE statement.

When records are described in the WORKING-STORAGE section

```
DATA DIVISION.
FILE SECTION.
FD  SALES-PERSON-FILE,
        .
        .
        .
01  SALES-PERSON-DATA          PIC X(80).
        .
        .
        .
WORKING-STORAGE SECTION.
        .
        .
        .
01  SALES-PERSON-MASTER-RECORD.
        .
        .
        .
01  SALES-PERSON-CURRENT-RECORD.
        .
        .
        .
PROCEDURE DIVISION.
        .
        .
        .
    READ SALES-PERSON-FILE,
        AT END . . .
    MOVE SALES-PERSON-DATA TO SALES-PERSON-MASTER-RECORD.
    READ SALES-PERSON-FILE,
        AT END . . .
    MOVE SALES-PERSON-DATA TO SALES-PERSON-CURRENT-RECORD.
        .
        .
        .
```

FIGURE 6-8. Processing Multiple Input Records

as in these examples it usually is required that they come after all 77-level items. ANS COBOL does not make this requirement, but most implementations of COBOL do (see Appendix A for details).

Because of the advantages of the READ/INTO and WRITE/FROM statements, they will be used for all examples in the remainder of the book. In the next chapter we will discuss a complete program that includes these statements.

CHAPTER 7

Report Output

One of the most common uses of computers is to prepare printed reports summarizing information related to the operation of an organization. All of the sample programs that we have discussed in previous chapters demonstrate this type of processing. In this chapter we explain additional details associated with preparing report output. These include COBOL elements necessary to space output lines, to control form movement, and to print headings.

7-1. SPACING PRINTED OUTPUT

When the WRITE statement illustrated in previous chapters is used, the computer prints each output record after advancing the paper in the printer one line. As a result, the printed output is single spaced. However, often we want to double or triple space the output. To double space the output we must instruct the computer to print the output record after advancing the paper two lines. Similarly, for triple-spaced output the computer prints after moving the paper up three lines.

In order to instruct the computer to advance the paper, we use the AFTER ADVANCING phrase in the WRITE statement. For example, to instruct the computer to double space the output we may use the statement:

```
WRITE REPORT-DATA FROM REPORT-RECORD
    AFTER ADVANCING 2 LINES.
```

In this statement the computer is told to print the output record after moving the paper up two lines from its current position. Notice that the AFTER ADVANCING phrase is part of the WRITE statement. Thus, the period that terminates the sentence comes after this phrase.

Within the AFTER ADVANCING phrase we may use any integer (whole number) from zero to some maximum number determined by the version of COBOL being used. (A common limit is 100. See Appendix A for details.) If zero is used the paper is not advanced before printing the line. This may be used to "overprint"; that is, to print new data on top of existing output. This is sometimes used to make patterns or graphs.

If the phrase

```
AFTER ADVANCING 1 LINES
```

is used then the effect is the same as without the AFTER ADVANCING phrase; the output is single spaced. Notice that the plural LINES is used and not LINE. Most versions of COBOL do not allow the singular form (see Appendix A for differences). In all versions, however, the word LINES (or LINE) may be left out completely.

We also may use a data name in the AFTER ADVANCING phrase. This name must be numeric and have a nonnegative integer value. For example, we might code:

```
WRITE REPORT-DATA FROM REPORT-RECORD
    AFTER ADVANCING SPACING-INDICATOR LINES.
```

In this case, the current value of the data name SPACING-INDICATOR is used to determine the number of lines to be advanced. The advantage of this technique is that we can vary the value of the data name during the execution of the program and thus change the spacing of the output if we want.

When the AFTER ADVANCING phrase is used in a program, it is usually required that it be used with *all* WRITE statements in the program. Although this is not a requirement of ANS COBOL, most implementations of COBOL make this a rule. Therefore, if any type of spacing is required other than single spacing, the AFTER ADVANCING phrase should be included with all WRITE statements.

A further requirement that is made in most versions of COBOL is that, when the AFTER ADVANCING phrase is used, there must be an extra character position specified at the beginning of each output record. This character position must be described by a filler with an alphanumeric picture. That is, the first entry in the record description should be:

```
05  FILLER        PIC X.
```

This character position is in addition to the others in the output record, and, thus, the record length is increased by one. Since we have been using 132 character output records in previous examples, the record length now becomes 133 characters. The RECORD CONTAINS clause in the FD entry must be modified to reflect this new record length. It becomes:

```
RECORD CONTAINS 133 CHARACTERS
```

This extra character position is not printed with the other characters in the output record. Printing actually begins with what is now the second character in the 133 position record. The purpose of the extra first position is to hold a character that tells the printer how to advance the paper. This character is put into the first position in the output record by the computer when the WRITE statement is executed. A different character is used for each type of advancing (i.e., single spacing, double spacing, etc.) and depends on what is specified in the AFTER ADVANCING phrase. When the output record reaches the printer, the first character is removed from the output record and is used to instruct the printer how to move the output paper.

This requirement for an extra character position in the output record is not specified in ANS COBOL and some versions of COBOL do not require it. However, since the most commonly used forms of COBOL do require an extra position we will use it in all examples. (Consult Appendix A for details on specific versions of COBOL.)

7-2. FORMS CONTROL

Most computer output paper consists of individual sheets of paper connected together along perforated top and bottom edges. This creates a continuous form that is moved through the printer. Figure 7-1 illustrates a continuous form output and the printer mechanism that controls it. This mechanism is called a *carriage* and is similar to a typewriter carriage. As the carriage rotates, the forms move up, exposing blank paper to the printing mechanism.

As we saw in the last section, the printer can be instructed to move

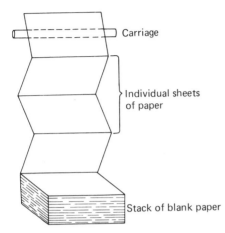

Carriage

Individual sheets of paper

Stack of blank paper

FIGURE 7-1. Continuous Form Output

up one, two, three, or more lines before printing an output record. This is accomplished by rotating the carriage the required number of lines. The printer also can be instructed to advance to the top of the next page. To control this type of advancing, a mechanism called a *forms-control tape* (or *carriage-control tape*) is usually used.

A forms-control tape is a piece of paper about an inch and a half wide and several feet in length. An example of part of a forms-control tape is shown in Figure 7-2. The tape is divided horizontally into lines that correspond with the possible print lines on an output form. These are numbered down the side of the form. Vertically the forms-control tape is divided into 12 *channels*. A rectangular hole may be punched in the tape at the intersection of any line and any channel. For example, in the tape shown in Figure 7-2, there is a punch in channel 1 at line 6 and a punch in channel 5 at line 17.

The tape is punched in channels that correspond with important lines in the output. Usually a channel 1 punch is used for the first printable line on the output page. That is, a channel 1 punch signifies the top of the page. Other channels are used to signify other lines in the output. For example, a channel 5 punch might be used at the beginning of the main body of the output (with headings appearing above).

After the tape is punched, it is formed into a loop and the ends are glued. It then is inserted into a mechanism that rotates in unison with the carriage. (The round holes down the center of the tape are used by this mechanism to rotate the tape.) Part of this mechanism senses where the holes are punched in channels in the tape. The computer then can be instructed to advance the paper until a hole in a particular channel is found. For example, if we say "advance to channel

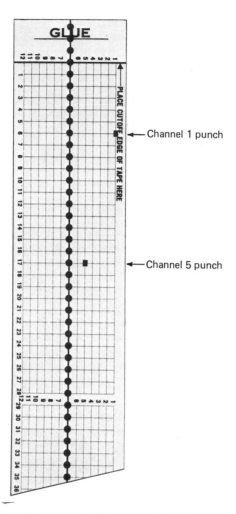

FIGURE 7-2. A Forms-Control Tape

1'' then we mean move the paper and forms-control tape in unison until a channel 1 punch is located in the forms-control tape. If the channel 1 punch corresponds with the top of the page then the effect of this instruction is to advance the forms to the top of the next page. Similarly, "advancing to channel 5" means move the paper and forms-control tape until a channel 5 punch is sensed.

In COBOL we tell the computer how we want the paper advanced with the AFTER ADVANCING phrase in the WRITE statement. To do this we first must assign a name to the various channel punches in the forms-control tape. This is accomplished in the SPECIAL-NAMES paragraph which appears in the CONFIGURATION section of the environment division. Each channel punch has a preassigned name that stands for it. Although there is no standard for these names, many computers use C01 for channel 1, C02 for channel 2, and so forth (see Appendix A for differences). In the SPECIAL-NAMES paragraph, we relate the appropriate channel name with a programmer-supplied name that can be used in the procedure division. We include a separate clause for each channel name that is used. For example, the following paragraph assigns names to the channel 1 punch and channel 5 punch:

```
SPECIAL-NAMES.
    C01 IS TO-TOP-OF-PAGE
    C05 IS TO-CHANNEL-5.
```

(Notice that a period only appears at the end of the entry, not at the end of each clause.) Names must be assigned only to channel punches that are actually punched. The programmer must know what forms-control tape is being used when his or her program is run and must code the SPECIAL-NAMES paragraph accordingly.

In the AFTER ADVANCING phrase of the WRITE statement, the special names associated with the channel punches may be used. For example, to advance the paper to the top of the page (channel 1) before writing the output we may use the statement:

```
WRITE REPORT-DATA FROM REPORT-RECORD
    AFTER ADVANCING TO-TOP-OF-PAGE.
```

Since the name TO-TOP-OF-PAGE is assigned to the channel 1 punch in the SPECIAL-NAMES paragraph, this statement advances the paper until a channel 1 punch is sensed in the forms-control tape and then prints the output record. Similarly, the following statement can be used to write an output record after advancing to a channel 5 punch:

```
WRITE REPORT-DATA FROM REPORT-RECORD
    AFTER ADVANCING TO-CHANNEL-5.
```

Notice that the names that are assigned in the SPECIAL-NAMES paragraph are selected so that they are understandable in the AFTER ADVANCING phrase.

7-3.   HEADINGS

In the programs that we have discussed in the previous chapters the output has consisted only of variable data. That is, the output fields were associated with data names in the program, and the values that were printed depended on the input and on the processing in the program. We also want to be able to print constant data; that is, data that do not change during processing. Usually this constant output takes the form of words and phrases that describe the variable output. For the reports that we have printed in the previous examples, such descriptive output usually consists of titles and headings for the columns of variable output data. In this section we discuss how heading output is coded in a COBOL program.

A heading is usually described in the WORKING-STORAGE section. The most common approach is to set up a complete output record for each line of heading output. We use an 01-level entry to give a name to the entire heading. Then we describe the heading with subordinate level entries using fillers instead of data names. For each entry there is a VALUE clause with either the figurative constant SPACES or a nonnumeric literal.

In Figure 7-3 we show how a simple heading line is described. In this case the heading consists only of the words COMMISSION REPORT beginning in print position 31. We use a VALUE clause with a nonnumeric literal to describe this part of the heading. To clear out the rest of the line we use VALUE clauses with the figurative constant SPACES. Since no variable data is printed on the line, data names are not needed and the word FILLER is used in each entry.

Notice that the entire record consists of 133 character positions. The extra position at the beginning is necessary for forms-control if the AFTER ADVANCING phrase is used. Actually, in this example, the first and second entries may be combined to read:

```
05 FILLER     PIC X(31) VALUE SPACES.
```

The fact that this puts a space in the first position is not important since the computer replaces the space with the appropriate character for advancing the paper.

With the heading coded in the WORKING-STORAGE we can use the WRITE/FROM statement to print the line. For example, we can code the following:

```
WRITE REPORT-DATA FROM HEADING-LINE
     AFTER ADVANCING TO-TOP-OF-PAGE.
```

```
01  HEADING-LINE.
    05  FILLER        PIC X.
    05  FILLER        PIC X(30)  VALUE SPACES.
    05  FILLER        PIC X(17)  VALUE 'COMMISSION REPORT'.
    05  FILLER        PIC X(85)  VALUE SPACES.
```

FIGURE 7-3. A Working Storage Description of a Heading Line

In this case the paper is advanced to the top of the page and then the heading line is printed.

Sometimes the heading to be printed is very long and cannot fit on one line in the WORKING-STORAGE section. When this happens, the heading can be broken into smaller pieces and a separate entry used for each piece. For example, if there is not enough room on the coding form for the heading in Figure 7-3, we can code two lines in the record description as follows:

```
05  FILLER        PIC X(11) VALUE 'COMMISSION '.
05  FILLER        PIC X(6)  VALUE 'REPORT'.
```

The result is the same either way.

Another approach that is used when the heading is very long is to continue the literal onto the next line of the coding form. As we have seen before, COBOL entries and sentences may be continued from one line to the next without any special consideration. However, when a nonnumeric literal is continued to another line, special coding is required. First, the literal must not be continued until the end of the line is reached. That is, we must fill out the line through column 72 before continuing to the next line. The literal is then continued on the next line starting anywhere in area B. To identify the beginning of the continued literal we must use a quotation mark, although there is no quotation mark at the end of the previous line. The rest of the literal is then coded. A final quotation mark must come at the end. Finally, we must put a hyphen in column 7 of the continued line.

As an example, consider the following entry:

```
    05  FILLER              PIC X(17) VALUE 'COMMIS
            'SION REPORT'.
```
column 7   column 72

Here we assume that in writing the literal we reached column 72 with the first S in the word COMMISSION. We then continued the literal on the next line with a hyphen in column 7 and a quotation mark to indicate the beginning of the next part of the literal.

These rules apply only to the continuation of nonnumeric literals. Numeric literals should not be split between lines. In general it is permissible to continue any entry or sentence to another line as long as the line is not broken in the middle of a word or numeric literal.

In the example of a heading line that we have shown in this section, no variable data is printed on the same line. However, it is permissible to have both variable and constant data on the same line. In such a case, any variable item is described with a data name and the appropriate picture in the record description. The constant data is specified using a FILLER and a VALUE clause as we have seen. An example of this situation is shown in Section 7-5.

7-4. LINE COUNTING

One of the problems associated with report output is what to do when the output takes more than one page. There is always a maximum number of lines that can be printed on a page. Usually this is between 50 and 60 lines. If there are more lines to be printed, then the report must be continued onto a new page. When printing reaches the end of a page most computers automatically skip to the top of the next page.

There are two problems with this automatic form of page advancing. One is that the headings are not automatically printed at the top of the page. Usually it is best to have the headings at the top of every page to make each page of output more readable. However, the program must include instructions for doing this. The second problem is that sometimes we do not want to print the maximum number of lines on each page. We may only want to print 30 or 40 lines on a page to allow for bigger margins and to make the output easier to read.

Because of these problems, we need some way of controlling the number of lines that are printed on each page. The most general technique that is used is to set up a special item to count the number of lines. Initially we assign the value zero to this item. Each time that a line is printed we add one to the item. Then we test to see if this item equals the number of lines that we wish to print. If it does, then we advance to the top of the next page, print the headings, and continue processing.

For example, assume that we have the following item described in the WORKING-STORAGE section:

```
77  WK-LINE-COUNTER              PIC 99.
```

As its name implies, this item is a line counter. At the beginning of each page it must be given an initial value of zero. We use a statement such as

```
MOVE ZERO TO WK-LINE-COUNTER
```

to accomplish this. Each time that a line is printed we add one to the line counter. This can be done with the following statement, which comes immediately after any WRITE statement:

```
ADD 1 TO WK-LINE-COUNTER.
```

With this form of the ADD statement the value one is added to the current value of the line counter each time that the statement is executed. At the beginning of the page WK-LINE-COUNTER is equal to zero. After the first line is printed, WK-LINE-COUNTER is increased to one. After the second line is printed it is equal to two. This continues for each line that is printed.

After each line is printed we must also test to see if the maximum number of lines for the page has been reached. The computer has no way of guessing this in advance, so we must make the test each time that the line counter is increased. For example, assume that we wish to print 40 lines on each page. Assume also that we have a module called WRITE-HEADINGS that contains all of the instructions necessary to advance to the top of the next page, print the headings, and reset the line counter to zero. Then the following IF statement can be used to test the line counter:

```
IF WK-LINE-COUNTER IS EQUAL TO 40
    PERFORM WRITE-HEADINGS-BEGIN
        THRU WRITE-HEADINGS-END.
```

In this statement, the line counter is tested to see if it is equal to 40. If it is, then the WRITE-HEADINGS module is performed. It is important that the line counter be reset to zero in the WRITE-HEADINGS module since a new page has been started and line counting must begin again from the top of the page. If the line counter is not equal to 40, then the PERFORM statement is bypassed.

Sometimes it is better to test if the line counter is *greater* than some value rather than equal to a value. The reason is that a problem arises with an equality test when the number of lines added may vary. For example, if we are at line 39 and for some reason we add two lines rather than one, the line counter will skip over 40 to 41. If we had tested the line counter for a value equal to 40 then the end of the page would not be detected. However, if the test were for a value greater than 39, then it would work in all cases.

Line counting is an important technique in programming for report output. Besides its use in controlling the number of lines printed on a page, it also can be used to control the placement of other sections of the output. For example, if a special part of the output is to begin at line 17, we can check the line counter for this line and perform the necessary output when it is reached. This often is used instead of a forms-control tape for this type of control.

7-5.   AN ILLUSTRATIVE PROGRAM

In Chapter 1 we showed the output of a sample program that included heading lines, detail lines, and a total line (see Figure 1-3). In this section we discuss the program that produces this output.

The purpose of the program is to calculate the new year-to-date sales and the new year-to-date returns for each salesperson. The new figures are found by adding the old year-to-date sales and returns to the current month's data. In addition, the new year-to-date net sales is computed by subtracting the new returns from the new sales. These calculations are performed for each salesperson, and a detail line is printed with the results.

We also need to calculate the total new year-to-date sales, returns, and net. These totals are found by accumulating the data as the new figures for each salesperson are calculated. There must be a field for each total, with an initial value of zero. Each time that a salesperson record is processed, the new sales, returns, and net are added to the totaling fields. In this way, the totals are accumulated until after the last record is processed when they can be printed.

In addition to printing the detail lines and the total lines, the program must print headings at the top of each page. (The layout of the report is shown in the print chart in Figure 1-10.) We want to print 40 detail lines per page, so we need a line counter.

To design the modular organization of the program, we first notice that there are three basic activities that must be performed — the headings must be printed, the detail part of the output must be produced, and the total output must be printed. Thus, we can start by dividing the program into a control module and three basic processing modules, as shown in Figure 7-4.

The WRITE-HEADINGS and WRITE-TOTALS modules do not need further subdivision. However, the DETAIL-PROCESS-LOOP module includes many activities. For each detail line printed we first must read an input record and then perform the necessary calculations using the input data. Thus, at a minimum we need three modules — one to read an input record; one to perform the calculations, including accumulating totals; and one to write an output record. However, since we are using a line counter, we need a fourth module to check the counter each time an output record is written. This module performs the WRITE-HEADINGS module if the line counter is equal to

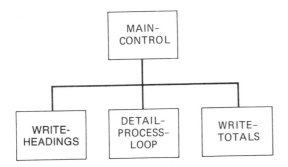

FIGURE 7-4. The First Level in the Modular Organization of the Sample Program

40. Adding these processing modules we get the module hierarchy diagram shown in Figure 7-5.

The complete listing of the sample program is shown in Figure 7-6. There are a number of things to notice in this program. First, in the CONFIGURATION section of the environment division we use the SPECIAL-NAMES paragraph to assign a name to the channel 1 punch on the forms control tape. We use this name in the AFTER ADVANCING phrase of the WRITE statement.

In the data division we describe all input and output records in

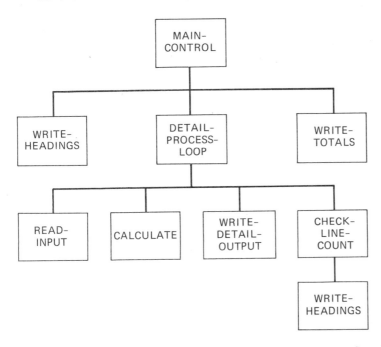

FIGURE 7-5. The Complete Module Hierarchy Diagram for the Sample Program

the WORKING-STORAGE section. The FILE section is used only for simple input and output records. Notice that the output record is 133 characters instead of 132 since the AFTER ADVANCING phrase is used. This is reflected not only in the PICTURE clause for this record, but also in the RECORD CONTAINS clause.

In the WORKING-STORAGE section a number of working items are defined. These include items for the new year-to-date sales, returns, and net. There are also three items for the total sales, total returns, and total net. Notice that these three items have initial values of zero, since they are used to accumulate totals. There is also a flag for the end-of-file condition and a line counter.

Besides the input record, there are three heading lines, a detail line, and a total line described in WORKING-STORAGE. All of the output records use the clause VALUE SPACES to blank out unused parts of the line. Notice how the nonnumeric literals are continued in the heading lines. In the total line we have both constant and variable data. The constant data is the word TOTALS. The variable data consists of the three totals to be printed. All of these are specified in the record description.

The procedure division is organized in the modular structure shown in Figure 7–5. It is suggested that the reader compare each module in the program listing with the module hierarchy diagram. In this way the structure of the program can be understood most easily.

In the WRITE-HEADINGS module the three heading lines are written after advancing to the top of the next page. After the third heading line is printed, it is necessary to print a blank line so that there is a double space before the first detail line. This is accomplished by moving SPACES to the REPORT-DATA record and then printing the record after advancing one line. When the first detail line is written, the printer advances another line (see the WRITE-DETAIL-OUTPUT module). Thus, there is double spacing between the last heading line and the first detail line. Finally, the line counter is set to zero in the WRITE-HEADINGS module.

The new data for the salesperson is calculated in the CALCULATE module. This data is also added to the total fields in this module. If this were not done at this time, the data would be destroyed when the next record is processed and totals could not be calculated. Thus, it is necessary to accumulate the totals as the records are processed.

The line count is checked each time that a record is written. In the WRITE-DETAIL-OUTPUT module, the value 1 is added to the line counter after the output record is written. Then the CHECK-LINE-COUNT module is performed. Since 40 detail lines are to be printed on each page, the line counter is tested to see if it is equal to 40. If it is, the WRITE-HEADINGS module is performed.

This program illustrates many of the basic elements of COBOL discussed in the first part of this book. In addition, it demonstrates a number of fundamental programming techniques. It is important that these elements and techniques be understood thoroughly before going on. In the next chapter we discuss the programming process in detail. Then, in Part III, we present many advanced elements and programming techniques used in COBOL.

```
IDENTIFICATION DIVISION.
PROGRAM-ID. SLS04.

ENVIRONMENT DIVISION.
CONFIGURATION SECTION.
SOURCE-COMPUTER. XYZ-1.
OBJECT-COMPUTER. XYZ-1.
SPECIAL-NAMES.
    C01 IS TO-TOP-OF-PAGE.
INPUT-OUTPUT SECTION.
FILE-CONTROL.
    SELECT SALES-PERSON-FILE
        ASSIGN TO CARD-READER.
    SELECT REPORT-FILE
        ASSIGN TO PRINTER.

DATA DIVISION.
FILE SECTION.
FD  SALES-PERSON-FILE,
    LABEL RECORDS ARE OMITTED,
    RECORD CONTAINS 80 CHARACTERS,
    DATA RECORD IS SALES-PERSON-DATA.
01  SALES-PERSON-DATA           PIC X(80).
FD  REPORT-FILE,
    LABEL RECORDS ARE OMITTED,
    RECORD CONTAINS 133 CHARACTERS,
    DATA RECORD IS REPORT-DATA.
01  REPORT-DATA                 PIC X(133).
WORKING-STORAGE SECTION.
77  WK-NEW-YTD-SALES            PIC 9(6)V99.
77  WK-NEW-YTD-RETURNS          PIC 9(5)V99.
77  WK-NEW-YTD-NET              PIC 9(6)V99.
77  WK-TOTAL-SALES              PIC 9(7)V99    VALUE ZERO.
77  WK-TOTAL-RETURNS            PIC 9(6)V99    VALUE ZERO.
77  WK-TOTAL-NET                PIC 9(7)V99    VALUE ZERO.
77  WK-EOF-FLAG                 PIC X          VALUE 'N'.
77  WK-LINE-COUNTER             PIC 99.
```

FIGURE 7-6. The Sample Program Source Listing (Part 1 of 4)

```
01   SALES-PERSON-RECORD.
     05   FILLER                          PIC XX.
     05   SP-NUMBER                       PIC XXXX.
     05   SP-NAME                         PIC X(18).
     05   FILLER                          PIC XX.
     05   SP-Y-T-D-SALES                  PIC 9(6)V99.
     05   SP-Y-T-D-RETURNS                PIC 9(5)V99.
     05   FILLER                          PIC XXXX.
     05   SP-CURRENT-SALES                PIC 9(5)V99.
     05   SP-CURRENT-RETURNS              PIC 9(4)V99.
     05   FILLER                          PIC X(22).
01   HEADING-LINE-1.
     05   FILLER                          PIC X(31)      VALUE SPACES.
     05   FILLER                          PIC X(25)      VALUE 'YEAR-TO-
-            'DATE SALES REPORT'.
     05   FILLER                          PIC X(77)      VALUE SPACES.
01   HEADING-LINE-2.
     05   FILLER                          PIC X(6)       VALUE SPACES.
     05   FILLER                          PIC X(27)      VALUE 'SALESPER
-            'SON       SALESPERSON'.
     05   FILLER                          PIC X(100)     VALUE SPACES.
01   HEADING-LINE-3.
     05   FILLER                          PIC X(8)       VALUE SPACES.
     05   FILLER                          PIC X(21)      VALUE 'NUMBER
-            '         NAME'.
     05   FILLER                          PIC X(16)      VALUE SPACES.
     05   FILLER                          PIC X(20)      VALUE 'SALES
-            '       RETURNS'.
     05   FILLER                          PIC X(10)      VALUE SPACES.
     05   FILLER                          PIC X(3)       VALUE 'NET'.
     05   FILLER                          PIC X(55)      VALUE SPACES.
01   DETAIL-LINE.
     05   FILLER                          PIC X(9)       VALUE SPACES.
     05   DL-NUMBER                       PIC XXXX.
     05   FILLER                          PIC X(6)       VALUE SPACES.
     05   DL-NAME                         PIC X(18).
     05   FILLER                          PIC X(5)       VALUE SPACES.
     05   DL-NEW-YTD-SALES                PIC ZZZ,ZZZ.99.
     05   FILLER                          PIC X(5)       VALUE SPACES.
     05   DL-NEW-YTD-RETURNS              PIC ZZ,ZZZ.99.
     05   FILLER                          PIC X(5)       VALUE SPACES.
     05   DL-NEW-YTD-NET                  PIC ZZZ,ZZZ.99.
     05   FILLER                          PIC X(52)      VALUE SPACES.
01   TOTAL-LINE.
     05   FILLER                          PIC X(33)      VALUE SPACES.
     05   FILLER                          PIC X(7)       VALUE
                                                         'TOTALS '.
     05   TL-TOTAL-SALES                  PIC Z,ZZZ,ZZZ.99.
     05   FILLER                          PIC XXXX       VALUE SPACES.
     05   TL-TOTAL-RETURNS                PIC ZZZ,ZZZ.99.
     05   FILLER                          PIC XXX        VALUE SPACES.
     05   TL-TOTAL-NET                    PIC Z,ZZZ,ZZZ.99.
     05   FILLER                          PIC X(52)      VALUE SPACES.
```

FIGURE 7-6. (Part 2 of 4)

```
PROCEDURE DIVISION.

MAIN-CONTROL-BEGIN.
    OPEN INPUT SALES-PERSON-FILE,
        OUTPUT REPORT-FILE.
    PERFORM WRITE-HEADINGS-BEGIN
        THRU WRITE-HEADINGS-END.
    PERFORM DETAIL-PROCESS-LOOP-BEGIN
        THRU DETAIL-PROCESS-LOOP-END
        UNTIL WK-EOF-FLAG IS EQUAL TO 'Y'.
    PERFORM WRITE-TOTALS-BEGIN
        THRU WRITE-TOTALS-END.
    CLOSE SALES-PERSON-FILE, REPORT-FILE.
MAIN-CONTROL-END.
    STOP RUN.

WRITE-HEADINGS-BEGIN.
    WRITE REPORT-DATA FROM HEADING-LINE-1
        AFTER ADVANCING TO-TOP-OF-PAGE.
    WRITE REPORT-DATA FROM HEADING-LINE-2
        AFTER ADVANCING 2 LINES.
    WRITE REPORT-DATA FROM HEADING-LINE-3
        AFTER ADVANCING 1 LINES.
    MOVE SPACES TO REPORT-DATA.
    WRITE REPORT-DATA
        AFTER ADVANCING 1 LINES.
    MOVE ZERO TO WK-LINE-COUNTER.
WRITE-HEADINGS-END.
    EXIT.

DETAIL-PROCESS-LOOP-BEGIN.
    PERFORM READ-INPUT-BEGIN
        THRU READ-INPUT-END.
    IF WK-EOF-FLAG IS EQUAL TO 'Y'
        GO TO DETAIL-PROCESS-LOOP-END.
    PERFORM CALCULATE-BEGIN
        THRU CALCULATE-END.
    PERFORM WRITE-DETAIL-OUTPUT-BEGIN
        THRU WRITE-DETAIL-OUTPUT-END.
    PERFORM CHECK-LINE-COUNT-BEGIN
        THRU CHECK-LINE-COUNT-END.
DETAIL-PROCESS-LOOP-END.
    EXIT.

WRITE-TOTALS-BEGIN.
    MOVE WK-TOTAL-SALES TO TL-TOTAL-SALES.
    MOVE WK-TOTAL-RETURNS TO TL-TOTAL-RETURNS.
    MOVE WK-TOTAL-NET TO TL-TOTAL-NET.
    WRITE REPORT-DATA FROM TOTAL-LINE
        AFTER ADVANCING 3 LINES.
WRITE-TOTALS-END.
    EXIT.
```

FIGURE 7-6. (Part 3 of 4)

```
READ-INPUT-BEGIN.
    READ SALES-PERSON-FILE INTO SALES-PERSON-RECORD
        AT END MOVE 'Y' TO WK-EOF-FLAG.
READ-INPUT-END.
    EXIT.


CALCULATE-BEGIN.
    ADD SP-CURRENT-SALES, SP-Y-T-D-SALES GIVING WK-NEW-YTD-SALES.
    ADD SP-CURRENT-RETURNS, SP-Y-T-D-RETURNS
        GIVING WK-NEW-YTD-RETURNS.
    SUBTRACT WK-NEW-YTD-RETURNS FROM WK-NEW-YTD-SALES
        GIVING WK-NEW-YTD-NET.
    ADD WK-NEW-YTD-SALES TO WK-TOTAL-SALES.
    ADD WK-NEW-YTD-RETURNS TO WK-TOTAL-RETURNS.
    ADD WK-NEW-YTD-NET TO WK-TOTAL-NET.
CALCULATE-END.
    EXIT.


WRITE-DETAIL-OUTPUT-BEGIN.
    MOVE SP-NUMBER TO DL-NUMBER.
    MOVE SP-NAME TO DL-NAME.
    MOVE WK-NEW-YTD-SALES TO DL-NEW-YTD-SALES.
    MOVE WK-NEW-YTD-RETURNS TO DL-NEW-YTD-RETURNS.
    MOVE WK-NEW-YTD-NET TO DL-NEW-YTD-NET.
    WRITE REPORT-DATA FROM DETAIL-LINE
        AFTER ADVANCING 1 LINES.
    ADD 1 TO WK-LINE-COUNTER.
WRITE-DETAIL-OUTPUT-END.
    EXIT.


CHECK-LINE-COUNT-BEGIN.
    IF WK-LINE-COUNTER IS EQUAL TO 40
        PERFORM WRITE-HEADINGS-BEGIN
            THRU WRITE-HEADINGS-END.
CHECK-LINE-COUNT-END.
    EXIT.
```

FIGURE 7-6. (Part 4 of 4)

CHAPTER 8

The Programming Process

At the end of Chapter 2 we briefly discussed the process of preparing a computer program. We mentioned five activities that make up the programming process. These activities are:

1. Understanding and defining the problem
2. Designing the program
3. Coding the program
4. Showing that the program is correct
5. Documenting the program

In this chapter we discuss each of these activities in detail.

The five activities in the programming process are not necessarily performed in sequence. In fact, several activities are usually taking place at the same time. For example, later we will see that documenting begins when we are trying to define and understand the problem. In addition, we can begin to show correctness of the program during the designing activity. The activities are listed not in the order in which they are *started*, but rather, in the order in which they are *finished*. For example, we cannot finish designing the program until we have finished understanding and defining the problem. However, we may have started the designing activity before the first activity is finished. Similarly, final coding cannot be completed until program design is done, showing that the program is correct cannot be finished until coding is completed, and documentation cannot be finalized until all other activities have been completed.

8-1. PROBLEM DEFINITION

The first activity in the programming process is to understand and carefully define the problem to be solved. The most difficult step often is recognizing that a problem exists for which a programmed solution is appropriate. However, it is usually not the programmer's responsibility to recognize the need for a program to solve a problem. Most often, the programmer receives a general statement of the problem, either verbally or in writing, and begins the programming process from that point.

At first the programmer should try to understand the problem as a whole. What is required by the problem? Usually this involves determining what output is to be produced. What data are available? Answering this question often involves determining what input data are to be processed. The programmer tries to get a general understanding of the problem as a whole without going into the details of the input and output layouts and the calculations.

In the preceding chapter we discussed a program that produces a year-to-date sales report. If we were just beginning to define that problem, we would start by determining that a program is needed to produce a report that lists the year-to-date sales, returns, and net for each salesperson and the totals for all salespeople. We would determine that the input available is the sales file.

After the programmer has a general understanding of the problem, he or she should refine the problem definition to include specific information about input and output layouts, calculations, and logical operations. For the year-to-date sales report we would obtain the input record layout (Figure 1-9) and the print chart for the report (Figure 1-10). We would determine what calculations are necessary to find the year-to-date sales, returns, and net.

The refinement of the problem definition should be continued until the programmer obtains sufficient detail to begin designing a solution. At the minimum, the problem definition must give the following:

1. What output is to be produced and its layout.
2. What input data is available and its layout.
3. What arithmetic calculations are to be performed.
4. What logical conditions affect processing.

Sometimes the programmer may have difficulty understanding a problem. When this happens, it often helps to try to isolate parts of the problem and to work with each part separately. Another approach is to think of a simpler but similar problem and to try to understand it first. The programmer may get some insight from the simpler problem that helps explain the more complex problem.

Some problems cannot be solved with a computer. In mathematics there are a number of problems that we know do not have solutions. In addition, some problems may be too large for a computer or may take too long to solve. Problems that cannot be solved do not often arise in business applications. However, we still must be careful in defining a problem to be sure that it is reasonable to attempt a programmed solution.

8-2. PROGRAM DESIGN

The objective of the program designing activity is to devise a plan for a program that solves the problem. This does not mean that the program is coded at this stage. Before coding is begun, a solution procedure should be devised. The procedure should, of course, be correct.

A procedure for solving a problem is called an *algorithm*. An algorithm is a set of instructions that, if carried out, results in the solution of a problem. Algorithms may be represented in many forms. For example, an algorithm may be written in English or using mathematical notation. A computer programming language also may be used to represent an algorithm.

During the program-designing activity, the first step is to select an algorithm that solves the problem. The second step is to decide how that algorithm is to be implemented on the computer. For example, the algorithm to produce a year-to-date sales report in the last chapter is fairly simple. It involves the following steps:

1. Print the headings.
2. For each salesperson:
   a. Read a sales record.
   b. Calculate new year-to-date sales, returns, and net and add the new figures to the totals.
   c. Print the data for the salesperson and increment the line counter.
   d. If the line counter equals 40, print the headings.
3. At the end, print the totals.

This is just one algorithm for this problem; there may be others. For any problem there are often several algorithms. The objective is to select the best algorithm that solves the problem. Which algorithm is "best" depends on tradeoffs between such factors as speed of execution, storage utilization, and algorithm understandability.

Sometimes it is difficult to devise an algorithm for a problem. When this happens, it often helps to think of a related problem and to try to develop an algorithm for it. Another approach is to simplify the problem by discarding some of the conditions; then try to develop an algorithm for the simpler version. Breaking the problem into parts and working with each part separately is also a good approach. Sometimes it is necessary to go back to the problem definition and to see if anything has been left out. Any of these approaches may help the programmer develop an algorithm for the problem.

After an algorithm is selected, the implementation of the algorithm for the computer must be devised. At this point, the structure of the data must be determined. Usually the input and output records are prescribed. However, the programmer must organize the working items. The development of the data structure is *not* independent of the development of the algorithm. As the algorithm is developed, the best way to organize the data must also be determined.

A flowchart may be used to help develop a computerized algorithm. The flowchart shows the processing logic in the algorithm. Often several flowcharts are drawn, so that different approaches can be compared.

If the program is to be designed in a modular fashion, two steps are involved. First, the general design of the program is prepared. This involves deciding what functions are to be performed by the program. Each function is then performed by a module. The result of this first step is a module hierarchy diagram. The second step in modular program design is to develop a detailed algorithm for each module. Here, a program flowchart is prepared that represents the processing logic in the module. Each module should have a single entry point and a single exit point and should perform one specific function in the program's logic.

One of the advantages of the modular approach is that, after the general design is prepared, the programmer need concentrate only on the detailed design of one module at a time. This greatly reduces the amount of program logic with which the programmer must be familiar at any one instant. Another advantage is that several programmers can work on different modules of the same program. Thus, the overall programming time may be reduced.

Modular design is a specific example of a more general technique known as *top-down program design.* (This is also called *stepwise program refinement.*) In top-down design, we start with the most general statement of the problem. For example, we may start with the statement:

Prepare a year-to-date sales report.

We then refine this statement by determining what things must be done to accomplish this. In this example we might come up with the following:

Produce the report headings.
Produce the detailed part of the report.
Produce the totals.

We then refine each of these statements in a similar manner. For example, the second statement might be refined to the following:

Read an input record.
Calculate new figures and totals.
Write a detail line.
Check the line counter.

We continue to refine these statements until we reach a point where we have a detailed design. The last step in top-down program refinement is to code the program.

We can see that top-down design leads naturally to a modular structure. However, it is not only for this reason that we use this approach. Top-down development allows us to think at different levels about how the problem should be solved. At each level we develop a more refined statement of how to solve the problem. This is one of the basic intellectual activities in program designing. As we will see in a later section, it is very much related to the activity of showing that the program is correct.

8-3. PROGRAM CODING — STRUCTURE AND STYLE

The objective during program coding is to produce a correctly coded program that is understandable. If the program has been properly designed, correctness follows by coding directly from the program flowcharts. Sometimes, during this activity, an error is discovered in the program's logic. When this happens the programmer must go back, correct the flowcharts, and, if necessary, correct the module hierarchy diagram. If a really serious error or misunderstanding is discovered, it may even be necessary to return to the problem definition and work forward again.

The most important thing, of course, is to produce a correct program. The program also should be as understandable and readable as possible. People other than the original programmer often look at the program. The programming manager may review the program to check for completeness and consistency with the problem definition and the programming standards of the organization. Other programmers may have to read the program to make corrections for errors that are not detected until after the program has been in use for a while. Modifications may be required because of changing requirements. For example, payroll programs have to be modified regularly because of changing tax structures. Sometimes it is decided to enhance the program so that it does more than was originally planned. In all of these situations, someone usually looks at the program several months or even years after it was originally coded. Even if the original programmer is given the task, he or she may have a difficult time remembering the program's logic unless it is clearly written out.

The basic problem in trying to understand a program is that there are really two versions of the program. One is a *static* version that is represented by the listing of the program on paper. The other is a *dynamic* form of the program that can only be understood by examining the logic that the program follows during execution. When a programmer reads a source listing, he or she is reading the static form of the program. As with a book, each statement is normally read in sequence from the top of the page down. The dynamic version may be different. For example, when a GO TO statement is encountered, the next statement in the dynamic version of the program (that is, the statement to which the program branches) is not the same as the next statement in the static version (which is the next statement in sequence). To understand the dynamic version, the programmer may have to jump all over the source listing instead of reading the program sequentially.

One of the basic principles of producing readable programs is to make the dynamic version of the program as close as possible to the static form. The program should execute from top to bottom just as it is read. The GO TO statement should be avoided unless in so doing the program's logic is even harder to understand. Generally, the GO TO statement should be used only to branch forward, down the program. A GO TO statement should *never* be used to branch from one module to another. Using simple structures like sequence, decision, and loop structures also helps make the program readable.

For modular programs, these principles apply within each module. A module should have only one entry and one exit point. Each module should be kept to a length that is read easily and can be understood in a few minutes. Usually this means that a module should be no longer than one page in the source listing (about 50 lines).

Following style conventions in coding can also help make the program more readable. We have mentioned a number of conventions in previous chapters. For example, selecting meaningful data names is important, and using prefixes to associate data names with records or to identify them as working items is helpful. Similarly, the naming conventions for the beginning and end of modules helps separate the parts of the procedure division.

Generally, each clause in an entry and each phrase in a statement should be coded on a separate line, although this is not necessary when the statement or entry is short enough to be written on one line. Words and numeric literals should not be split between lines. Indentation of subordinate statements, clauses, and phrases helps identify related parts of the program. All elements of the program that belong to the same logical group should be indented by the same amount. If modular programming is used, the procedure division should be organized with the main control module first, followed by the modules at the next level in the module hierarchy diagram, and so forth through the program. Blank lines should be left between modules.

Following the ideas on program structure and style presented in this section and in previous chapters helps make the program more readable and understandable. As a result, it is easier to correct errors in the program and to make modifications and enhancements to the program.

8-4. PROGRAM CORRECTNESS

In Chapter 2 we discussed the three types of errors that can occur in a program. These are compilation errors, execution errors, and logic errors. Compilation errors are detected by the computer during the compilation of the program. An error message is printed for each compilation error. To correct such errors, the programmer must interpret the error message and make appropriate changes in the source program. Usually compilation errors result from the misuse of the programming language. Since these errors are detected by the computer, they are usually easy to correct.

Execution errors occur during the execution of the program. The program must have no serious compilation errors in order to be executed. Therefore, any execution error is the result of some condition that can be detected only during execution. A common execution error is sometimes called a "data check" and usually results from incorrectly punched input data. For example, if a numeric input field is accidentally punched with an alphabetic character, then a "data check" error occurs if that field is used in an arithmetic calculation. When such an error is detected, the computer normally stops execution of the program and prints an error message. There are other types of execution errors, but, in all such errors, a message explaining the cause of the error is printed. It is the programmer's responsibility to interpret the error message and to make the necessary correction.

If the program compiles and executes without errors, it still may not be correct. Errors may exist in the logic of the program. These are the most difficult errors to detect. The usual approach is to make up some test data and to determine by hand what output is expected from the data. Then the program is run with the test data, and the actual output is compared with the expected output. If the outputs do not agree, then there is an error that must be located and corrected.

A testing procedure such as this only shows the *presence* of errors, not their *absence*. To show that a program is correct we must show that under all circumstances the program produces the correct result. To do this by using test data would require running the program with all possible combinations of data and comparing the output with the expected output calculated by hand. In addition to being an enormous task, this would be senseless, since then we would have all possible output calculated by hand and there would be no need for a program (except, perhaps, to check our hand calculations). Thus, we need some other way of showing that the program is logically correct.

It is sometimes possible to prove that a program is correct in a mathematical sense. However, this approach is usually too complex and tedious for the average programmer. However, we can informally "prove" a program's correctness by following a top-down design process. Recall that in this approach we start with a general statement of the problem and then refine this statement by determining what things must be done to accomplish it. At each "level" in the top-down design we refine the statements of the previous level until we reach the coded program. To show that a program is correct, we need to show that each refinement accomplishes the task specified at the previous level.

As an example, consider the problem:

Prepare a year-to-date sales report.

We assume that this is a correct definition of the problem and begin by refining it into the statements:

Produce the report headings.

Produce the detailed part of the report.

Produce the totals.

We can say that the program is correct at this level because we know that to produce the year-to-date sales report we only have to do the three things listed above. We then refine each of these three things separately and show that each refinement is a correct way of accomplishing the task that is being described. Thus we can refine the second statement to the following:

Read an input record.

Calculate new figures and totals.

Write a detail line.

Check the line counter.

Then the program is correct at this level. At some further level, we may refine the program by drawing a set of flowcharts. If everything is correct to this point, then the flowcharts are correct (assuming that we have not made an error in drawing the flowcharts). Finally, we code the program from the flowcharts, and, if there are no coding errors, the coded program is logically correct.

This method of showing program correctness through stepwise refinement is a very important part of programming. Most programmers do this even though they may not think they are "proving" that the program is correct. However, if this is done carefully and explicitly, then the chance of serious logic errors in the program is greatly reduced. Thus, the development of the program is the most important step in the programming process.

Even if a program is developed in the manner described here, logic errors may occur. Often small things are forgotten or a logical step in the development is passed over too quickly. Therefore, a thorough testing of the program should be performed to try to force out any hidden errors. The programmer should be merciless in his or her testing of the program. Some organizations have a different programmer do the testing so that the original programmer is not tempted to pass over possible weaknesses just to get the job done. The objective of program testing is to force errors to reveal themselves.

If the program is written in a modular fashion, then each module can be tested separately. Sometimes testing can begin on an incomplete program by inserting "dummy" modules for incomplete parts of the program. After the modules are tested separately the interaction between the modules can be tested. Pairs of modules can be tested, then three modules at a time, until finally the entire program is tested as a whole.

The first tests of the program should be simple, to make sure that the program works in the simplest cases. Obvious errors such as misspelling of headings or alignment of columns can be corrected at this point. Then more complex tests can be performed. Eventually, every statement in the program should be executed at least once using test data and the results compared with the expected output.

Special tests should be made with the first and last input records. Errors often occur when unusual conditions appear at the beginning or end of processing. Tests should be made to see what happens when there is too much or too little data. Fields that contain zeros and negative values should be included in the test data. Repeated and missing values also should be included. The maximum and minimum value for each field should be tested. All error conditions must be tested.

When an error is detected, it is necessary to locate the cause of the error in the program. Testing each module separately as suggested earlier helps isolate errors. Some versions of COBOL have special features that help locate logical errors. These are not features of standard ANS COBOL, but have been implemented in a number of versions.

One of these special debugging features provides a "trace" of the logical flow of the program during execution. The trace lists the number or name of each paragraph as it is executed. (Most compilers number the lines of the program in the source listing. The number corresponding to the line containing the paragraph name is printed when the trace feature is used with some computers. See Appendix A for differences.)

To start the trace feature, the statement

```
READY TRACE
```

is inserted at any point in the procedure division. When the statement is encountered during the execution of the program, the trace feature is turned "on." From that point on, the computer prints the number or name of each paragraph as it is executed, along with any other output. By following the trace in the output listing, the programmer usually can locate the paragraph that is being executed at the time that the error occurs. To turn off the trace feature, the statement

```
RESET TRACE
```

may be used.

Another special debugging feature that appears in some versions of COBOL is the EXHIBIT statement. This statement can be used to print the value of a data name without printing an entire record. The simplest form of the statement consists of the words EXHIBIT

NAMED followed by one or more data names. For example, the following statement prints the values of two working items:

```
EXHIBIT NAMED WK-AMOUNT, WK-TOTAL.
```

Each time that this statement is encountered during the execution of the program the data names and their current values are printed along with the other output.

Another form of the EXHIBIT statement prints the value of an item only if the value has changed from the previous time the statement was executed. In this form of the statement, the words EXHIBIT CHANGED NAMED are used followed by a list of data names. For example, consider the statement:

```
EXHIBIT CHANGED NAMED WK-AMOUNT, WK-TOTAL.
```

The first time this statement is encountered, all values are considered to be changed, and hence all values are printed. Each subsequent time that the statement is encountered, a comparison of the current value of each item is made with the previous value. If the values are different, the new value is printed along with the data name; otherwise no printing takes place. Only those values that change are printed. The EXHIBIT statement is especially useful for printing the values of items that are not part of output records. If the programmer suspects an error in one of these items, he or she can check the exhibited values. If this is combined with the trace feature, it is often possible to pinpoint the error.

The features discussed in this section can help locate errors in a program. However, if a program has been developed by following a logical, top-down approach, these errors should be at a minimum. It is the programmer's responsibility to take whatever steps are necessary to guarantee that his or her program is correct. A program is correct when there are no logic errors as well as no compilation and execution errors.

8-5. PROGRAM DOCUMENTATION

Documentation of a program serves the purpose of providing information so that others can understand how to use the program and how the program works. Documentation of how to use the program is provided mainly for the computer operators. This often is called *operator* or *user documentation*. It includes instructions for setting up the computer to run the program, what input to use, and what to do with the output. Documentation on how the program works is provided for other programmers in case errors must be corrected or modifications in the program need to be made. This usually is called *program documentation*. In this section we are concerned with this type of documentation.

Program documentation begins during the problem definition activity. Any written specifications of the program prepared at this stage are part of the documentation. For example, record and report layouts are part of the problem definition and should be included in the final program documentation. During program planning, module hierarchy diagrams and flowcharts are prepared. These, too, should be included in the final documentation. Listings of the test data used and sample outputs also should be part of the program documentation.

This type of documentation is external to the source program. Much of the documentation can be included within the program itself. In fact, because of the Englishlike syntax of COBOL, the source listing provides excellent documentation. There are, however, other things that may be included in the source program to improve its self-documenting characteristics.

There are several special paragraphs that may be included in the identification division for documentation purposes. These are the AUTHOR, INSTALLATION, DATE-WRITTEN, DATE-COMPILED, and SECURITY paragraphs. (The DATE-COMPILED paragraph is not allowed in all versions of COBOL. In addition, practically all implementations of COBOL include a REMARKS paragraph in the identification division, although this is not standard in ANS COBOL. See Appendix A for details.) In these paragraphs the programmer may supply any descriptive information and comments that are desired. If the DATE-COMPILED paragraph is used, the computer replaces the comment with the current date. An example of a complete identification division for the sample program in Chapter 7 is shown in Figure 8-1.

Descriptive comments may be included anywhere in the program by putting an asterisk (*) in column 7. When this is done, the entire line is treated as a comment and printed in the source listing. Anything

```
IDENTIFICATION DIVISION.
PROGRAM-ID. SLS04.
AUTHOR. ROBERT C NICKERSON.
INSTALLATION. C & E PRODUCTS, INC.
DATE-WRITTEN. SEPTEMBER 1976.
DATE-COMPILED.
SECURITY. THIS PROGRAM IS FOR INTERNAL USE ONLY.
```

FIGURE 8-1. A Complete Identification Division

may be written on a comment line. (Some versions of COBOL have other ways of including comments. See Appendix A for details.)

Usually, comments appear in the identification and procedure divisions. In the identification division comments are used to provide a brief summary of the overall function of the program. In the procedure division a comment should be included at the beginning of each module to explain the function of the module. Other comments should appear anywhere that an extra description of the processing is needed. One good practice is to write the comments for each module before actually coding the statements in the module. This can be done during the top-down design activity. Then the comments can be reviewed to be sure that the program's logic makes sense before coding begins. An example of a module with comments is shown in Figure 8-2.

The lines in the source program can be sequenced by using columns 1 through 6 of the coding form. Columns 1, 2, and 3 are used for the page number. The first page of the coding form is numbered 001, the second is 002, and so forth. Columns 4, 5, and 6 are used for the line number within the page. Initially lines should be numbered by tens. That is, the first line on a page is numbered 010, the second 020, and so on. The reason for this is so that, subsequently, lines may be inserted in the program without destroying the sequence. For example, assume that we needed to add a line between the fourth and fifth lines of the second page. These lines would be numbered 002040 and 002050. The new line to be inserted would be given a number halfway between — that is, 002045.

Page and line numbers are printed along with the source listing. However, their main function is to provide a means of resequencing the program if necessary. For example, if a source program that is punched in cards is accidentally dropped so that the cards get shuffled, the sequence numbers can be used to rearrange the cards. (A

```
CALCULATE-BEGIN.
*
*     THIS MODULE CALCULATES THE NEW YEAR-TO-DATE SALES,
*     RETURNS, AND NET. THESE NEW FIGURES ARE THEN
*     ADDED TO THE TOTAL FIELDS.
*
      ADD . . .
             .
             .
             .
CALCULATE-END.
   EXIT.
```

FIGURE 8-2. An Example of Comments for a Module

card sorter, found in many data processing installations, can be used for this.)

Each line of the source program also can be provided with identification. Columns 73 through 80 may contain any identifying information about the program. The information does not affect processing, but is printed in the source listing. Usually, each line in the program is given the same identifying information. Often, the program name is used for this purpose. Then, if the program is accidentally mixed up with another program, it is easy to separate the two.

The internal documentation of the source program that has been described here is an important part of the overall program documentation. It should be developed as the program is coded. If subsequent changes are made in the coded program, the internal documentation should be changed at the same time. If this rule is carefully followed, then the most current version of the program will have the most up-to-date documentation.

The source listing, with the internal documentation described above, must be included in the final program documentation. We have mentioned other things that should be in the documentation such as record and report layouts. The following is a list of the documentation for a program:

1. Program summary or abstract
2. Requirements chart
3. Program narrative
4. Module hierarchy diagram
5. Program flowcharts
6. Record layouts (i.e., card layouts)
7. Report layouts
8. List of test data and sample output
9. Summary of error messages and accounting controls
10. Source program listing

The purpose of the *program summary* is to provide a brief statement of the overall function of the program. This is often the same as the summary that appears in the identification division. Figure 8-3 shows a sample program summary for the year-to-date sales report program.

The *requirements chart** is a graphical description of the input and output requirements of the program. The chart shows at a glance what is required to run the program. This chart is also included in

*A requirements chart is a specific type of *system flowchart* and is often referred to by this name.

PROGRAM SUMMARY

　　The purpose of this program is to prepare the year-
to-date sales report. Input consists of the sales data
file for the current month. The new year-to-date sales,
returns, and net are calculated for each salesperson.
Totals are accumulated for all salespeople. The report
lists the new data for each salesperson and the totals.

FIGURE 8-3. A Sample Program Summary

the operator's documentation. Figure 8-4 shows an example of a
requirements chart. In this example there is only one input and output
file. However, some programs may have numerous input and output
files. For example, Figure 8-5 shows a requirements chart for a program with two input files and three output files. The symbols that
are used in requirements charts are summarized in Figure 8-6.

　　The *program narrative* is a written description of the program's
logic. It is necessary only if there is unusual processing in the program. Still, some organizations require a narrative description of the
processing in every program. However, if the source program contains proper comments, this should not be necessary. In fact, the

FIGURE 8-4. A Requirements Chart for a Program with One Input File and One
　　　　　　Output File

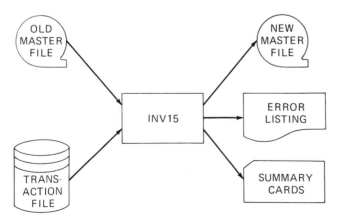

FIGURE 8-5. A Requirements Chart for a Program with Multiple Input and
　　　　　　Output Files

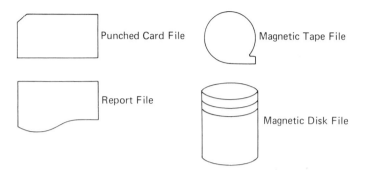

FIGURE 8-6. Symbols Used in a Program Requirements Chart

narrative has a tendency to become out-of-date if the program is changed often. In general, a narrative description should be provided for any module that performs unique or complex processing.

The complete set of documents should be bound together with a title page and a table of contents. There should be one binder for each program, and the entire library of program documentation should be under the control of one or more documentation librarians. If a program is changed, it is important that the documentation be updated. No programmer should ever consider his or her job done until the final documentation is prepared or appropriately modified.

8-6. CONCLUSION

Computer programming is a process that includes several activities. One of the common misconceptions is that writing the program is all that is involved in programming. However, as we have seen, this activity, which is usually called coding, is only one part of the whole programming process. When we use the word "programming" we mean the whole set of activities associated with preparing a computer program. This includes the five activities discussed in this chapter.

The approach to programming that is discussed in this book is commonly called *structured programming*. There is a lot of disagreement about what is meant by structured programming; a single definition does not exist. However, most people agree that structured programming involves a systematic process that results in programs that are easily understood, maintained, and modified, and that can be shown to be correct.

In this book we emphasize designing programs in a top-down manner. This approach leads to modular programs that are easy to understand and to change. In addition, top-down design helps us show the correctness of the program. The structure and style rules discussed in the text also aid in producing readable and correct programs.

Structured programming is really just good programming. By following the guidelines set down in this book, the programmer can produce good, correct programs.

PART THREE

Advanced
COBOL Programming

Format Notation

Throughout Part III we use a standard notation to describe the syntax of the elements of the COBOL language. COBOL reference manuals also use this notation. The notation shows precisely the format of each element and makes clear such characteristics as which words are reserved, which words are programmer-supplied, and what parts are optional.

As an example of the use of this notation, consider the WRITE statement as we have described it in previous chapters. The following is the general form of this statement expressed in the format notation:

WRITE record-name [FROM identifier-1]

$$\left[\text{AFTER ADVANCING} \left\{ \begin{matrix} \begin{Bmatrix} \text{identifier-2} \\ \text{integer} \end{Bmatrix} \text{LINES} \\ \text{mnemonic-name} \end{matrix} \right\} \right]$$

In this notation, uppercase words (that is, those written in all capital letters) are COBOL reserved words. Lowercase words identify information that must be supplied by the programmer. Thus, in the WRITE statement, the words WRITE, FROM, AFTER, ADVANCING, and LINES are reserved words and must be coded exactly as shown. However, the programmer must supply information in the statement in place of record-name, identifier-1, identifier-2, integer, and mnemonic-name. (An identifier is simply a data name. An integer is a whole number. Mnemonic — pronounced *new-monic* — means "memory aid-

160

ing." In the WRITE statement, a mnemonic-name refers to a name specified in the SPECIAL-NAMES paragraph.)

If an uppercase word is underlined, then it is required if the portion in which it appears is used. Uppercase words that are not underlined are optional. Thus, in the example, the words WRITE, FROM, and AFTER are required, while the words ADVANCING and LINES need not be used.

Any part that is enclosed in square brackets, [ ], may be included or omitted depending on the requirements of the program. In the WRITE statement, the FROM phrase and the AFTER ADVANCING phrase are optional. Within an optional part, underlined reserved words are required only if that part is used.

Braces, { }, are used to enclose vertical lists of alternative elements. That is, the programmer must select one of the elements in the list to be included in that portion of the program. For example, if the AFTER ADVANCING phrase is used, the programmer must use either an identifier or an integer followed optionally by the word LINES, or a mnemonic name must be used.

As another example of the use of the format notation consider the following:

$$\underline{ADD} \begin{Bmatrix} \text{identifier-1} \\ \text{literal-1} \end{Bmatrix} , \begin{Bmatrix} \text{identifier-2} \\ \text{literal-2} \end{Bmatrix} \begin{bmatrix} , \text{identifier-3} \\ , \text{literal-3} \end{bmatrix} \cdots$$
$$\underline{GIVING} \text{ identifier-m}$$

This is one form of the ADD statement discussed in Chapter 4. Notice that the words ADD and GIVING are required reserved words. The programmer must supply either an identifier or a numeric literal for each value to be added, except in the GIVING part, in which only an identifier may be used. At least two identifiers or literals are required after the word ADD. A third identifier or literal is shown as being optional. The series of dots after this is called an *ellipsis* and indicates that the previous part of the format may be repeated. Thus, in the ADD statement we may use any number of identifiers or literals as long as there are at least two.

Commas or semicolons shown in a general format are always optional. In some versions of COBOL these characters are interchangeable. (See the Chapter 3 reference in Appendix A for details.) In the ADD statement, commas may be used in the positions shown.

The format notation discussed here is a convenient way of representing the general form of the parts of a COBOL program. The notation is used for elements in all divisions of a COBOL program. The programmer must be familiar with this notation in order to read and understand COBOL reference manuals.

CHAPTER 9

Advanced Data Description

In this chapter we discuss a number of advanced features of COBOL that are used to describe data. Most of the discussion refers to elements that appear in the data division of a program. Often these elements can be used to improve the programmer's efficiency and to provide greater versatility. The sections in this chapter may be read in any order.

9-1. QUALIFICATION OF DATA NAMES

In the examples in previous chapters, a unique name is used for each data item. This is necessary so that the programmer has a way of identifying each item. However, it is possible to use the same name for several items in a program. For example, Figure 9-1 shows a description for the sales record discussed in Section 6-1. However, in this record description the name SALES is used in two places. The name appears in the Y-T-D-DATA group and the CURRENT-MONTH-DATA group. Similarly, the name RETURNS is used twice in this record description.

When a name is specified more than once in the data division it must be *qualified* whenever it is used in the procedure division. Qualification of a data name involves using one or more *qualifiers*

162

```
01  SALES-PERSON-RECORD.
    05  SALES-PERSON-ID.
        10  CODE.
            15  REGION          PIC XX.
            15  NUMBER          PIC XXXX.
        10  NAME                PIC X(18).
    05  CLASSIFICATION.
        10  QUOTA               PIC X.
        10  COMMISSION          PIC 9.
    05  Y-T-D-DATA.
        10  SALES               PIC 9(6)V99.
        10  RETURNS             PIC 9(5)V99.
    05  DATE.
        10  MONTH               PIC XX.
        10  YEAR                PIC XX.
    05  CURRENT-MONTH-DATA.
        10  SALES               PIC 9(5)V99.
        10  RETURNS             PIC 9(4)V99.
    05  FILLER                  PIC X(22).
```

FIGURE 9-1. A Record Description

with the name. A qualifier consists of the word IN or OF followed by the name of a group item. The group item must contain the name being qualified. For example, to identify the year-to-date sales in Figure 9-1 we could use:

```
SALES OF Y-T-D-DATA
```

Similarly, the current month's sales could be identified by:

```
SALES OF CURRENT-MONTH-DATA
```

In these examples, the phrase following the word SALES is a qualifier. Either the word IN or OF may be used in the qualifier; there is no difference in the meaning of these words.

The purpose of qualification is to specify precisely which item is being identified. Whenever a name that is not unique is used in the procedure division, it must be qualified. For example, if we wished to add the year-to-date sales and the current month's sales we could code the following:

```
ADD SALES OF Y-T-D-DATA, SALES OF CURRENT-MONTH-DATA
    GIVING WK-NEW-YTD-SALES.
```

Sometimes several qualifiers are required to identify an item. For example, if the name SALES also is used in another record description it may be necessary to qualify it as follows:

```
SALES OF Y-T-D-DATA IN SALES-PERSON-RECORD
```

In this example, two qualifiers are required to uniquely specify the data item.

Each qualifier must include the name of a group item that contains the item being qualified. That is, each qualifier must be successively higher in the same hierarchy of data. For example, the name NUMBER in Figure 9-1 may be qualified as follows:

```
NUMBER OF CODE OF SALES-PERSON-ID IN SALES-PERSON-RECORD
```

This qualification would be necessary if NUMBER were used in another record description in a similar hierarchy of data.

Only enough qualifiers are required to make the name unique. For example, it only may be necessary to qualify the NUMBER field as follows:

```
NUMBER IN SALES-PERSON-RECORD
```

This qualification of NUMBER may be used if it is sufficient to uniquely distinguish the item. However, additional qualification may be used even though it is not needed.

The main purpose of qualification is to uniquely identify an item of data. However, qualification also is used to make the program more understandable. Some programmers qualify all data names to make it clear to which record the item belongs. In previous chapters we have used prefixes with data names for a similar reason. Which approach is used depends on the personal taste of the programmer.

9-2. REDEFINING DATA

Sometimes it is useful to refer to a data item by two different names. For example, in a data processing application, two types of records may be identical except for one field. In the data division we could have two complete record descriptions. However, since all of the fields are the same except for one, it is easier to describe the record once and give two names to the one field that is different. This can be accomplished by using the REDEFINES clause.

As a simple example, consider the situation in which an input file contains names and addresses. One type of record has a person's name in the first 20 columns. Another record type has the person's address in these columns. Thus, these are two types of records with the same layout but different data in the first field. Using a REDE-FINES clause we can describe the records as follows:

```
01   NAME-ADDRESS-RECORD.
     05   NAME                        PIC X(20).
     05   ADDRESS REDEFINES NAME      PIC X(20).
     05   FILLER                      PIC X(60).
```

The second 05-level entry contains a REDEFINES clause. It says that ADDRESS and NAME refer to the first 20 columns. We can use either data name in the program for the data in this field.

When the REDEFINES clause is used, it must come immediately after the item being redefined. It always has the general form:

level-number data-name-1 REDEFINES data-name-2

Data-name-2 must be the name of the item in the immediately preceeding data description. The level number must be the same as for data-name-2. The effect is that both data names refer to the same item.

The REDEFINES clause may be used to give a different picture to an item. For example, in a payroll application, a field may refer to either the employee's monthly salary or his hourly pay rate depending on how the employee is paid. The following might be used to describe this field.

```
05   SALARY                          PIC 9999.
05   HOURLY-RATE REDEFINES SALARY    PIC 99V99.
```

In this example, SALARY has the picture 9999, while HOURLY-RATE has the picture 99V99. However, both names refer to the same field.

An elementary item may be redefined as a group item by using a REDEFINES clause. For example, in the sales record discussed in Section 6-1, the first six columns contain the salesperson's identifying code. This code is divided into two parts. The first two columns identify the salesperson's region and the last four columns give the person's number. In a program we may wish to refer to the entire field with a numeric picture and to subfields with alphanumeric pictures. The following accomplishes this:

```
10   SP-CODE-NUMBER        PIC 9(6).
10   SP-CODE REDEFINES     SP-CODE-NUMBER.
     15   SP-REGION        PIC XX.
     15   SP-NUMBER        PIC XXXX.
```

In this example, the REDEFINES clause is used for a group item. Elementary items subordinate to the group item contain the necessary PICTURE clauses.

A VALUE clause can be used with an item being redefined. However, it cannot be used with the redefining item — that is, with the item containing the REDEFINES clause. For example, we could use the following to give two names and pictures to a field with an initial value of zero:

```
77  WK-AMOUNT        PIC 99V99   VALUE ZERO.
77  WK-DATA REDEFINES WK-AMOUNT
                     PIC 999V9.
```

The reason that the VALUE clause is not allowed with the REDEFINES clause is so that the programmer cannot inadvertantly give two different values to the same item.

Since data names refer to areas in internal storage, the effect of the REDEFINES clause is to give two names and pictures to the same area of storage. With this in mind, it is easy to understand the rules associated with the REDEFINES clause. To summarize:

1. The REDEFINES clause must be the first clause following the item being redefined.
2. It must have the same level number as the item being redefined.
3. The VALUE clause may not be used with the REDEFINES clause.

9-3. CONDITION NAMES

Condition names are special data names that can be used to check for certain conditions in the program. As an example, assume that an input file contains two types of records — master records and transaction records. The records are distinguished from one another by a one-column field that contains an M (for master) or T (for transaction). Within the procedure division, we must be able to determine what type of record has been read.

One obvious way of determining the record type is to test for an M or T in the RECORD-TYPE-CODE field. For example, we could use the following IF statement:

```
IF RECORD-TYPE-CODE IS EQUAL TO 'M'
    PERFORM MASTER-PROCESS-BEGIN
        THRU MASTER-PROCESS-END.
```

By using condition names, we can shorten the IF statement and make the program easier to code.

There must be one condition name for each possible value of the item. These names are given level number 88 and come immediately after the item's description in the data division. A VALUE clause is used with each condition name to associate a value with the name. A PICTURE clause is not used with a condition name. For example, to specify condition names for the record-type condition we would use the following:

```
05  RECORD-TYPE-CODE        PIC X.
    88  MASTER-RECORD-TYPE            VALUE 'M'.
    88  TRANS-RECORD-TYPE             VALUE 'T'.
```

Two condition names are specified in this example. The first, MASTER-RECORD-TYPE, stands for the condition that the record-type code has the value M. The second condition name, TRANS-RECORD-TYPE, indicates the condition that the type code is equal to T.

In the procedure division, we can use condition names in IF statements to test for the existence of the condition. For example, to test if the record-type code is M in the above example we may use the following:

```
IF MASTER-RECORD-TYPE
    PERFORM MASTER-PROCESS-BEGIN
        THRU MASTER-PROCESS-END.
```

Notice that only the condition name appears after the word IF. If the field associated with the condition name has the value of the condition name, then the condition is true and the statements in the IF statement are executed. Otherwise, the condition is false and the statements in the IF statement are not executed. Similarly, we could test for a transaction record in this example with the following statement:

```
IF TRANS-RECORD-TYPE
    PERFORM TRANS-PROCESS-BEGIN
        THRU TRANS-PROCESS-END.
```

When condition names are used, the literal in the VALUE clause must be the same length and type as the picture of the item being described. In the above example, the item is a one-character alphanumeric field. Therefore, we use single-character nonnumeric literals with the condition names. If appropriate, numeric values may be used and larger fields are allowed. As many condition names as are needed may be used but all condition names must be specified immediately after the item associated with the condition.

Condition names may be specified either in the FILE section or in the WORKING-STORAGE section. In fact, these are the only items that can have VALUE clauses in the FILE section.

Besides making the program easier to code and to understand, condition names make it easier to modify the program. If the values that indicate the condition change and condition names are not used, then all IF statements that test for the condition must be changed. However, when condition names are used, it is necessary only to modify the VALUE clauses associated with the condition names.

9-4. ADVANCED EDITING

In Chapter 3 we discussed the use of zero suppression and the insertion of commas and decimal points in the pictures of printed output items. The purpose of this editing is to make printed output more understandable. There are a number of other ways that output can be edited. In this section we discuss several advanced editing techniques.

Currency Symbols

The dollar sign ($) normally is used as a currency symbol in the United States. It may be included in the picture of an output item and thus printed along with the output data. For example, assume that the following item description is included in an output record:

```
    05   A-AMOUNT                PIC $ZZ,ZZZ.99.
```

The dollar sign that appears in the picture is printed each time that the output record is written. For example, if the value to be printed is 0458372, then the output printed is $ 4,583.72. Notice that the dollar sign takes a full printed position and must be included in the count of the number of characters in the line. Suppressed zeros to the right of the dollar sign are replaced with blank spaces.

In this example, the dollar sign is *fixed* because it always is printed in the same position in the output record. Sometimes it is desirable to have the dollar sign printed just ahead of the first digit, with no intervening spaces. This is called a *floating* dollar sign, because it "floats" in ahead of the number. To include a floating dollar sign in the output, dollar signs are used in the item's picture instead of the zero suppression character Z. For example, the following item description includes a floating dollar sign:

```
    05   B-AMOUNT                PIC $$$,$$$.99.
```

In effect, the dollar sign in the item's picture indicates both zero suppression and insertion of a floating dollar sign.

In this example of a floating dollar sign, the value 0458372 is printed as $4,583.72, with no space between the dollar sign and the first digit. The value 0002530 is printed as $25.30. The dollar sign in the item's picture not only suppresses any lead zeros but also any unnecessary comma.

When using a floating dollar sign, there must be one extra dollar sign at the beginning of the item's picture. In the above example, we have assumed that the output value has no more than five digits to the left of the decimal point. However, six dollar signs are included in the picture. The extra dollar sign is necessary for the case where the maximum number of digits is to be printed. For example, the value 1032565 is printed as $10,325.65. Without the extra dollar sign in the item's picture there would not be sufficient space to print all of the output characters in this example.

The number of positions required for the field is the total count of characters in the item's picture. This is true no matter what value is printed. Thus, in the above example, ten print positions are required even though some may contain blanks.

Asterisk Protection

Asterisk protection (also called *check protection*) involves inserting asterisks in place of suppressed zeros. For example, the output ****38.59 includes asterisk protection. The reason asterisk protection is used is that with such protection it is difficult to alter the output. This is important in checks to avoid forgeries.

To use asterisk protection, the asterisk (*) is included in the output item's picture instead of the zero suppression symbol Z. For example, the following item description includes asterisk protection:

```
05  C-AMOUNT              PIC **,***.99.
```

In effect, the asterisks cause lead zeros to be suppressed and to be replaced by asterisks. In addition, if the comma is suppressed it is replaced by an asterisk.

A fixed dollar sign may be used with asterisk protection. The following item description illustrates this:

```
05  D-AMOUNT              PIC $**,***.99.
```

For example, the value of 0458372 would be printed as $*4,583.72.

Signed Numbers

A numeric item may have a negative value in a program. For example, an input value may be punched as a negative number on a card (see Section 1-6), or the result of a calculation may be negative. If an item may have a negative value, then the item's picture must indicate this. This is done by using the symbol S (for *signed*) as the first character in the item's picture. For example, the following item description indicates that the item may be signed:

```
05  E-AMOUNT              PIC S9(5)V99.
```

The S in the item's picture is not counted as a character position, but must be included if the item possibly can be negative.

In the examples in previous chapters, the S is not used in numeric pictures. For all of these examples, the numeric value of the item is assumed to be positive. In fact, if an S is not used and the value is negative, then the computer removes the sign and stores a positive number. Because of this, it usually is best to indicate that every numeric item may be signed.

For numeric edited items, the symbol S is not used. Instead several special editing characters may be included in the item's picture. If one of these editing characters is not included and the value to be printed is negative, then the actual value printed will appear as a positive number, without a sign. Hence, it is important to include the necessary editing characters if an item may be negative.

In many applications in accounting, a negative amount is called a *credit* and is written with the characters CR to the right. To include this type of editing in the output, these characters are used in the item's picture. For example, the following item description indicates editing with the CR symbol:

```
05  F-AMOUNT              PIC ZZ,ZZZ.99CR.
```

If the amount to be printed is negative, then the characters CR are printed. For example, the number -0012550 is printed as 125.50CR. However, if the amount is positive, then CR is not printed. Instead, two blank spaces are left in the output. Thus the number +0012550 is printed as 125.50 , with two spaces on the right.

Whether or not the characters CR are printed, two print positions must be allowed in the output record. If the output is negative, these positions contain the characters CR. If the value is positive, these positions are left blank.

In some situations, a negative amount may indicate a *debit* instead of a credit. In this case, the programmer can use the symbol

DB in the item's picture. For example, the following item description includes these symbols:

    05   G-AMOUNT   PIC ZZ,ZZZ.99DB.

The rules for DB are the same as for CR. If the amount is negative, the characters DB are printed; otherwise, two blank spaces are left in the output.

A positive or negative sign may be printed in the output by including a plus or minus sign in the item's picture. If a plus sign is used in the picture, then a plus sign is printed if the item is positive and a minus sign is printed if the item is negative. For example, in the following item description a plus sign is used:

    05   H-AMOUNT   PIC +ZZ,ZZZ.99.

If the amount is +0825637 then + 8,256.37 is printed. An amount of -3204500 is printed as -32,045.00. If a minus sign is included in the item's picture, then a blank space is left in the output if the item is positive, but a minus sign is printed if the item is negative. For example, the following item description uses a minus sign for editing:

    05   I-AMOUNT   PIC -ZZ,ZZZ.99.

An amount of +0825637 is printed as 8,256.37, while the value -3204500 is printed as -32,045.00.

In these examples, the plus or minus sign appears in a fixed position to the left of the number. The sign occupies a full print position whether or not it is printed. A plus or minus sign also may be included to the right of the number. The following item description illustrates the use of a plus sign in this position:

    05   J-AMOUNT   PIC ZZ,ZZZ.99+.

In this case, a plus sign is printed on the right if the amount is positive and a minus sign is printed if it is negative. If a minus sign is used on the right, then a blank space is left if the item is positive, while a minus sign is printed on the right if it is negative. This is illustrated in the following item description:

    05   K-AMOUNT   PIC ZZ,ZZZ.99-.

A floating plus or minus sign may be used in the same way as a floating dollar sign. Either a plus or a minus sign is used in place of the zero suppression symbol Z. This is illustrated in the following examples:

```
05  L-AMOUNT              PIC +++,+++.99.
05  M-AMOUNT              PIC ---,---.99.
```

For example, if the value to be printed is +0002535, then in the first example the output is +25.35, while in the second case the value printed is 25.35 without a sign. If the amount is -0010375, then the output appears as -103.75 in either case. Notice that when using a floating sign, an extra character position must be included to the left so that there are sufficient positions in the field to print the largest value.

Insertion Characters

It is possible to insert blanks and zeros in an item in the same way that commas and decimal points are inserted. The symbol 0 is used to insert zeros and B is used to include blanks. For example, the following item description shows three zeros in the picture:

```
05  N-AMOUNT              PIC Z,ZZZ,000.
```

If the value moved to this field is 1234, then the output printed is 1,234,000.

To insert blanks, the character B is included wherever a blank is desired. The following example indicates that three blanks should be inserted:

```
05  O-AMOUNT              PIC Z9B99B99.
```

If the value to be printed is 030977, then the output would be 3 09 77. Often this is used to separate the parts of a date. Another use is to set off the CR symbol. For example, the following item description indicates that a blank should be inserted before the CR:

```
05  P-AMOUNT              PIC ZZ,ZZZ.99BCR.
```

An amount of -0012550 would be printed as 125.50 CR.

Date Editing

In some versions of COBOL, dates may be edited by including a slash (/) in the output item's description. This is shown in the following example:

```
05  DATE            PIC Z9/99/99.
```

If the date to be printed is 030977 then the output would be 3/09/77.

This feature is not available in all versions of COBOL (see Appendix A for details).

The BLANK WHEN ZERO Clause

An output value of zero is printed when using any of the typical editing patterns that we have illustrated previously. For example, consider the following description:

```
05  Q-AMOUNT          PIC ZZ,ZZZ.99.
```

If the amount is zero then the output .00 is printed. Sometimes it is desirable to leave a blank space if the value is zero. This often improves the readability of reports containing long lists of numbers. To do this, the BLANK WHEN ZERO clause is used. This is shown in the following example:

```
05  R-AMOUNT          PIC ZZ,ZZZ.99  BLANK WHEN ZERO.
```

In this case, any nonzero value is printed in the normal way. However, if the value is zero, then blank spaces are left in the output. Notice that the BLANK WHEN ZERO clause is part of the item's description entry. Thus, a period comes after this clause and not after the PICTURE clause.

The JUSTIFIED RIGHT Clause

In Section 6-3 we discuss the effect of item length on the MOVE statement. If the sending item is shorter than the receiving item, then the data is left-justified in the receiving item, and the extra positions on the right are filled with blanks. If the sending item is longer than the receiving item, then the data is left-justified, and additional characters on the right are truncated.

By using the JUSTIFIED RIGHT clause, these rules are reversed. This clause appears only with alphanumeric items. The following example shows how it is used:

```
05  R-FIELD           PIC X(9)  JUSTIFIED RIGHT.
```

If R-FIELD in this example is used as the receiving item in a MOVE statement, then the data that is moved is *right-justified*. If the sending item is shorter than the receiving item, then extra positions on the left are filled with blanks. If the sending item is longer than R-FIELD, then extra characters on the left are truncated.

9-5. FIGURATIVE CONSTANTS

In previous chapters we have mentioned two figurative constants. These are ZERO (also spelled ZEROS or ZEROES) and SPACE (or SPACES). ZERO represents either the number zero or one or more occurrences of the character 0. SPACE is used for one or more spaces or blanks. There are several other figurative constants that can be used in COBOL. In this section we discuss these.

The figurative constant LOW-VALUE (or LOW-VALUES) represents the lowest value in the computer's collating sequence. This value always appears first in any sorted list of the values that can be stored by the computer. (With most computers, the LOW-VALUE is a series of binary zeros. See Chapter 12 for a discussion of binary numbers.)

The highest value in the computer's collating sequence is represented by the figurative constant HIGH-VALUE (or HIGH-VALUES). This is the last value in any sorted list of the values that the computer can store. (HIGH-VALUE is usually a series of binary ones.)

The figurative constant QUOTE (or QUOTES) represents one or more occurrences of the quotation mark (either " or '). This literal cannot be used in place of the quotation marks that must enclose a nonnumeric literal. Normally it is used to produce a quotation mark in printed output.

The final figurative constant is the word ALL followed by a nonnumeric literal enclosed in quotation marks. The meaning is that the literal is to be repeated until the field is filled. For example, the following item description contains the ALL figurative constant in the VALUE clause:

```
05  A-FIELD          PIC X(5) VALUE ALL '*'.
```

The effect of this example is that the five character positions reserved for A-FIELD are filled with asterisks. This is equivalent in this example to using the nonnumeric literal '*****' in the VALUE clause. As another example, consider the following:

```
05  B-FIELD          PIC X(6) VALUE ALL 'AB'.
```

In this case, the value ABABAB is stored in the area reserved for B-FIELD. (Some versions of COBOL only allow single character literals in the ALL figurative constant. See Appendix A for details.)

All of the figurative constants in COBOL may be used any place in a program where a nonnumeric literal can appear. This includes the VALUE clause, the IF statement, and the MOVE statement. Only the figurative constant ZERO may be used in place of a numeric literal.

CHAPTER 10

Advanced Procedure Description

Most of this chapter is devoted to elements of COBOL that are used in the procedure division. These elements include advanced features for input/output, arithmetic, and logical processing. The proper use of these features can increase the programmer's efficiency and versatility. The sections in this chapter may be read in any order.

10-1. SPECIAL FORMS OF INPUT AND OUTPUT

In Part II we limited our discussion of I/O processing to punched card input and printed output. In later chapters we will discuss magnetic tape and disk input and output. In this section we describe several other forms of input and output and how they are used.

Punched Card Output

Sometimes it is necessary to punch the results of processing into cards rather than to print the output. When punched card output is needed, a file must be assigned to the card punch with a SELECT entry in the environment division. For example, assume that the name associated with the card punch device is CARD-PUNCH. Then the following SELECT entry could be used to assign a file, named CARD-FILE, to this device:

```
SELECT CARD-FILE
    ASSIGN TO CARD-PUNCH.
```

(Appendix A gives examples of device names used for card punches with different computers.)

In the data division, an FD entry is required for each punched card file, just as one is needed for other input and output files. Label records always are omitted with punched card output files. The record length is usually 80 characters. The following is an example of an FD entry and record description for a punched card file:

```
FD  CARD-FILE,
    LABEL RECORDS ARE OMITTED,
    RECORD CONTAINS 80 CHARACTERS,
    DATA RECORD IS CARD-DATA.
01  CARD-DATA     PIC X(80).
```

In the procedure division, the punched card file must be opened as an OUTPUT file. Thus, the OPEN statement for the file described in the previous FD entry would be

```
OPEN OUTPUT CARD-FILE.
```

To cause punched card output to be produced, the WRITE statement is used. The statement has the same format for punched card output as for printed output. For example, the following statement may be used for the card file described in the previous FD entry:

```
WRITE CARD-DATA FROM CARD-RECORD.
```

In this example, the FROM option indicates that the output record's description is in the WORKING-STORAGE section. Notice that the AFTER ADVANCING phrase is not used in this example. Usually this phrase is not needed for punched card output. However, with some computers it can be used to control the movement of cards in the card punch. (Refer to the appropriate reference manual for details.)

It is important to notice that the WRITE statement does not indicate what type of output is to be produced. The same form is used for both printed output and punched output. The computer knows what form of output is to be produced by the SELECT entry. This entry connects the file name with a specific output device.

Console Typewriter Input and Output

With many computer systems a special I/O device called a *console typewriter* is available. This device is connected to the CPU and is very much like an electric typewriter. It can be used for printed output or for keyed input. When used for output, it prints one character at a time across the paper just like a typewriter. It is much slower than the printer used with most computers. For input, each character must be keyed by the computer operator. It only goes as fast as the person using it.

Because the console typewriter is so much slower than most other I/O devices, it usually is used only for short communications between the program and the computer operator. Often, error messages are printed on the console typewriter so that the operator can correct the error condition. Sometimes the operator is required to supply a small amount of input data such as the date. This type of input and output is most appropriate for the console typewriter.

For input from the console typewriter, the ACCEPT statement is used. This statement has the form:

<u>ACCEPT</u> data-name <u>FROM</u> mnemonic-name

The data-name must be the name of an item described in the WORKING-STORAGE section. Files are *not* used for console typewriter input and output. The item may be either an elementary item or a group item.

The mnemonic-name is supplied by the programmer. It must be associated with the computer's name for the console typewriter through the SPECIAL-NAMES paragraph of the environment division. For example, assume that the computer uses the name CONSOLE for the console typewriter. Then the following SPECIAL-NAMES paragraph assigns the mnemonic-name TYPEWRITER to this device:

```
SPECIAL-NAMES.
    CONSOLE IS TYPEWRITER.
```

(See Appendix A for console typewriter names used with different computers.) The name TYPEWRITER can now be used in the ACCEPT statement to refer to the console typewriter.

As an example of the use of the ACCEPT statement, assume that the following item is specified in the WORKING-STORAGE section:

```
01  TRANS-DATE.
    05  TD-MONTH    PIC 99.
    05  TD-DAY      PIC 99.
    05  TD-YEAR     PIC 99.
```

The computer operator must supply the data for this item. To accept this data the following statement would be used:

```
ACCEPT TRANS-DATE FROM TYPEWRITER.
```

When an ACCEPT statement is executed, the computer usually prints a message on the console typewriter indicating that input from the typewriter is needed. It then stops execution of the program. At this point, the computer operator must type the appropriate data and then press a button to restart the program. In the example shown above, the computer operator must type six digits for the date. The program gets the data that is typed and stores it in the item identified in the ACCEPT statement. It then continues processing.

For console typewriter output, the DISPLAY statement is used. The general form of this statement is as follows:

$$\underline{\text{DISPLAY}} \begin{Bmatrix} \text{data-name-1} \\ \text{literal-1} \end{Bmatrix} \begin{bmatrix} \text{, data-name-2} \\ \text{, literal-2} \end{bmatrix} \dots \underline{\text{UPON}} \text{ mnemonic-name}$$

Any data name in this statement must refer to an item in WORKING-STORAGE. The item may be an elementary item or a group item. The mnemonic name in this statement must be associated with the computer's name for the console typewriter in the SPECIAL-NAMES paragraph.

The following is an example of a simple DISPLAY statement:

```
DISPLAY WK-AMOUNT UPON TYPEWRITER.
```

When this statement is executed, the current value of the item named WK-AMOUNT is displayed. The name TYPEWRITER must appear in the SPECIAL-NAMES paragraph.

Numeric and nonnumeric literals also may be used in the DISPLAY statement. For example, the following statement causes an error message to be typed on the console typewriter:

```
DISPLAY 'DATA ERROR - JOB TERMINATED' UPON TYPEWRITER.
```

Several fields and literals may be displayed using one DISPLAY statement. The following example illustrates this:

```
DISPLAY 'TRANSACTION DATE ' TRANS-DATE UPON TYPEWRITER.
```

In this example the nonnumeric literal is printed first, followed by the current value of the item named TRANS-DATE.

10-2. ADVANCED ARITHMETIC PROCESSING

The basic arithmetic statements in COBOL are the ADD, SUBTRACT, MULTIPLY, and DIVIDE statements. These are described in Chapter 4. With these statements most types of arithmetic processing can be accomplished. In this section we describe additional features that can be used with these statements and discuss a new statement that can be used for complex arithmetic processing.

Rounding

The number of places to the right of the decimal point in the result of an arithmetic calculation may be more than the number of places specified in the picture of the result field. For example, assume that there is a field named PRINCIPAL and one named INTEREST, each with two places to the right of the decimal point. To calculate INTEREST we multiply PRINCIPAL by .05 as follows:

```
MULTIPLY PRINCIPAL BY .05 GIVING INTEREST.
```

If PRINCIPAL is 81.93, then the result of multiplication by .05 is 4.0965. Since INTEREST has only two places to the right of the decimal point, the last two digits in the calculated amount are dropped (we say they are *truncated*) and the result stored for INTEREST is 4.09.

Notice in this example that it would be more accurate to store 4.10 for INTEREST. However, when using the basic forms of the arithmetic statements, the result is not rounded off before it is stored. Rather, extra places to the right of the decimal point always are truncated.

To accomplish rounding in situations such as this, COBOL allows the ROUNDED option with all arithmetic statements. This consists of using the word ROUNDED after the result field in the statement. For example, to cause the result to be rounded in the previous multiplication we would use the statement:

```
MULTIPLY PRINCIPAL BY .05 GIVING INTEREST ROUNDED.
```

If the principal were 81.93 as before, then the result stored for INTEREST would be 4.10.

When using the ROUNDED option, the word ROUNDED comes immediately after the name of the result field in the arithmetic statement. If the GIVING phrase is used, then ROUNDED comes after the field named in this phrase. If GIVING is not used, then ROUNDED follows the name of the result field. For example, in the following ADD statement, the ROUNDED option is used without the GIVING phrase:

```
ADD A-AMOUNT TO B-AMOUNT ROUNDED.
```

In this example, the values of A-AMOUNT and B-AMOUNT are added and the result is rounded to the number of decimal positions in B-AMOUNT. Then the rounded result is stored in B-AMOUNT.

Size Errors

If the number of places to the *left* of the decimal point in the result of a calculation is greater than the number specified in the result field's picture, then a *size error* occurs. For example, assume that INTEREST in the previous calculation has the picture 9V99. If PRINCIPAL has a value greater than 200.00, then a size error will occur during the multiplication. For example, if PRINCIPAL is 250.00, then the result of the multiplication is 12.5000. This result has two places to the left of the decimal point, while the picture associated with INTEREST has only one.

When a size error occurs, the value stored in the result field is unknown. To avoid this situation, the SIZE ERROR option may be used in the arithmetic statement. This option consists of the phrase ON SIZE ERROR followed by one or more statements. The phrase comes at the end of the arithmetic statement, after the ROUNDED option if it is used. The statements in the SIZE ERROR phrase are executed if a size error occurs; otherwise, they are not executed.

As an example, assume that there is a module called ERROR-ROUTINE that is to be performed in the event of a size error. The calculation of the interest can then be coded as follows:

```
MULTIPLY PRINCIPAL BY .05 GIVING INTEREST ROUNDED
    ON SIZE ERROR
        PERFORM ERROR-ROUTINE-BEGIN
            THRU ERROR-ROUTINE-END.
```

In this example, the SIZE ERROR option includes a PERFORM statement for the ERROR-ROUTINE module. The effect of this statement is that, if a size error occurs during the execution of the multiplication, the PERFORM statement is executed. If a size error does not occur, this statement is bypassed.

Sometimes when a size error occurs, the program simply prints an error message explaining the error and stops execution. At other times an attempt is made to correct the error. When a size error occurs in a statement with the SIZE ERROR option the result field is unchanged from its previous value. This must be taken into account in any error-processing routine.

The SIZE ERROR option may be used with any arithmetic statement. It always comes as the last phrase in the statement.

The COMPUTE Statement

When it is necessary to perform an arithmetic calculation using the basic arithmetic statements, each step of the calculation must be coded in a separate statement. For complex calculations, this form of coding may require a large number of statements. The amount of coding often can be reduced by using the COMPUTE statement. This statement indicates the calculations that are to be performed in an algebralike expression. More than one operation can be coded in the statement. Thus, complex calculations can be coded using one COMPUTE statement.

The general form of the COMPUTE statement is as follows:

<u>COMPUTE</u> data-name = arithmetic-expression

The effect of this statement is that the arithmetic expression on the right of the equal sign is evaluated, and the result is assigned to the data name on the left of the equal sign. For example, consider the following COMPUTE statement:

```
COMPUTE A-FIELD = B-FIELD + C-FIELD - D-FIELD.
```

The expression on the right of the equal sign indicates that the values of B-FIELD and C-FIELD should be added and the value of D-FIELD should be subtracted from the result. The final value is then assigned to A-FIELD.

The arithmetic expression on the right of the equal sign of a COMPUTE statement may be a data name, a numeric literal, or an expression involving several names and literals. A COMPUTE statement with only a single data name or literal on the right is equivalent to a MOVE statement. For example, the following COMPUTE statement has only the numeric literal 0 on the right of the equal sign:

```
COMPUTE A-AMOUNT = 0.
```

In effect, this statement is equivalent to the following:

```
MOVE 0 TO A-AMOUNT.
```

More complex arithmetic expressions use *arithmetic operators* to indicate the type of calculation that is to be performed. The arithmetic operators that are used in COBOL and their meanings are as follows:

+ addition
– subtraction or negation
* multiplication
/ division
** exponentiation

Whenever any of these operators is used, the value of the data names or literals on either side of the operator is used in the calculation. For example, the expression

```
B-FIELD + C-FIELD
```

means add the value of B-FIELD and the value of C-FIELD. Notice that the symbol for multiplication is an asterisk (*). Thus the expression

```
PRINCIPAL * .05
```

means multiply the value of PRINCIPAL by .05. The slash means the value on the left is to be divided by the value on the right. For example, the expression

```
A-AMOUNT / 2
```

means divide the value of A-AMOUNT by 2. Exponentiation means raising to a power. It is indicated by two asterisks in succession. Thus, to raise the value of B-AMOUNT to the second power we would use the expression:

```
B-AMOUNT ** 2
```

The minus sign may be used to indicate either subtraction or negation. For subtraction, the second value is subtracted from the first. Thus the expression

```
E-FIELD - D-FIELD
```

means subtract the value of D-FIELD from the value of E-FIELD. To negate a value, the minus sign is used in front of a data name or literal with nothing to the left. Thus the expression

```
- X-VALUE
```

means form the negative of X-VALUE. A minus sign used in this manner is called a *unary* minus sign. (Some versions of COBOL also allow a unary plus sign; see Appendix A.)

For arithmetic expressions involving several arithmetic operators, the order in which the operations are performed becomes important. In COBOL the order is as follows:

1. All unary minus signs are evaluated
2. All exponentiation is performed
3. All multiplication and division is performed left to right
4. All addition and subtraction is performed left to right

For example, consider the following expression:

```
- A ** 2 + B * 3.5 / C - 5.0
```

This expression is evaluated in the following order:

1. The negative of A is computed
2. The result from step 1 is raised to the second power
3. The value of B is multiplied by 3.5 and the result is divided by C
4. The results from steps 2 and 3 are added, and then the value 5.0 is subtracted to get the final result

In algebraic notation, the expression appears as:

$$(-A)^2 + \frac{B \times 3.5}{C} - 5.0$$

Within an arithmetic expression, parentheses may be used to change the order of operations. When this is done, any expression in parentheses is evaluated first, before operations outside of the parentheses are performed. For example, consider the following modification of the previous example:

```
- (A ** 2 + B) * 3.5 / (C - 5.0)
```

The expression A ** 2 + B is enclosed in parentheses and is evaluated before the other operations are performed. Thus, the value of A is raised to the second power and the result is added to B. Then the expression C - 5.0 is evaluated, since it is enclosed in parentheses. Next, the unary minus is evaluated; and, finally, the multiplication and division operations are performed. The result in algebraic notation is as follows:

$$\frac{-(A^2 + B) \times 3.5}{C - 5.0}$$

Expressions in parentheses may be imbedded in other parenthetic expressions. When this is done, the computer evaluates the expression in the innermost parentheses first, then the expression in the next level of parentheses, and so on until all operations have been performed. For example, consider the following:

```
- (A ** (2 + B) * 3.5) / (C - 5.0)
```

In algebraic notation this expression is evaluated as follows:

$$\frac{-(A^{2+B} \times 3.5)}{C - 5.0}$$

Notice that, whenever parentheses are used, they must appear in pairs: for every left parenthesis there must be a matching right parenthesis.

Unlike algebra, operations may not be implied. That is, an arithmetic operator must always be used to indicate what operation is to be performed. For example, 3K is invalid and must be coded as 3 * K. Similarly, parentheses may not be used to imply multiplication. For example, (A + B)(B + C) is not valid and must be written

```
(A + B) * (B + C)
```

Arithmetic operators always must be preceeded by a space and followed by a space. There is one exception to this. When a unary minus sign (or unary plus sign, if permitted) is used after a left parenthesis, a space is usually not allowed after the parenthesis. This is not true for all versions of COBOL. Refer to Appendix A for differences.

Within an arithmetic expression, only numeric items or numeric literals may be used. Numeric-edited items, nonnumeric literals, and alphanumeric items may never appear in an arithmetic expression.

After the value of the arithmetic expression in a COMPUTE statement is evaluated, it is assigned to the data name on the left of the equal sign. It is important to recognize that the equal sign does not mean equality in COBOL. Rather, it means *assignment*. That is, the equal sign tells the computer to assign the value of the expression to the data name on the left. Therefore, there always must be a single data name — and never an arithmetic expression — on the left of the equal sign. In addition, statements that normally are invalid in algebra are correct in COBOL. For example, the statement

```
COMPUTE K = K + 1
```

is valid. It means that 1 is added to the current value of K and the result is assigned to K, replacing its old value. Thus, the value of K is increased by one. If K is 5 before this statement is executed, then it is 6 after execution. Similarly, the following statement causes the current value of A to be replaced by a value that is five times as large:

```
COMPUTE A = 5.0 * A
```

The data name on the left of the equal sign in the COMPUTE statement may be either a numeric item or a numeric-edited item. If it is a numeric-edited item, then the name may not be used in any arithmetic expression or another calculation.

The ROUNDED option and SIZE ERROR option may be used with the COMPUTE statement. The ROUNDED option is used after the data name on the left of the equal sign. The SIZE ERROR phrase comes at the end of the statement. For example, the following COM-PUTE statement contains both of these options:

```
COMPUTE A ROUNDED = B + C - D
    ON SIZE ERROR
        PERFORM ERROR-ROUTINE-BEGIN
            THRU ERROR-ROUTINE-END.
```

10-3. ADVANCED MODULE CONTROL

In Chapter 5 we described two forms of the PERFORM statement. With the simplest form, a module is performed once. For example, the statement

```
PERFORM CALCULATIONS-BEGIN
    THRU CALCULATIONS-END.
```

causes the module named CALCULATIONS to be performed a single time. With the PERFORM-UNTIL statement, a module is repeatedly executed until a specific condition occurs. Thus, the statement

```
PERFORM PROCESS-LOOP-BEGIN
    THRU PROCESS-LOOP-END
    UNTIL WK-EOF-FLAG IS EQUAL TO 'Y'.
```

causes the PROCESS-LOOP module to be performed over and over
until the end-of-file flag is equal to Y. In this section we describe two
other forms of the PERFORM statement that can be used to repeatedly
execute a module.

The PERFORM/TIMES Statement

Sometimes it is necessary to perform a module a specific number of
times. In this case, the PERFORM/TIMES statement may be used.
For example, assume that it is necessary to perform the CALCULA-
TIONS module exactly ten times. Then the following statement can be
used:

```
PERFORM CALCULATIONS-BEGIN
    THRU CALCULATIONS-END
    10 TIMES.
```

The last phrase of this statement indicates the number of times that the
module is to be performed. In effect, this statement creates a loop
containing the module, which is executed the number of times indicated.

Either a numeric literal or a data name may be used in the TIMES
phrase. If a data name is used, it must be numeric and have a positive
integer value. For example, assume that there is a field named WK-
LOOP-COUNT that indicates the number of times that the CALCULA-
TIONS module should be performed. Then the following PERFORM
statement can be used to repeatedly execute this module the required
number of times:

```
PERFORM CALCULATIONS-BEGIN
    THRU CALCULATIONS-END
    WK-LOOP-COUNT TIMES.
```

The PERFORM/VARYING Statement

In the PERFORM/VARYING statement, the value of a numeric data
name is varied each time that the module is performed. The data name,
its initial value, and the amount by which it is varied are specified
in the VARYING phrase of the statement. In addition, the statement

gives the condition that indicates when repetition of the module should be stopped.

The general form of the simplest PERFORM/VARYING statement is as follows:

PERFORM paragraph-name-1
    THRU paragraph-name-2
    VARYING data-name-1 FROM $\left\{\begin{array}{l}\text{literal-1}\\ \text{data-name-2}\end{array}\right\}$ BY $\left\{\begin{array}{l}\text{literal-2}\\ \text{data-name-3}\end{array}\right\}$
    UNTIL condition

The effect of this statement is to cause the computer to repeatedly perform the indicated paragraphs. Before executing the paragraphs the first time, data-name-1 is given the FROM value (that is, the value of literal-1 or data-name-2). The condition is then tested and, if it is true, the computer continues to the next statement after the PER-FORM statement. The condition can be any conditional expression that may be used in an IF statement. If the condition is false, the paragraphs are executed. Then the BY value (i.e., the value of literal-2 or data-name-3) is added to the value of data-name-1 and the condition is tested again. This continues until the condition becomes true.

As an example of the PERFORM/VARYING statement, consider the following:

```
PERFORM CALCULATIONS-BEGIN
    THRU CALCULATIONS-END
    VARYING WK-COUNTER FROM 1 BY 1
    UNTIL WK-COUNTER IS GREATER THAN 10.
```

In this statement, the data name WK-COUNTER is used to count the number of times that the CALCULATIONS module is performed. Initially, this item is given the value of 1. After each execution of the module, WK-COUNTER is increased by 1. The condition is tested just before the module is executed each time. If the condition is false, the module is executed; if it is true, the computer proceeds to the next statement following the PERFORM/VARYING statement.

In this example, the condition tested is whether the value of WK-COUNTER is greater than ten. Since WK-COUNTER is initially 1 and is increased by 1 each time that the module is performed, this item counts the number of times that the module is performed. The first time that the module is performed, WK-COUNTER is equal to 1; the second time that the module is performed, this item is equal to 2. This continues through the tenth time that the module is performed, during which WK-COUNTER is equal to 10. After this tenth time, WK-COUNTER is increased to 11. At this point, the condition is true and the module is no longer repeated. Thus, this PERFORM/-VARYING statement causes the CALCULATIONS module to be performed exactly ten times.

The advantage of using the PERFORM/VARYING statement for this type of processing instead of the PERFORM/TIMES statement is that the VARYING option allows the programmer to specify a data name that may be used in the module. A data name that counts the number of times that the module is performed often is needed for some processing within the module. (In Chapter 11 we will discuss the use of this technique in processing tables of data.)

Another advantage of the PERFORM/VARYING statement is that the FROM value and the BY value may be any integer value (except that the BY value may not be zero). Because of this we can use this statement to count in increments of 2s, 3s, or whatever and may even count backward. For example, using the phrase

```
VARYING WK-COUNTER FROM 0 BY 2
UNTIL WK-COUNTER IS GREATER THAN 50
```

counts from zero to 50 by 2s. Similarly, the phrase

```
VARYING WK-COUNTER FROM 10 BY -1
UNTIL WK-COUNTER IS EQUAL TO 0
```

counts backward from 10 to 1. The only restriction is that the FROM value and the BY value must have integer values. These values also may be given by data names. For example, in the following phrase, the current values of the data names are used for the FROM and BY values:

```
VARYING WK-AMOUNT FROM INIT-VALUE BY INCREMENT
UNTIL WK-AMOUNT IS GREATER THAN TEST-VALUE
```

The condition tested in the PERFORM/VARYING statement need not be related to the data name specified in the VARYING phrase. Any valid condition is acceptable. For example, the following statement causes an input module to be performed until the end-of-file flag is equal to Y:

```
PERFORM READ-INPUT-BEGIN
    THRU READ-INPUT-END
    VARYING WK-CARD-COUNT FROM -1 BY 1
    UNTIL WK-EOF-FLAG IS EQUAL TO 'Y'.
```

The VARYING phrase indicates that the item named WK-CARD-

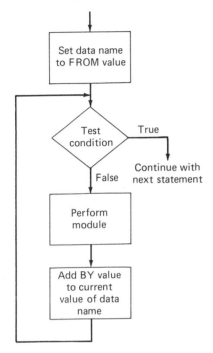

FIGURE 10-1. Flowchart Logic for the PERFORM/VARYING Statement

COUNT is to be initialized to -1 and increased by 1 each time that the module is performed. After the condition becomes true, this item will contain a count of the number of cards read.

It is important to remember the order in which the various steps in the PERFORM/VARYING statement are performed. The flowchart in Figure 10-1 summarizes the processing of this statement. Notice that the condition is tested before the module is performed, and that the data name is modified after the module is executed.

There are other forms of the PERFORM/VARYING statement that are used for complex processing. These are discussed in Chapter 11.

10-4. ADVANCED LOGICAL PROCESSING

In Chapter 4 we described the use of relation conditions in the IF statement. Relation conditions also are used in the UNTIL phrase of the PERFORM statement. Other conditions may be tested in the IF statement and used in the PERFORM statement. In Section 9-3 we described the use of condition-name conditions. In general, the condition in an IF or PERFORM statement is called a *conditional expression*. Relation conditions and condition-name conditions are specific types of conditional expressions. In this section we describe several other types of conditional expressions. We also discuss advanced forms of the IF statement.

Class Conditions

A class condition is used to test whether the value of a data name is numeric or alphabetic. A value is *numeric* if it contains solely numeric characters (that is, 0, 1, 2, . . . , 9) and possibly a sign. An item is *alphabetic* if it consists of only alphabetic characters (that is, A, B, C, . . . , Z) and spaces. Any other combination of characters is neither alphabetic nor numeric.

To test if a data name is numeric the class condition

data-name IS <u>NUMERIC</u>

is used. For example, the following IF statement causes a processing module to be performed if the item named IN-FIELD is numeric:

```
IF IN-FIELD IS NUMERIC
    PERFORM PROCESS-A-BEGIN
        THRU PROCESS-A-END.
```

The class condition for an alphabetic item is of the form:

data-name IS <u>ALPHABETIC</u>

The following IF statement uses this condition:

```
IF IN-DATA IS ALPHABETIC
    PERFORM PROCESS-B-BEGIN
        THRU PROCESS-B-END.
```

Either of the class conditions may be combined with NOT to test for the opposite conditions. Thus, the condition

data-name IS <u>NOT</u> <u>NUMERIC</u>

is true if the item is not of the numeric class. Similarly, the condition

data-name IS <u>NOT</u> <u>ALPHABETIC</u>

tests for the absence of an alphabetic item.

Whenever the NUMERIC condition is used, the item should have a numeric or alphanumeric picture. For the ALPHABETIC condition, the item should have an alphanumeric picture.

Class conditions often are used as one type of test to validate input data. Input validation involves determining if the input data conforms to the specifications for the program. For example, fields that are supposed to contain numeric values should be tested to be sure that no data errors have occurred. Other data validation tests involve determining whether values are within the expected ranges and whether the records are in the proper order.

Sign Conditions

A numeric item may be tested with a sign condition to determine if it is positive, negative, or zero. The sign condition is of the form:

$$\text{data-name IS} \left\{ \begin{array}{l} \underline{\text{POSITIVE}} \\ \underline{\text{NEGATIVE}} \\ \underline{\text{ZERO}} \end{array} \right\}$$

For example, the following PERFORM statement uses a sign condition in the UNTIL phrase:

```
PERFORM PROCESS-C-BEGIN
    THRU PROCESS-C-END
    UNTIL WK-AMOUNT IS NEGATIVE.
```

In this case, the module is performed until the item named WK-AMOUNT is less than zero.

The opposite of these conditions can be tested by including the word NOT. The condition has the following form:

$$\text{data-name IS } \underline{\text{NOT}} \left\{ \begin{array}{l} \underline{\text{POSITIVE}} \\ \underline{\text{NEGATIVE}} \\ \underline{\text{ZERO}} \end{array} \right\}$$

Complex Conditions

All of the conditional expressions discussed so far are called *simple conditions* because they each test for a single condition. It is possible to combine simple conditions with the words AND and OR to form complex conditions. This way, several conditions can be tested in one statement. The words AND and OR are called *logical operators*.

As an example of a complex condition, consider the following IF statement:

```
IF A-FIELD IS EQUAL TO B-FIELD
    AND B-FIELD IS NOT ZERO
    GO TO PROCESS-END.
```

In this example, a relation condition and a sign condition are tested. If both are true, then the GO TO statement is executed. If either condition is false or both are false, then the GO TO statement is bypassed.

The following statement illustrates the use of OR in a complex condition:

```
IF C-DATA IS LESS THAN 25
    OR C-DATA IS GREATER THAN 50
    PERFORM ERROR-RTN-BEGIN
        THRU ERROR-RTN-END.
```

In this example, two relation conditions are tested. If one or the other or both are true, then the ERROR-RTN module is performed. If both are false, then the PERFORM statement is not executed.

The AND logical operator always indicates that the complex condition is true if both simple conditions are true. However, if one or the other or both of the simple conditions is false, the AND operator indicates that the complex condition is false. The OR logical operator gives a true value if one or the other or both of the simple conditions is true. Otherwise, a false value is indicated.

Several AND and OR operators can be used in one expression. For example, the following conditional expression includes two AND operators and one OR operator:

```
A-FIELD IS EQUAL TO 10 AND B-FIELD IS ZERO
OR A-FIELD IS LESS THAN 5 AND B-FIELD IS POSITIVE
```

When several logical operators are used in one expression, the AND operators are evaluated first and then the OR operators. The order can be changed by using parentheses. Expressions within parentheses are evaluated first, before evaluating operators outside of the parentheses. For example, the following conditional expression uses the same basic form as the previous example, but it is evaluated in a different order because of the use of parentheses:

```
A-FIELD IS EQUAL TO 10
    AND (B-FIELD IS ZERO OR A-FIELD IS LESS THAN 5)
    AND B-FIELD IS POSITIVE
```

Other more complex conditions can be formed using logical operators. However, complex expressions are difficult to understand. In general, only a simple condition or a complex condition with a single logical operator should be used. If it is essential to use a more complex expression, parentheses should be included to set off the various parts of the expression and make the order of evaluation very clear.

Nested IF Statements

Within an IF statement, either after the conditional expression or in the ELSE phrase, other IF statements may be used. When such a structure is used, we say that the IF statements are *nested*. Not all versions of COBOL allow nested IF statements. (See Appendix A for differences.)

Figure 10-2 shows a general form with two nested IF statements.

```
IF condition-1
    statement-1
      .
      .
      .
    IF condition-2
        statement-2
          .
          .
          .
    ELSE
        statement-3
          .
          .
          .
ELSE
    statement-4
      .
      .
      .
    IF condition-3
        statement-5
          .
          .
          .
    ELSE
        statement-6
          .
          .
          .
```

FIGURE 10-2. The General Form for Nested IF Statements

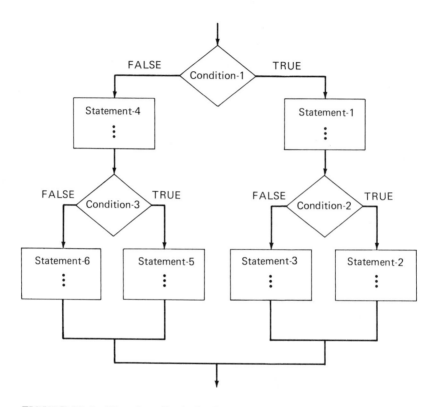

FIGURE 10–3. Flowchart Logic for Nested IF Statements

This statement is executed as follows: First condition-1 is tested. If it is true then the following is done:

1. Statement-1 and all of the following statements up to the next IF are executed.
2. Condition-2 is tested. If it is true, then statement-2 and all of the following statements up to the ELSE are executed. If condition-2 is false, then statement-3 and the statements that follow it are executed.
3. The computer goes on to the next sentence in sequence (assuming that no branch statement has been executed).

On the other hand, if condition-1 is false, then the computer proceeds as follows:

1. Statement-4 and the statements following it, up to the next IF, are executed.
2. Condition-3 is tested and, if it is true, then statement-5 and

```
IF A-FIELD IS GREATER THAN B-FIELD
    ADD 5 TO A-FIELD
ELSE
    IF A-FIELD IS EQUAL TO B-FIELD
        ADD 10 TO A-FIELD
    ELSE
        ADD 15 TO A-FIELD.
```

FIGURE 10-4. An Example of a Nested IF Statement

the statements up to the final ELSE are executed. If condition-3 is false, then the statements after the ELSE and up to the final period are executed.

3. If no branch statement has been executed, the computer goes on to the next sentence in sequence.

This logic is illustrated in the flowchart in Figure 10-3.

In the form shown in Figure 10-2 there are two nested IF statements. Additional IF statements may be nested, adding more "levels" to the logic. Simpler structures result from using fewer nested IF statements. For example, Figure 10-4 shows an IF statement with only one other IF statement nested in the ELSE part.

We can see from this discussion that nested IF statements can be quite complex. In general, it is best to avoid nested IF statements since they often can lead to errors. If a nested IF statement must be used, a form similar to that shown in Figure 10-4 is the easiest to understand. Nesting beyond one "level" makes a very complex structure.

Indentation becomes especially important when using nested IF statements. The statements that are to be performed under different conditions should be carefully indented to show their relationship to the conditions.

10-5. MULTIPLE PATH BRANCHING

As we have seen in Chapter 3, the GO TO statement can be used to branch from one point in the program to another. Another statement that may be used for branching is the GO TO/DEPENDING statement. With this statement, several branches can be specified; the computer selects one of the branches at the time of execution, depending on the value of a data name.

The GO TO/DEPENDING statement has the following general form:

GO TO paragraph-name-1, paragraph-name-2, . . .
DEPENDING ON data-name

(The word TO in this statement is optional in some versions of CO-
BOL; see Appendix A.) After the words GO TO is a list of names of
paragraphs to which the program may branch. The computer selects
one of the paragraphs, depending on the value of the data name. If
the data name is equal to 1, the computer branches to the first paragraph named. If the data name has a value of 2, the second paragraph
name is selected. Similarly, if the data name equals 3, then the computer branches to the third paragraph listed in the statement. This
continues for as many paragraph names as are listed in the statement.
In other words, the computer branches to one of the paragraphs depending on the value of the data name.

As an example of a GO TO/DEPENDING statement consider the
following:

```
GO TO CALC-A, CALC-B, CALC-B,
    CALC-C, CALC-C, CALC-D, CALC-C
    DEPENDING ON IN-CODE.
```

In this example the computer branches to the paragraph named CALC-
A if IN-CODE is equal to 1. If IN-CODE is 2 or 3, the computer branches
to the CALC-B paragraph. When IN-CODE is 4, 5, or 7, the CALC-C
paragraph is selected. The computer branches to CALC-D if IN-CODE
is equal to 6. Notice that the paragraph names need not be unique.
Depending on the requirements of the program, paragraph names
may be repeated in the GO TO/DEPENDING statement.

If the value of the data name is outside of the range for the number
of paragraphs listed, the computer does not branch. Instead, processing
continues with the next statement in sequence. Thus, in the last example, if IN-CODE is less than 1 or greater than 7, no branching takes
place.

The data name that is used in the GO TO/DEPENDING statement must be numeric with no decimal positions. As a result, it always has an integer value.

Figure 10-5 shows a flowchart of the logic in the previous example. This flowchart demonstrates how the decision symbol is used
to represent multiple path branching. Notice that each path leaving
the symbol is labeled with the condition that it represents.

The GO TO/DEPENDING statement can be used effectively in
some processing situations. However, because it is similar in effect
to a regular GO TO statement, we must be careful in its use. In general,
the GO TO/DEPENDING statement should only be used to branch
within a module. It should never be used to branch out of one module

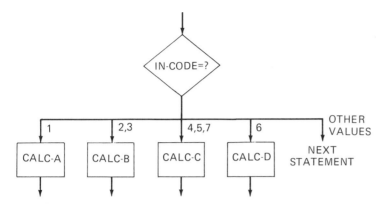

FIGURE 10-5. A Flowchart for a GO TO/DEPENDING Statement

to another. All the paragraphs named should be located farther down the module from the GO TO/DEPENDING statement. The statement never should be used to create a loop.

Often the GO TO/DEPENDING statement is used to select which of several paragraphs within a module is to be executed. The program logic usually indicates that after the selected paragraph is executed the other paragraphs should be bypassed. In order to do this, a GO TO statement at the end of each selected paragraph is necessary. Without this statement, the computer automatically would go on to the next paragraph in sequence. Usually this GO TO statement causes the computer to branch to the end paragraph of the module. An example of this is shown in Figure 10-6. The last GO TO statement in this example is not essential. However, it is a good idea to include this statement, since then additional paragraphs can be added without the possible error of forgetting to include the necessary GO TO statement.

10-6. SECTIONS IN THE PROCEDURE DIVISION

As we have seen, the environment and data divisions of a COBOL program are divided into sections. The procedure division may also contain sections. Sections in the procedure division are given names that are user-defined words following the same rules as paragraph names. A section begins with the name of the section, followed by the word SECTION and a period. The section contains all paragraphs and sentences up to the beginning of the next section or to the end of the program.

The advantage of using sections in the procedure division is that the entire section can be executed using a PERFORM statement.

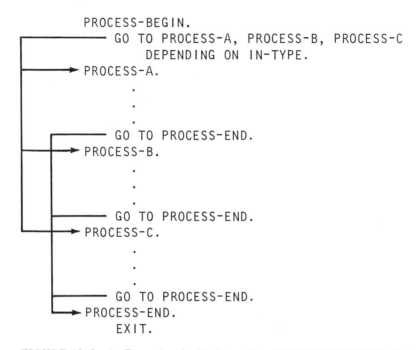

```
        PROCESS-BEGIN.
            GO TO PROCESS-A, PROCESS-B, PROCESS-C
                DEPENDING ON IN-TYPE.
        PROCESS-A.
                .
                .
                .
            GO TO PROCESS-END.
        PROCESS-B.
                .
                .
                .
            GO TO PROCESS-END.
        PROCESS-C.
                .
                .
                .
            GO TO PROCESS-END.
        PROCESS-END.
            EXIT.
```

FIGURE 10-6. An Example of a Module with a GO TO/DEPENDING Statement

For example, consider a section that has the form shown in Figure
10-7. This section has the name CALCULATIONS. To perform all of
the paragraphs in this section, the following PERFORM statement
may be used:

```
PERFORM CALCULATIONS.
```

Notice that when a section name is used in a PERFORM statement,
the word SECTION does not appear. In addition, it is not necessary
to name the first and last paragraphs that are to be performed. By
giving only the name of the section in the PERFORM statement, the
entire section of the procedure division is performed.

A section name also may be used in a GO TO statement. For
example, the statement

```
GO TO CALCULATIONS.
```

causes the computer to branch to the beginning of the CALCULA-
TIONS section. Notice again that the word SECTION is not used in
this statement.

When sections are used in the procedure division, the entire division
should be divided into sections. Usually each module is a separate

```
CALCULATIONS SECTION.
CALCULATIONS-BEGIN.
       .
       .
       .
CALC-A.
       .
       .
       .
CALC-B.
       .
       .
       .
CALCULATIONS-END.
     EXIT.
```

FIGURE 10-7. An Example of a Procedure Division Section

section. Then each PERFORM statement names a section that is to be performed.

10-7. CHARACTER PROCESSING

Most of the processing that we have described so far has involved numeric data. The arithmetic statements are used primarily for this type of processing. Logical operations involve numeric and nonnumeric data. In this section we discuss several statements that are used to process nonnumeric, or character, data.

The EXAMINE Statement

The most widely available statement for character processing is the EXAMINE statement. It is included in the 1968 version of ANS CO-BOL and most implementations use it, but it is not part of the 1974 ANS version (see Appendix A for details).

There are several forms of the EXAMINE statement. In the simplest form, the statement is used to count, or *tally*, the number of occurrences of certain characters in a field. The general form of this statement is as follows:

$$\underline{\text{EXAMINE}} \text{ data-name } \underline{\text{TALLYING}} \left\{ \begin{array}{l} \underline{\text{UNTIL FIRST}} \\ \underline{\text{ALL}} \\ \underline{\text{LEADING}} \end{array} \right\} \text{literal}$$

One of the three options UNTIL FIRST, ALL, and LEADING must be used. The data name may be either numeric or alphanumeric. The literal must be a single character and may be either numeric or non-numeric. However, if the data name is numeric, then the literal must also be numeric. Similarly, an alphanumeric data name requires a nonnumeric literal.

If the UNTIL FIRST option is used, then the computer examines the value of the data name from left to right and counts the number of characters until the first occurrence of the literal in the field. For example, consider the following statement:

```
EXAMINE A-FIELD TALLYING UNTIL FIRST '*'.
```

In this case, the value of A-FIELD is examined and the number of characters until the first asterisk is counted. If A-FIELD has the value ABC*D*E, then the EXAMINE statement counts three characters before the first asterisk. The count from the EXAMINE statement is stored in a special numeric item named TALLY. This item is not defined by the programmer. It is automatically part of the program. After an EXAMINE statement is executed, the name TALLY may be used to refer to the count.

With the ALL option of the EXAMINE statement, the count represents the number of occurrences of the literal in the field. For example, the statement

```
EXAMINE B-DATA TALLYING ALL 2.
```

counts the number of occurrences of the digit 2 in the item named B-DATA. This value is assigned to the special item named TALLY.

The LEADING option is used to count the number of occurrences of the literal until some other character appears. The field is examined left to right, and TALLY is assigned the count of the number of leading characters that are the same as the literal. Thus, the statement

```
EXAMINE C-ITEM TALLYING LEADING 0.
```

counts the number of leading 0s in C-ITEM. If C-ITEM has the value 0000123, then after execution of this statement TALLY is equal to 4.

Figurative constants (except ALL) may be used in the EXAMINE statement instead of a literal. Thus the previous example may be coded:

```
EXAMINE C-ITEM TALLYING LEADING ZEROS.
```

The EXAMINE statement also may be used to replace certain

occurrences of a character in a field by another character. The general form of this statement is as follows:

EXAMINE data-name

$$\underline{\text{REPLACING}} \begin{Bmatrix} \underline{\text{ALL}} \\ \underline{\text{LEADING}} \\ \underline{\text{FIRST}} \\ \underline{\text{UNTIL FIRST}} \end{Bmatrix} \text{literal-1} \underline{\text{BY}} \text{ literal-2}$$

In this statement, one of the options ALL, LEADING, FIRST, and UNTIL FIRST must be selected. Literal-1 and literal-2 must be single character literals or figurative constants. They must be numeric or nonnumeric, depending on whether the data name is numeric or alphanumeric.

With the ALL option, each occurrence of literal-1 in the data name is replaced by literal-2. For example, the statement

```
EXAMINE D-FIELD
    REPLACING ALL SPACES BY ZEROS.
```

causes all spaces in D-FIELD to be replaced by zeros. The LEADING option is used to replace all leading occurrences of literal-1 by literal-2. The field is examined left to right and all occurrences of literal-1 up to the first character that is not the same as literal-1 are replaced by literal-2. With the FIRST option, only the first occurrence of literal-1 is replaced by literal-2. Finally, the UNTIL FIRST option is used to replace all characters up to the first occurrence of literal-1 with literal-2.

The final version of the EXAMINE statement allows both tallying and replacing. This statement has the form:

$$\underline{\text{EXAMINE}} \text{ data-name } \underline{\text{TALLYING}} \begin{Bmatrix} \underline{\text{UNTIL FIRST}} \\ \underline{\text{ALL}} \\ \underline{\text{LEADING}} \end{Bmatrix} \text{literal-1}$$

$$\underline{\text{REPLACING}} \ \underline{\text{BY}} \text{ literal-2}$$

The TALLYING part of this statement operates as before. In addition, all characters that are counted are replaced by literal-2.

The INSPECT Statement

The INSPECT statement replaces the EXAMINE statement in the 1974 version of ANS COBOL. Figure 10–8 shows several forms of the INSPECT statement. The main difference when using the INSPECT statement for tallying is that the special item named TALLY is not

INSPECT data-name-1 TALLYING data-name-2

$$\text{FOR} \left\{ \begin{array}{l} \text{ALL} \\ \text{LEADING} \end{array} \right\} \text{literal}$$

INSPECT data-name-1 TALLYING data-name-2

FOR CHARACTERS BEFORE literal

INSPECT data-name

$$\text{REPLACING} \left\{ \begin{array}{l} \text{ALL} \\ \text{LEADING} \\ \text{FIRST} \end{array} \right\} \text{literal-1 BY literal-2}$$

INSPECT data-name

REPLACING CHARACTERS BY literal-1 BEFORE literal-2

FIGURE 10-8. Some Forms of the INSPECT Statement

used. Instead, the programmer must supply a data name after the word TALLYING. This name must be specified in the data division. After execution of the INSPECT statement this name is assigned the tally.

In the INSPECT statement, the UNTIL FIRST option of the EXAMINE statement is replaced by the more descriptive phrases shown in the second and fourth forms in Figure 10-8. The ALL, LEADING, and FIRST options are the same. The entire REPLACING phrase in the third and fourth forms may be used after the TALLY-ING phrase of the first and second forms. There are a number of other variations in the INSPECT statement. Refer to the appropriate reference manual for details.

The STRING and UNSTRING Statements

The STRING statement is used to bring together two or more fields into one field. A group of characters sometimes is called a *string*. The process of putting together two strings of data, one after the other, to form one long string is called *concatenation*. The STRING statement is used in COBOL to concatenate two or more strings of data. It is available in only a few versions of COBOL (see Appendix A).

The simplest form of the string statement is as follows:

STRING data-name-1, data-name-2, ... DELIMITED BY SIZE
        INTO data-name-n

The data names used in the STRING statement normally refer to alphanumeric items. The effect of this statement is to concatenate the items named after the word STRING and to store the result in the field named after the word INTO. For example, the following statement concatenates the contents of three fields:

```
STRING A-FIELD, B-FIELD, C-FIELD DELIMITED BY SIZE
       INTO D-FIELD.
```

Assume that A-FIELD is two characters in length with the value AB, B-FIELD contains four characters with the value 1234, and C-FIELD is three positions with the value XYZ. Concatenating these three fields yields the value AB1234XYZ. If D-FIELD is nine positions in length, then it receives the entire concatenated string. If D-FIELD is less than nine positions, then extra characters on the right are truncated. If D-FIELD is longer than nine positions, then the entire concatenated string is stored left-justified in D-FIELD with the extra positions on the right unchanged.

The UNSTRING statement performs the opposite function of the STRING statement. That is, the UNSTRING statement breaks a long character string into two or more substrings. The UNSTRING statement is available in only a few versions of COBOL.

The simplest form of the UNSTRING statement is as follows:

UNSTRING data-name-1 INTO data-name-2, data-name-3, ...

The effect of this statement is to store the first part of data-name-1 in data-name-2, the second part of data-name-1 in data-name-3, and so forth. The length of each part is determined by the lengths of data-name-2, data-name-3, and so on.

As an example of the UNSTRING statement consider the following:

```
UNSTRING D-FIELD INTO X-FIELD, Y-FIELD.
```

Assume that X-FIELD and Y-FIELD are four and five positions in length respectively, and that D-FIELD is nine characters with the value AB1234XYZ. After execution of this statement, X-FIELD has value AB12 and Y-FIELD is equal to 34XYZ.

The STRING and UNSTRING statements discussed in this section are the simplest forms of these statements. Several other options are available with each of these statements. Refer to the appropriate reference manuals for details.

10-8.   THE LIBRARY FEATURE

COBOL is a very wordy programming language in comparison to other languages. Because of this characteristic, COBOL programs are fairly easy to understand. However, in addition they are usually very long and tedious to code. Programmers are always looking for ways of reducing the amount of coding required in a COBOL program.

One way of reducing the amount of work necessary to code a COBOL program is to use parts of other programs. Often parts of several programs are identical. This is especially true with record descriptions. For example, several programs may process the same input record, and thus all can use the same record description.

A segment of a program that is to be used in another program usually is stored in a special file on a magnetic tape or disk called a *library*. (Sometimes this is called a *source-statement library* or a *source-program library*.) In the library there usually are many commonly used segments of programs. Each program segment in the library is given a name called a *library name*. The library name usually is assigned by the person who stored the program segment in the library.

To include a program segment from the library, the programmer uses a COPY statement in his or her COBOL program. The general form of this statement is as follows:

<u>COPY</u> library-name.

The effect of this statement is to copy the program segment with the indicated name from the library into the program at the point where the COPY statement is located. The library segment that is copied is considered part of the source program and is compiled along with the remainder of the program.

In most versions of COBOL, the COPY statement can be used only in certain restricted situations. These are summarized in Figure

Environment Division:

```
SOURCE-COMPUTER. COPY library-name.
OBJECT-COMPUTER. COPY library-name.
SPECIAL-NAMES. COPY library-name.
FILE-CONTROL. COPY library-name.
```

Data Division:

```
FD   file-name COPY library-name.
01   record-name COPY library-name.
```

Procedure Division:

```
paragraph-name. COPY library-name.
section-name SECTION. COPY library-name.
```

FIGURE 10-9. Uses of the COPY Statement

10-9. For example, assume that there is an entry in the library that contains the data division description of the salesperson record. This entry has the name SLSRC and consists of the level numbers, field names, and pictures for this record. Instead of coding this information in the data division, we can copy it from the library. The following entry in the data division accomplishes this:

```
01   SALES-PERSON-RECORD COPY SLSRC.
```

The programmer can use the data names in this record description exactly as if the entries are coded directly in the program.

Besides record descriptions, another common use of the COPY statement is to copy modules from the library. Often, common processing modules are used in several programs. If such a module is stored in the library the first time it is coded, the module can be used by other programmers.

Most versions of COBOL print the copied library entry along with the source listing. This way, the programmer has a complete listing of the program.

In some versions of COBOL the COPY statement is not restricted to the uses shown in Figure 10-9. In this case, the COPY statement may appear practically anywhere in the program. However, the statement always must be terminated by a period. This unrestricted use of the COPY statement is not available in all versions of COBOL (see Appendix A for differences).

CHAPTER 11

Table Processing

In many programs, tables of data are needed. For example, income tax tables are used in payroll programs. Pricing tables often are used in merchandising applications. Many programs use tables to tabulate or summarize the results of processing. In this chapter we discuss how tables are processed in COBOL. The reader must be familiar with the REDEFINES clause (Section 9-2) and the PERFORM/VARY-ING statement (Section 10-3) in order to understand this chapter.

11-1. TABLE CONCEPTS

A *table* is a list of data that is identified in a COBOL program by a single name. For example, Figure 11-1 shows a table of commission rates that might be used in the sales application discussed in previous chapters. The commission classification code comes from the input record for the salesperson (see column 26 in the card layout in Figure 1-9). The commission paid to the salesperson is a percentage of the salesperson's net sales. The commission rate depends on the sales-person's commission classification code as shown in the table in Figure 11-1.

In a COBOL program, each table is given a name that stands for the entire table. A table name is like other data names in COBOL. (In the next section we will see how table names are specified in a

Commission Classification Code	Commission Rate
1	.000
2	.010
3	.025
4	.050
5	.075
6	.100
7	.125
8	.150

FIGURE 11-1. A Table of Commission Rates

program.) The table of commission rates in Figure 11-1 may have the name COMMISSION-RATE.

Each value in a table is called an *element* of the table or an *entry* in the table. The elements of the table are numbered beginning with 1. In the commission rate table, the elements have the same numbers as the commission classification code. For example, the first element of the commission rate table has the value .000 and corresponds to commission classification code 1. Similarly, the fifth element has the value .075 and the eighth element has the value .150.

In order to identify a particular element of a table, we use the table name followed by the element number enclosed in parentheses. This number in parentheses is called a *subscript*. For example, to identify the first element of the commission table we use the name

COMMISSION-RATE (1)

Similarly the fifth and eighth elements are referred to by the names

COMMISSION-RATE (5)

and

COMMISSION-RATE (8)

The number in parentheses in these examples is the subscript and refers to an element of the table.

A table name with a subscript may be used like any other data name in a COBOL program. For example, we can calculate the commission for a salesperson with a commission classification code of 5 using the following statement:

```
MULTIPLY WK-NET-CURRENT-SALES BY COMMISSION-RATE (5)
     GIVING WK-COMMISSION.
```

We can also use subscripted table names in MOVE statements, IF statements, and practically any other place that a data name may appear in a program.

A subscript also may be a data name. For example, we can use the name SP-COMM-CLASS, which is the name for the input field containing the commission classification code. Thus, the subscripted table name

```
COMMISSION-RATE (SP-COMM-CLASS)
```

may be used to refer to an element of the commission rate table that depends on the value of SP-COMM-CLASS. If this field is 1, then the first element is identified; if it is 2, then the second element is referred to; and so on.

The process of locating an element of a table often is called *table look-up* or *table search*. Using the name of the table followed by a subscript is a form of table look-up. Given the subscript, the program "looks up" the corresponding element of the table. Another form of table look-up involves finding the subscript given the table *element*. For example, we may wish to know the commission classification code for the rate .025. This involves searching the table until the appropriate rate is found. In the next section we will see other examples of table look-up.

The type of table that is illustrated in this section often is called a *one-level* or *single-level* table. COBOL also allows two- and three-level tables. In the next section we will discuss one-level table processing in detail. In the following section we will describe multilevel tables and their processing.

11-2. ONE-LEVEL TABLES

Tables are specified in the data division of a COBOL program by using the OCCURS clause. This clause identifies a table name and indicates how many elements are in the table. The OCCURS clause has the general form:

OCCURS integer TIMES

The integer gives the number of elements in the table. This must be a positive whole number.

The OCCURS clause must appear with an item description entry that has a level number between 02 and 49. The name of the item in the description is the table name. The PICTURE clause gives the picture of each element of the table. For example, the following entry may be used to define the eight-element commission rate table:

```
05  COMMISSION-RATE       PIC V999    OCCURS 8 TIMES.
```

In this example, the table name is COMMISSION-RATE. The OCCURS clause indicates that there are eight elements in this table. The PICTURE clause specifies that each element has the picture V999.

Because the OCCURS clause cannot appear with an 01 level entry, the table specification with this clause must be a subordinate entry in a record description. Sometimes this entry is part of an input record description. Often, however, each table is defined as a separate record in the WORKING-STORAGE section. For the commission rate table this may be accomplished as follows:

```
01  COMMISSION-RATE-TABLE.
    05  COMMISSION-RATE       PIC V999    OCCURS 8 TIMES.
```

In this example, the group item named COMMISSION-RATE-TABLE refers to the entire table of data. However, this name is *not* used to refer to individual elements of the table. The name COMMISSION-RATE with a subscript is used for this purpose.

When an OCCURS clause is used, a table is defined in the data division. However, this definition of the table does not assign values to the elements in the table. Later we will see how this is done. For now we will assume that the appropriate values have been assigned to the table and discuss how the table is processed.

In the previous section we saw how subscripts are used to refer to the elements of a table. When an item is defined with an OCCURS clause it always must be used with a subscript. That is, we never can use a table name in a COBOL program without a subscript. The subscript may be a numeric literal or a numeric data name. The value of the subscript must be a whole number within the range specified by the OCCURS clause. For example, in the commission rate table, the subscript must be an integer value from 1 to 8.

Most versions of COBOL require that a space be included between the table name and the left parenthesis enclosing the subscript. However, no space may appear after the left parenthesis or before the right parenthesis. These restrictions are not made in all versions of COBOL (see Appendix A).

In the last section we describe how subscripted table names may be used in statements in a COBOL program. Often an entire table needs to be processed in some manner. For example, we may wish to find the total of all of the elements of a table or set each element of the table to some initial value. When this type of processing is necessary, a loop usually is used to process the table one element at a time. The PERFORM/VARYING statement can be most useful in this situation.

As an example of the use of the PERFORM/VARYING statement, assume that we have a table named DATA-VALUE that contains 50 elements. We need to find the total of the 50 values in this table and to store the result in an item named WK-VALUE-TOTAL. Figure 11-2 shows how this might be done. In this example, the TOTAL-VALUES module is performed in a loop. The item named WK-SUB is used as a subscript for the DATA-VALUE table. This item must be defined with a numeric picture with no decimal positions. The PERFORM/VARYING statement uses this same name in the VARYING phrase. After WK-VALUE-TOTAL is initialized to zero, the PERFORM/VARYING statement sets WK-SUB to 1. Then the TOTAL-

```
PROCEDURE DIVISION.
        .
        .
        .
    MOVE ZERO TO WK-VALUE-TOTAL.
    PERFORM TOTAL-VALUES-BEGIN
        THRU TOTAL-VALUES-END
        VARYING WK-SUB FROM 1 BY 1
        UNTIL WK-SUB IS GREATER THAN 50.
        .
        .
        .
TOTAL-VALUES-BEGIN.
    ADD DATA-VALUE (WK-SUB) TO WK-VALUE-TOTAL.
TOTAL-VALUES-END.
    EXIT.
```

FIGURE 11-2. An Example of Table Processing Using the PERFORM/VARYING Statement

```
PROCEDURE DIVISION.
    .
    .
    .
    PERFORM ZERO-TABLE-BEGIN
        THRU ZERO-TABLE-END
        VARYING WK-SUB FROM 1 BY 1
        UNTIL WK-SUB IS GREATER THAN 25.
    .
    .
    .
ZERO-TABLE-BEGIN.
    MOVE ZERO TO DATA-AMOUNT (WK-SUB).
ZERO-TABLE-END.
    EXIT.
```

FIGURE 11-3. Initializing a Table Using the PERFORM/VARYING Statement

VALUES module is performed. As a result, DATA-VALUE (1) is added to WK-VALUE-TOTAL. Then WK-SUB is increased to 2 and the module is performed again. This time DATA-VALUE (2) is added to WK-VALUE-TOTAL. Thus, after two executions of the TOTAL-VALUES module, WK-VALUE-TOTAL is equal to the sum of the first two elements of the table. Processing continues in this manner until the fiftieth element of the table is added to WK-VALUE-TOTAL. Thus, at the end of processing, WK-VALUE-TOTAL is equal to the sum of the 50 elements in the DATA-VALUE table.

In order to assign initial values to the elements of a table, several techniques are possible. One of the problems with initializing tables is that the VALUE clause cannot be used along with the OCCURS clause. The reason for this is that the OCCURS clause defines many items, while the VALUE clause gives only one value. Thus, other techniques must be used to initialize the elements of a table.

The PERFORM/VARYING statement may be used when each element of a table is to be initialized to the same value. For example, assume that we need to assign an initial value of zero to each element of the 25-element table named DATA-AMOUNT. Figure 11-3 shows how this might be done.

Often, the initial values for the elements of a table are contained in one or more data cards. When this is the case, properly defining an input record sometimes solves the initialization problem. For example, assume that the eight elements of the commission rate table are contained in the first eight three-column fields of a punched card, with no spaces between the fields. We then could define an input record in the WORKING-STORAGE section as follows:

```
01  COMMISSION-RATE-TABLE.
    05  COMMISSION-RATE        PIC V999    OCCURS 8 TIMES.
    05  FILLER                 PIC X(56).
```

The first 24 columns of the card contain the table values. The 56-character FILLER is necessary to account for all 80 columns of the punched card. In order to read this record we could use the following statement:

```
READ SALES-PERSON-FILE INTO COMMISSION-RATE-TABLE
    AT END . . .
```

After execution of this statement, the commission rate table is available for processing in the program.

A table also may be initialized in the WORKING-STORAGE section. However, since the VALUE clause cannot be used with the OCCURS clause, the initial values must be specified first and then redefined as a table. Figure 11-4 illustrates this approach. First, a record is defined with a filler for each element of the table. The fillers are assigned the initial values for the table using VALUE clauses. Then this record is redefined as a table. The OCCURS clause is used in this part of the specification.

Whether the initial values of a table are specified in WORKING-STORAGE or read from an input card depends on the requirements of the problem. If the table values vary from time to time, then the input technique should be used. Extra input is required each time the program is run. However, this is more desirable than changing the values for the table in WORKING-STORAGE. If the table values are constant, then initializing the values in WORKING-STORAGE is more desirable.

In the examples that we have discussed so far, the table name always has been an elementary item. However, this is not essential.

```
01  COMMISSION-RATE-VALUES.
    05  FILLER                 PIC V999 VALUE .000.
    05  FILLER                 PIC V999 VALUE .010.
    05  FILLER                 PIC V999 VALUE .025.
    05  FILLER                 PIC V999 VALUE .050.
    05  FILLER                 PIC V999 VALUE .075.
    05  FILLER                 PIC V999 VALUE .100.
    05  FILLER                 PIC V999 VALUE .125.
    05  FILLER                 PIC V999 VALUE .150.
01  COMMISSION-RATE-TABLE REDEFINES COMMISSION-RATE-VALUES.
    05  COMMISSION-RATE        PIC V999 OCCURS 8 TIMES.
```

FIGURE 11-4. Initializing a Table in the WORKING-STORAGE Section

The name associated with a table may define a group item. In such a case, a subscript may be used with the names of the elementary items in the group to identify the subparts of the table element.

As an example of the use of a group item in a table definition, consider the pricing table shown in Figure 11-5. This table has six elements. Each element consists of a product's identification code and its price. To define this table, it is necessary to use a group item for each element. The group item contains an elementary item for the product code and an elementary item for the price. The following data description entries accomplish this:

```
01  PRICING-TABLE
      05  PRICE-DATA              OCCURS 6 TIMES.
          10  PRODUCT-CODE        PIC XX.
          10  PRODUCT-PRICE       PIC 99V99.
```

The OCCURS clause must appear with the name of the group item. This clause indicates the number of elements in the table. The elementary item descriptions give the picture of each part of the table elements.

When a table is defined using a group item entry, any reference to the group name or the names of the elementary items must be subscripted. For example, to identify the third element of the table we would use the name PRICE-DATA (3). This name refers to the entire entry containing the product code and the price. To identify the parts of this element separately we would use the subscripted names PRODUCT-CODE (3) and PRODUCT-PRICE (3).

Product Code	Product Price
A1	1.25
A5	7.00
C3	3.98
C8	12.50
D1	.75
E7	6.39

FIGURE 11-5. A Pricing Table

Table look-up for this type of table usually requires special processing. Normally we are given the value of one of the elementary items and we must look up the other. For example, we may be given product code C3 and asked to find the corresponding price. Sometimes the product is not in the table. In this case, special error processing must be performed.

Figure 11-6 shows an example of table look-up for the situation described here. In this example, we assume that an item named IN-PRODUCT-CODE is an input field containing the product code for a product that we wish to locate in the table. When this product is found, the PROCESS-ROUTINE module is to be performed. If the product code is not in the table, then the ERROR-ROUTINE module is to be performed. The end-of-search flag is used to signal either that the product has been found or that the end of the table has been reached without finding the product. The PERFORM/VARYING

```
PROCEDURE DIVISION.
        .
        .
        .
    MOVE 'N' TO WK-END-OF-SEARCH-FLAG.
    PERFORM TABLE-SEARCH-BEGIN
        THRU TABLE-SEARCH-END
        VARYING WK-SUB FROM 1 BY 1
        UNTIL WK-END-OF-SEARCH-FLAG IS EQUAL TO 'Y'.
        .
        .
        .
TABLE-SEARCH-BEGIN.
    IF PRODUCT-CODE (WK-SUB) IS EQUAL TO IN-PRODUCT-CODE
        PERFORM PROCESS-ROUTINE-BEGIN
            THRU PROCESS-ROUTINE-END
        MOVE 'Y' TO WK-END-OF-SEARCH-FLAG
        GO TO TABLE-SEARCH-END.
    IF WK-SUB IS EQUAL TO 6
        PERFORM ERROR-ROUTINE-BEGIN
            THRU ERROR-ROUTINE-END
        MOVE 'Y' TO WK-END-OF-SEARCH-FLAG.
TABLE-SEARCH-END.
    EXIT.
```

FIGURE 11-6. A Table Look-up Routine

statement uses this flag to indicate that the TABLE-SEARCH module should no longer be performed.

The type of table look-up that is illustrated in this example is sometimes called a *sequential search*. This is because the program goes through the table elements in sequence from the beginning of the table examining each element in turn. The search ends either when the desired element is found or when the end of the table is reached without finding the wanted element.

Another type of table look-up is called a *binary search*. For this type of look-up, the field that is examined in the table must be in ascending or descending sequence. The program searches by looking in the *middle* of the table first. The program determines whether the desired element is above or below the middle and then searches the appropriate half of the table. Next the program examines the middle of the indicated half and determines whether the wanted element is above or below this point in the table. Each time that the program makes a comparison it cuts the part of the table under consideration in half. This process continues either until the desired element is located or until it can be determined that the element is not in the table.

Binary search is very fast for some types of tables. The table must be arranged so that the field that is searched is in ascending or descending sequence. If this is not the case, a sequential search must be used. Sequential search is fast if the desired element is toward the beginning of the table but is slow otherwise. Because binary search can be used in many situations, some versions of COBOL provide special statements for this type of table look-up. These statements are explained in the appropriate reference manuals.

11-3. MULTILEVEL TABLES

In a one-level table the elements vary with one factor. For example, in the one-level pricing table shown in Figure 11-5, the price varies with the product code. In some situations, tables are needed in which two or more factors are used to specify an element. A price table in which the price depends on the product code and the size is an example of a two-level table. If the price depends on three factors such as product code, size, and color, then a three-level table is needed. In this section we discuss two-level and three-level tables.

Size:

		1	2	3
	1	1.10	1.25	1.39
Product Code:	2	6.85	7.25	7.75
	3	14.90	16.05	17.20
	4	3.85	3.98	4.19

FIGURE 11-7. A Two-level Pricing Table

Two-level Tables

Figure 11-7 shows a simple two-level pricing table. The price for a product depends on the product code and the size. This table lists the prices of four products in three sizes each. For example, the price of product 3 in size 2 is 16.05. The price of product 1 in size 3 is 1.39.

To define a two-level table in a COBOL program, each level must be specified with an OCCURS clause. First the number of *rows* in the table is specified in a data description entry. Then the number of *columns* is given in a subordinate entry. For example, the following entries may be used to specify the two-level pricing table:

```
05  PRODUCT-NUMBER                           OCCURS 4 TIMES.
    10  PRODUCT-PRICE      PIC 99V99          OCCURS 3 TIMES.
```

The first entry gives the number of products; the second gives the number of sizes for each product. The second entry also contains the PICTURE clause that gives the picture of each element of the table.

The table name that is used to identify the elements of a table is the name in the last entry in the table description. Thus, in the previous example, the table name is PRODUCT-PRICE. To identify an element of a two-level table, *two* subscripts must be used after the table name. The first subscript gives the *row* number and the second gives the *column* number of the desired element in the table. These subscripts must be enclosed in parentheses and separated by a comma with a space after the comma. (Some versions of COBOL do not require a comma with multiple subscripts. See Appendix A

Size:

	1	2	3
1	(1,1)	(1,2)	(1,3)
2	(2,1)	(2,2)	(2,3)
3	(3,1)	(3,2)	(3,3)
4	(4,1)	(4,2)	(4,3)

Product Code:

FIGURE 11-8. The Subscripts for the Elements of the Two-level Pricing Table

for differences.) For example, to identify the price of product 3 in size 2 we use the name PRODUCT-PRICE (3, 2). Similarly, the name for the table element containing the price of product 1 in size 3 is PRODUCT-PRICE (1, 3). The complete list of subscripts for the pricing table is shown in Figure 11-8.

In order to assign values to the elements of a two-level table, data may be read from input records or assigned in the WORKING-STOR-AGE section. In the latter case, the data must be organized by rows. That is, the data for the first row must be given before the data for the second row and so forth. For the pricing data, this means that the prices for the three sizes for the first product must be listed first, followed by the prices for the second product, then the third product's prices, and finally the data for the last product. Then the data for the table are redefined and the OCCURS clauses for the table are given. This is illustrated in Figure 11-9.

When a two-level table must be processed in a loop, a special form of the PERFORM/VARYING statement may be used. This statement has the form:

PERFORM paragraph-name-1
    THRU paragraph-name-2
    VARYING data-name-1 FROM literal-1 BY literal-2
    UNTIL condition-1
    AFTER data-name-2 FROM literal-3 BY literal-4
    UNTIL condition-2

This statement causes a module to be performed with *two* data names

```
01  PRICING-TABLE-VALUES.
    05  PRODUCT-1-VALUES.
        10  FILLER          PIC 99V99 VALUE 1.10
        10  FILLER          PIC 99V99 VALUE 1.25.
        10  FILLER          PIC 99V99 VALUE 1.39.
    05  PRODUCT-2-VALUES.
        10  FILLER          PIC 99V99 VALUE 6.85.
        10  FILLER          PIC 99V99 VALUE 7.25.
        10  FILLER          PIC 99V99 VALUE 7.75.
    05  PRODUCT-3-VALUES.
        10  FILLER          PIC 99V99 VALUE 14.90.
        10  FILLER          PIC 99V99 VALUE 16.05.
        10  FILLER          PIC 99V99 VALUE 17.20.
    05  PRODUCT-4-VALUES.
        10  FILLER          PIC 99V99 VALUE 3.85.
        10  FILLER          PIC 99V99 VALUE 3.98.
        10  FILLER          PIC 99V99 VALUE 4.19.
01  PRICING-TABLE REDEFINES PRICING-TABLE-VALUES.
    05  PRODUCT-NUMBER                  OCCURS 4 TIMES.
        10  PRODUCT-PRICE   PIC 99V99 OCCURS 3 TIMES.
```

FIGURE 11-9. Initializing the Two-level Pricing Table in WORKING-STORAGE

varying. In effect, this statement produces a loop within a loop. The *outer* loop causes data-name-1 to vary from the value of literal-1 by the amount of literal-2 until condition-1 is true. The *inner* loop is executed each time that the outer loop is performed. In this loop, data-name-2 is varied from an initial value of literal-3 by the value of literal-4 until condition-2 is true. Each time that the inner loop is executed, the module named in the statement is performed. This logic is summarized in the flowchart in Figure 11-10. The FROM and BY values in this statement also may be given by data names if the values of the names are integer.

As an example of this form of the PERFORM/VARYING statement, assume that we have defined the following table in WORKING-STORAGE:

```
05  DATA-ROW                        OCCURS 10 TIMES.
    10  DATA-VALUE   PIC 9(5)V99     OCCURS 5 TIMES.
```

This table consists of ten rows and five columns. It is necessary to initialize all elements of this table to zero. Figure 11-11 shows how this may be done. In this example, the data name WK-SUB-1 in the PERFORM statement is varied from 1 to 10 and is used as the first subscript for the table name in the processing module. The data name

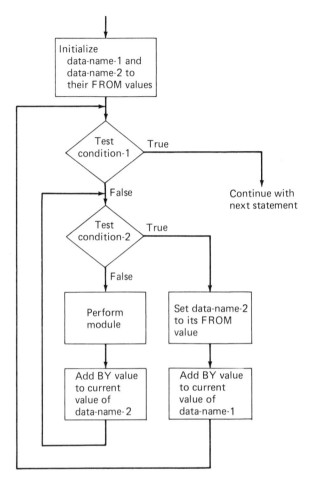

FIGURE 11-10. Flowchart Logic for the PERFORM/VARYING Statement that Varies Two Data Names

WK-SUB-2 is used as the second subscript. It is varied from 1 to 5 by the PERFORM statement.

Three-level Tables

In a three-level table, the elements depend on three factors. Figure 11-12 shows a simple three-level pricing table. In this case, the price depends on the product code, the size, and the color. For example, the price of a product with product code 3, in size 2, and with color code 2 is 17.36.

```
PROCEDURE DIVISION.
      .
      .
      .
    PERFORM INITIALIZE-TABLE-BEGIN
        THRU INITIALIZE-TABLE-END
        VARYING WK-SUB-1 FROM 1 BY 1
        UNTIL WK-SUB-1 IS GREATER THAN 10
        AFTER WK-SUB-2 FROM 1 BY 1
        UNTIL WK-SUB-2 IS GREATER THAN 5.
      .
      .
      .
INITIALIZE-TABLE-BEGIN.
    MOVE ZERO TO DATA-VALUE (WK-SUB-1, WK-SUB-2).
INITIALIZE-TABLE-END.
    EXIT.
```

FIGURE 11-11. Initializing a Two-level Table Using a PERFORM/VARYING Statement

		Color 1			Color 2		
		Size 1	Size 2	Size 3	Size 1	Size 2	Size 3
	1	1.10	1.25	1.39	1.19	1.34	1.47
Product Code:	2	6.85	7.25	7.75	7.35	7.80	8.25
	3	14.90	16.05	17.20	15.89	17.36	18.45
	4	3.85	3.98	4.19	4.05	4.24	4.39

FIGURE 11-12. A Three-level Pricing Table

To define a three-level table, three OCCURS clauses are required. For example, the three-level pricing table is specified by the following entries:

```
05  PRODUCT-NUMBER                        OCCURS 4 TIMES.
    10  PRODUCT-SIZE                      OCCURS 3 TIMES.
        15  PRODUCT-PRICE   PIC 99V99     OCCURS 2 TIMES.
```

The first OCCURS clause gives the number of products, the second specifies the number of sizes, and the third gives the number of colors. The PICTURE clause appears with the last entry and gives the picture of each element in the table.

When a three-level table is used, *three* subscripts are required to identify each element. The name in the last entry in the table description is used as the table name, followed by the subscripts in parentheses. For example, to identify the price of the third product in size 2 and color 2 we use the name PRODUCT-PRICE (3, 2, 2). The first subscript gives the product code, the second represents the size, and the third gives the color code.

The processing techniques for one- and two-level tables may be extended to three-level tables. The PERFORM/VARYING statement for three-level table processing has the form:

PERFORM paragraph-name-1
    THRU paragraph-name-2
    VARYING data-name-1 FROM literal-1 BY literal-2
    UNTIL condition-1
    AFTER data-name-2 FROM literal-3 BY literal-4
    UNTIL condition-2
    AFTER data-name-3 FROM literal-5 BY literal-6
    UNTIL condition-3

With this statement, three data names are varied. The flowchart logic for the statement is shown in Figure 11-13. The FROM and BY values in this statement may be given by data names instead of literals.

Figure 11-14 shows an example of the use of the PERFORM/VARYING statement to initialize the elements of a three-level table to zero. In this example the table is named DATA-AMOUNT. The first subscript is varied from 1 to 10; the second subscript, from 1 to 5; and the third subscript, from 1 to 8.

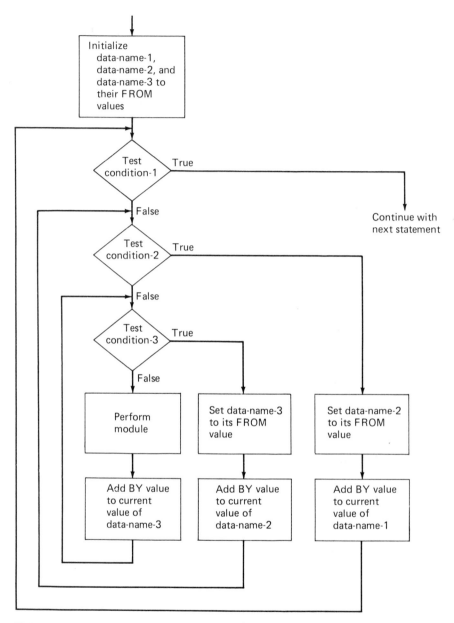

FIGURE 11-13. Flowchart Logic for the PERFORM/VARYING Statement that Varies Three Data Names

```
PROCEDURE DIVISION.
        .
        .
        .
    PERFORM ZERO-TABLE-BEGIN
        THRU ZERO-TABLE-END
        VARYING WK-SUB-1 FROM 1 BY 1
        UNTIL WK-SUB-1 IS GREATER THAN 10
        AFTER WK-SUB-2 FROM 1 BY 1
        UNTIL WK-SUB-2 IS GREATER THAN 5
        AFTER WK-SUB-3 FROM 1 BY 1
        UNTIL WK-SUB-3 IS GREATER THAN 8.
        .
        .
        .
ZERO-TABLE-BEGIN.
    MOVE ZERO TO DATA-AMOUNT (WK-SUB-1, WK-SUB-2, WK-SUB-3).
ZERO-TABLE-END.
    EXIT.
```

FIGURE 11-14. Initializing a Three-level Table Using a PERFORM/VARYING
Statement

CHAPTER 12

Internal Data
Representation

In order to use the COBOL programming language, little knowledge of the internal organization of a computer is needed. In fact, in previous chapters we have discussed only briefly the physical characteristics of a computer. However, some familiarity with the computer's internal structure will help us to understand certain features of COBOL. Of most use is an understanding of the way data is represented in the internal storage of a computer. In this chapter we discuss internal data representation and its relationship to COBOL.

12-1. DATA REPRESENTATION

Humans usually represent data by using *characters*. In the Western world, the character set consists of *alphabetic characters* (A, B, . . . , Z), *numeric characters* (0, 1, . . . , 9), and a number of *special characters* ($, + / etc.). Computers, however, cannot use human characters to represent data. A computer's internal storage is composed of a large number of electromagnetic circuits. Each circuit has only two conditions or *states* — "on" and "off." An example of a common electronic circuit that has only two states is a light bulb. Like a circuit in a computer, a light bulb can be only on or off. There are 50 to 60 common characters used by humans to represent data. If a single circuit in a computer were used to represent any character, then that circuit would have to have 50 to 60 different states. However, because a computer's circuit is a two-state device, it is not possible to represent any human character with a single circuit.

How, then, do computers store data? The answer is that computers use a series of electromagnetic circuits in a particular pattern of on/off states to represent data. A computer processes data (that is, characters) by converting the data to its two state representation. For output, the computer converts the results of its processing from the two-state internal representation to human characters.

Data represented in this two-state manner are said to be in the *binary mode*. For ease of presenting data in the binary mode on paper, the digit "1" is used to represent the "on" state and the digit "0" is used for the "off" state. The characters "1" and "0" are called the *binary digits*, or *bits*. Internally, all data are stored as bits.

12-2. NUMBER SYSTEMS

In order to understand how data is represented in the binary mode, it is necessary first to consider number systems. A *number system* is a way of expressing quantities. Most humans use the *decimal number system*. However, most computers use the *binary number system*.

The Decimal Number System

Consider the decimal number 285. What does this number really mean? We can think of 285 as 200 plus 80 plus 5. But 200 is 2 times 100, 80 is 8 times 10, and 5 is 5 times 1. Finally, 100 is 10 times 10 or 10^2, 10 is 10^1, and 1 is 10^0. Thus, 285 can be interpreted as follows:

$$285 = 200 + 80 + 5$$
$$= (2 \times 100) + (8 \times 10) + (5 \times 1)$$
$$= (2 \times 10^2) + (8 \times 10^1) + (5 \times 10^0)$$

(It is appropriate at this time to review briefly the concept of raising a number to a power. Any number raised to a power means to multiply the number by itself the number of times specified in the power; that is, use the number as a factor the number of times given by the power. For example, 6^4 means use 6 as a factor 4 times:

$$6^4 = 6 \times 6 \times 6 \times 6 = 1296$$

As other examples consider the following:

$$10^2 = 10 \times 10 = 100$$
$$10^3 = 10 \times 10 \times 10 = 1000$$
$$10^4 = 10 \times 10 \times 10 \times 10 = 10000$$
$$2^2 = 2 \times 2 = 4$$
$$2^3 = 2 \times 2 \times 2 = 8$$
$$2^4 = 2 \times 2 \times 2 \times 2 = 16$$
$$2^5 = 2 \times 2 \times 2 \times 2 \times 2 = 32$$

A number raised to the first power is just that number. For example, 6^1 is 6, 10^1 is 10, and 2^1 is 2. Finally, a number raised to the zero power is one. This is true for any number except zero [0^0 is indeterminate]. For example, 6^0 is 1, 10^0 is 1, and 2^0 is 1).

As another example of a decimal number, consider 4096:

$$4096 = 4000 + 000 + 90 + 6$$
$$= (4 \times 1000) + (0 \times 100) + (9 \times 10) + (6 \times 1)$$
$$= (4 \times 10^3) + (0 \times 10^2) + (9 \times 10^1) + (6 \times 10^0)$$

Notice how the digit zero is used to hold a place in the number without adding value to the number. In this example zero holds the 100s place. But since zero times any number is zero, it does not increase the value of the number.

These examples illustrate the basic concepts of a number system. A number system is composed of a set of *digits*. In the decimal number system the digits are 0, 1, 2, 3, 4, 5, 6, 7, 8, and 9. The number of digits is called the *base* of the number system. There are ten digits in the decimal number system because the base of the system is ten. (The word *decimal* means ten.) A *number* is a quantity that is represented by a *numeral* composed of a string of digits. For example, the decimal numeral 285 is composed of digits that are acceptable in the decimal number system. This numeral represents the number two-hundred eighty-five. The digits in a numeral occupy positions that have value. The *position values* (also called *place values*) of a number system are successive powers of the base. Considering only whole numbers, the rightmost position has a value of the base to the zero power, the next position to the left has a value of the base to the first power, the next position has a value of the base to the second power, and so forth. Thus, the position values for the decimal number system are as follows:

$$\ldots 10^5 \quad 10^4 \quad 10^3 \quad 10^2 \quad 10^1 \quad 10^0$$

A numeral is interpreted in a number system as the sum of the products of the digits in the numeral and their corresponding position values. Thus, 285 is interpreted as a decimal number as follows:

Digits:	2	8	5
Position values:	10^2	10^1	10^0
Interpretation:	$(2 \times 10^2) + (8 \times 10^1) + (5 \times 10^0)$		

The interpretation of the numeral is found by multiplying the digits in the numeral by their corresponding position values and then adding the results. Notice that the rightmost digit occupies the 10^0 position, and that the position values increase to the left.

As another example, consider 4096:

Digits:	4	0	9	6
Position values:	10^3	10^2	10^1	10^0
Interpretation:	$(4 \times 10^3) + (0 \times 10^2) + (9 \times 10^1) + (6 \times 10^0)$			

Note how the digit zero serves the purpose of holding a place in the numeral without adding value to the number.

In summary, a number system is composed of a set of digits. The base of the system is the number of digits that are acceptable in the system. The position values are successive powers of the base. A numeral is a string of digits that represents a number or quantity. A numeral can be interpreted as the sum of the products of the numeral's digits and their position values.

Although we have made a distinction between a numeral and a number, the distinction is rarely made in practice. Most often we use the word "number" whether we mean the "quantity" or the representation of the quantity by a "numeral." This practice will be followed in the remainder of this chapter. The meaning of the term should be evident from the context in which it is used.

The Binary Number System

Computers do not use the decimal number system to express quantities. Since a computer uses two-state electronic circuits, it requires a number system that has only two digits. Such a system is the *binary number system*.

The base of the binary number system is two. The digits of the binary number system are 0 and 1. These are the binary digits or bits that correspond to the "on" and "off" states of a computer's circuits. The position values are successive powers of the base:

$$\ldots 2^5 \quad 2^4 \quad 2^3 \quad 2^2 \quad 2^1 \quad 2^0$$

A number in any number system can be composed only of digits acceptable to the system. Thus, a binary number can be composed only of the digits 1 and 0. For example, 10011 is a binary number (read "one zero zero one one"). To interpret a binary number, each digit is multiplied by its corresponding position value and the results are totaled. Thus, the binary number 10011 can be interpreted as follows:

$$
\begin{array}{lccccc}
\text{Digits:} & 1 & 0 & 0 & 1 & 1 \\
\text{Position values:} & 2^4 & 2^3 & 2^2 & 2^1 & 2^0 \\
\text{Interpretation:} & (1 \times 2^4) & + (0 \times 2^3) & + (0 \times 2^2) & + (1 \times 2^1) & + (1 \times 2^0)
\end{array}
$$

Since the position values are expressed in the decimal system, such an interpretation results in converting the binary number to its equivalent in the decimal number system:

$$
\begin{aligned}
10011 &= (1 \times 2^4) + (0 \times 2^3) + (0 \times 2^2) + (1 \times 2^1) + (1 \times 2^0) \\
&= (1 \times 16) + (0 \times 8) + (0 \times 4) + (1 \times 2) + (1 \times 1) \\
&= 16 + 0 + 0 + 2 + 1 \\
&= 19
\end{aligned}
$$

Thus, 10011 in the binary number system is equivalent to 19 in the decimal number system.

A special notation is sometimes used to distinguish numbers in different number systems. In this notation, the base of the number system is written as a subscript immediately following the number. Thus 10011_2 is a base 2 or binary number and 19_{10} is a base 10 or decimal number. This notation, while not required, is important when there may be confusion about the base of the number. For example, consider the number 10. This may represent a decimal number ("ten") or a binary number ("one zero"). However, 10_{10} is not equivalent to 10_2 ($10_2 = (1 \times 2^1) + (0 \times 2^0) = 2_{10}$). Therefore, to avoid confusion, this special notation is used to indicate what type of number is being expressed.

As a final example, consider the binary number 110101. This number can be interpreted as follows:

$$
\begin{array}{lcccccc}
\text{Digits:} & 1 & 1 & 0 & 1 & 0 & 1 \\
\text{Position values:} & 2^5 & 2^4 & 2^3 & 2^2 & 2^1 & 2^0 \\
\text{Interpretation:} & (1 \times 2^5) & + (1 \times 2^4) & + (0 \times 2^3) & + (1 \times 2^2) & + (0 \times 2^1) & + (1 \times 2^0) \\
& = (1 \times 32) & + (1 \times 16) & + (0 \times 8) & + (1 \times 4) & + (0 \times 2) & + (1 \times 1) \\
& = 32 & + 16 & + 0 & + 4 & + 0 & + 1 \\
& = 53
\end{array}
$$

Thus, 110101_2 is equivalent to 53_{10}.

Decimal to Binary Conversion

So far we have only considered conversion of a binary number to its decimal equivalent. The inverse process, that of converting a decimal number to its binary equivalent, is also important. There are a number of quick techniques for doing this. The technique discussed here, while not the fastest, is based on the underlying nature of number systems.

To convert a decimal number to its binary equivalent, the largest power of two that is less than or equal to the decimal number is found first. Then the maximum significant position value in the binary equivalent of the decimal number is that power of two. Working backwards toward 2^0, the next significant position value is found. This value is the next power of two that is less than or equal to the original decimal number minus the position value that has already been used. This continues until the 2^0 position is reached, or until the remainder from subtracting significant position values from the original number is zero.

For example, consider the decimal number 21. The largest power of two that is less than or equal to 21 is 2^4 or 16. Thus, there is 1 $\times$ 2^4 in 21. Subtracting 2^4 from 21 leaves 5. The largest power of two that is less than or equal to 5 is 2^2 or 4; there is 1×2^2 in 5. Subtracting 2^2 from 5 leaves 1. The largest power of two that is less than or equal to 1 is 2^0 or 1; there is 1×2^0 in 1. Subtracting 1 from 1 leaves 0 and there are no more significant position values. Thus, in 21 there is 1×2^4, 1×2^2, and 1×2^0. The intermediate position values (2^3 and 2^1) are held by the digit 0. Therefore, the binary equivalent of 21_{10} is 10101_2. These calculations can be summarized as follows:

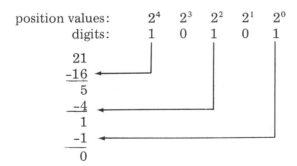

As another example, consider the decimal number 54. The largest power of two that is less than or equal to 54 is 2^5 or 32. Working backwards from 2^5 to 2^0, we get the following:

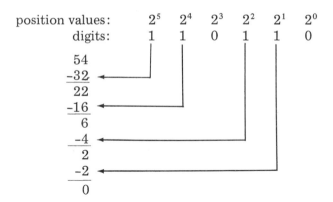

Thus 54_{10} is equivalent to 110110_2.

Hexadecimal Notation

One of the problems that the programmer faces when using binary numbers is that these numbers are often very long. As a result, they are difficult to read, write, and remember. For example, the binary number

1011010100101110

is 16 bits in length and is equivalent to the five digit decimal number 46,382. To try to remember this binary number is very difficult. Even copying the number leads to errors because of the repetitive use of 1s and 0s. The programmer could convert all binary numbers to their decimal equivalents and use these decimal numbers. But, as we have seen, the conversion process takes time and also leads to errors.

When a programmer must work with binary numbers, the usual procedure is to use a shorthand notation for the numbers. The notation is such that it is easy to convert the binary number to its equivalent in the shorthand notation and to convert back. The programmer can use the shorthand notation for any work that he or she needs to do with binary numbers.

There are several shorthand notations that are used for binary numbers. One of the most common is called *hexadecimal notation*. Actually, this notation is a number system with a base of 16 (hexadecimal means 16). However, we don't need to understand it as a number system to see how it is used as a notation for binary numbers.

In hexadecimal notation there are 16 digits. These digits correspond to the decimal numbers 0 through 15. The first ten hexadecimal digits are the same as the decimal digits 0, 1, . . . , 9. For the remaining six hexadecimal digits we use the first six letters of the alphabet A, B, C, D, E, and F. In other words, the hexadecimal digit A corresponds to the decimal number 10, B is equivalent to 11, and so forth up to the hexadecimal digit F, which is equal to the decimal number 15. Notice that we could have used any other six symbols for these six hexadecimal digits. However, we could not have used 10, 11, ..., 15 since these are not individual symbols but rather combinations of other digits. By convention, however, the first six letters of the alphabet are used for the last six hexadecimal digits.

The reason that hexadecimal digits are used as a shorthand notation for binary numbers is because any four bit binary number can be represented by a hexadecimal digit. For example, the four bit binary number 1010 is equivalent to the decimal number 10, which, as we have said, is equal to the hexadecimal digit A. The largest four bit binary number is 1111, which is 15 in the decimal number system and F in hexadecimal notation. Some four bit binary numbers require 0s in the lead positions. For example, 0011 is equal to 3 in the decimal number system and is 3 in hexadecimal notation. The binary number 0000 is 0 in both the decimal and hexadecimal systems. Figure 12-1 shows a complete list of hexadecimal digits and their equivalents in the binary and decimal number systems.

To use hexadecimal numbers as a shorthand notation for long binary numbers we arrange the bits of the binary number into groups of four. Then we write down the equivalent hexadecimal digit for each group. For example, the binary number given at the beginning of this section is converted to hexadecimal notation as follows:

$$1011\ 0101\ 0010\ 1110$$
$$B\quad 5\quad 2\quad E$$

Thus B52E is the hexadecimal notation for the 16 bit binary number.

To convert a hexadecimal number to its equivalent binary number we reverse the process. For each hexadecimal digit, we write the equivalent four bit binary number. For example, consider the hexadecimal number 40AF7. Since this number has five digits, the equivalent binary number will have five times four or 20 digits. The conversion is as follows:

$$4\quad 0\quad A\quad F\quad 7$$
$$0100\ 0000\ 1010\ 1111\ 0111$$

Hexadecimal notation is used by many computers when printing binary numbers. In addition, reference manuals often use this notation to explain the internal data representation of the computer. We will use hexadecimal notation in a number of examples in this chapter.

Decimal	Binary	Hexadecimal
0	0000	0
1	0001	1
2	0010	2
3	0011	3
4	0100	4
5	0101	5
6	0110	6
7	0111	7
8	1000	8
9	1001	9
10	1010	A
11	1011	B
12	1100	C
13	1101	D
14	1110	E
15	1111	F

FIGURE 12-1. Decimal–Binary–Hexadecimal Equivalence

12-3. INTERNAL DATA REPRESENTATION

Computers use the binary number system or some variation of it to represent data in their internal storage. In general, a computer's internal storage is composed of a large number of electromagnetic circuits. The individual circuits are grouped to form *storage locations*. Each storage location is a group of several computer circuits. By setting the circuits in a storage location to a particular pattern of on/off states, a value can be stored. Later, the computer can examine the pattern of on/off states to determine what value is stored at the storage location.

As a simple analogy, consider a sequence of four light bulbs. In Figure 12-2 the light bulbs are shown in the pattern on-off-off-on. Using binary digits, this represents 1001 or the decimal number 9. A different pattern of on/off states (i.e., bits) represents different

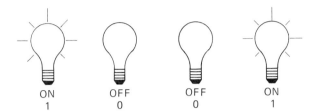

ON   OFF   OFF   ON
1   0   0   1

FIGURE 12-2. Internal Data Representation — The Light Bulb Analogy

data. Of course, computers don't use light bulbs for their internal storage, but the idea is the same; a pattern of bits, stored in a series of computer circuits, is used to represent data.

As we have seen, there are two major types of data that are used in COBOL. *Numeric data* consists of numbers that are manipulated arithmetically. For example, in the sales analysis application the year-to-date sales is numeric data because it is used in various calculations. *Alphanumeric data* consists of letters, numbers, and special characters that are not processed arithmetically. A salesperson's name is an example of alphanumeric data. A street address is alphanumeric data even though it may contain some numbers; the numbers in the address normally are not used in arithmetic calculations.

Internally, computers represent different types of data in different ways. In order to execute a COBOL program, a computer must be able to store alphanumeric data and numeric data. In this section we discuss how these types of data are stored in a computer. This section considers only the internal data representation that is used by the IBM System/360 and System/370 computers. However, the basic principles can be extended to almost all computers. Some of the differences for other computers are discussed in Appendix A.

Alphanumeric Data

Alphanumeric data consists of alphabetic, numeric, and special characters. In the IBM System/360 and System/370, an alphanumeric character is stored as a sequence of eight bits. That is, each character is assigned a unique, eight bit code that represents the character. For example, the letter A is represented by the code 11000001 or C1 in hexadecimal notation; the letter K is represented by 11010010 (D2 in hexadecimal notation); the number 5 is 11110101 (F5 in hexadecimal notation); the decimal point is represented by 01001011 (4B in hexadecimal notation). There is a unique eight bit pattern for each alphanumeric character.

This code is called the Extended Binary Coded Decimal Interchange Code or EBCDIC. It is a standard code that has been adopted by many computer manufacturers. There are a total of 256 different configurations of eight bits, but not all are used in the EBCDIC code. However, all of the characters used in COBOL have a unique representation in this code.

The EBCDIC code is related to the Hollerith card code. Recall from Chapter 1 that, in the Hollerith code, each alphabetic character is represented by two punches, one in the zone area of the punched card and the other in the digit area. For example, the letter A is a 12-punch (a zone punch) and a 1-punch. In the EBCDIC code, the first four bits usually represent the zone punch and the last four bits represent the digit punch. For example, a 12-punch is 1100 (or C in hexadecimal notation) in EBCDIC. Since the letter A is a 12-punch and a 1-punch, it is represented in EBCDIC by a code consisting of 1100 for the zone part and 0001 for the digit part. The same pattern applies to the other alphabetic characters. No zone punch is used for numeric characters. In EBCDIC, the absence of a zone punch is represented by 1111 (F in hexadecimal notation). Hence, the EBCDIC code for the digit 5 consists of 1111 for the zone part and 0101 for the digit part.

Although the EBCDIC code uses binary digits to represent alphanumeric characters, the computer does not confuse an alphanumeric character with a true binary number. For example, if the computer is told that 11000001 represents an alphanumeric character in the EBCDIC code, it interprets it as the letter A. If this pattern of eight bits is interpreted as a true binary number, it is equivalent to the decimal number 193. This is especially important when considering the numeric characters. For example, 5 is represented in the EBCDIC code as 11110101. However, if this pattern is interpreted as a true binary number, it is equivalent to the decimal number 245. Thus, the way in which a series of bits is interpreted depends on whether the bits are supposed to represent alphanumeric data or numeric data.

In the IBM System/360 and System/370, each storage location is composed of eight bits. An eight bit storage location is often referred to as a *byte*. Bytes are the basic building blocks of internal storage. Each byte is given a unique number, called an *address*, to identify it. The computer locates data in storage by specifying the address of the byte or bytes where the data is stored. The internal storage capacity is measured in terms of the number of bytes that can be stored. For example, one common model of the IBM System/370 has a capacity of about 146,000 bytes.

Numeric Data

There are two types of numeric data that are used commonly in COBOL on the IBM System/360 and /370. These are *binary data* and *packed decimal data.* A third type, called *floating-point data*, also is available but rarely is used. We only consider binary and packed decimal data in this book.

Binary data are the simplest type of numeric data. Internally, each binary item is represented by a binary number. Each number is stored in a fixed number of bits that depends on the item's length. If the item is one to four decimal digits in length, then 16 bits or two bytes are used to store the data. If the item is five to nine decimal digits, then 32 bits (four bytes) are used. An item that is 10 to 18 decimal digits requires 64 bits (eight bytes) of internal storage. For example, assume that we wish to store the decimal number 25 as binary data. In the binary number system, 25 is 11001. However, since 25 has two digits, 16 bits are required to store this number. Hence, 25 is represented internally as

$$0000000000011001$$

or 0019 in hexadecimal notation. The significant part of the number is stored on the right, with zeros filling in the lead positions.

A configuration of a fixed number of bits that are used to represent numeric data is called a *word*. In the IBM System/360 and 370, each word is 32 bits. Since internal storage is composed of eight bit bytes, four consecutive bytes are required to form a word. Two bytes are called a *half-word* and eight bytes are called a *double-word*. Binary data is stored internally in half-words, full words, or double-words depending on the length of the item being stored.

The difference between numeric and alphanumeric data can be understood more clearly at this point. As a 16 bit true binary number, 25 is represented as shown above. As alphanumeric data, however, 25 appears as follows:

$$11110010 \quad 11110101$$

(This is F2F5 in hexadecimal notation.) The first byte represents 2 in the EBCDIC code; the second byte is 5. In this form, the data cannot be used in arithmetic calculations. It can only be stored in the computer's internal storage and retrieved when needed. However, as a binary number, the data can be used in arithmetic processing.

A binary item can be either positive or negative. In a binary number requiring 16, 32, or 64 bits, the sign is represented by the first bit. If the first bit is 0, then the number is positive; if the first bit is 1, then the sign is negative. In fact, negative numbers are stored in a special manner known as *two's complement form*. To form the two's complement of a binary number, the number is first inverted (that is, all of the 1 bits are changed to 0s and all of the 0 bits are changed to 1s) and then 1 is added. The result is the negative of the original number in two's complement form. For example, –25 is formed as follows:

                0000000000011001   (+25 as a true binary number)
                1111111111100110   (invert the number)
                            +1   (add 1)
                1111111111100111   (–25 in two's complement)

Note that the first bit (the sign bit) is a 1, indicating a negative number in two's complement form. Internally, all negative binary numbers are represented in two's complement form.

The other type of numeric data used on the IBM systems is packed decimal data. This representation of data is related to the EBCDIC code. Recall that in EBCDIC, each character requires eight bits or one byte. Thus, the number 138 in EBCDIC is

                11110001 11110011 11111000

This is F1F3F8 in hexadecimal notation. Numbers, when represented in EBCDIC, sometimes are called *zoned decimal data*. In zoned decimal data, the first four bits of each byte are 1111 (hexadecimal F), except possibly for the last byte. The first four bits of the last byte of a zoned decimal item are used to represent the sign of the number. If there is no sign, then 1111 (hexadecimal F) is used in these positions. A number with this configuration is treated as if it were a positive number. If the number is negative, then 1101 (D in hexadecimal) is used for the first four bits of the last byte. For example, –138 is represented in zoned decimal as

                11110001 11110011 11011000

or F1F3D8 in hexadecimal notation. If the number has a plus sign, then 1100 (C in hexadecimal notation) is used for the sign bits. Thus +138 is represented as

                11110001 11110011 11001000

or F1F3C8 in hexadecimal notation.

Zoned decimal data cannot be used in calculations. In fact, zoned decimal data are considered alphanumeric data and not numeric data. However, zoned decimal data can be converted to *packed decimal data* very easily and in this form the data can be used in calculations. To convert a zoned decimal item to a packed decimal item, the first four bits of each byte except the last are discarded, and the remaining four bits are stored, or packed, two per byte. This pattern is followed for all bytes in the item except for the last. In the last byte, the sign is represented in the first four bits. This is not discarded, but is interchanged with the last four bits and stored in the last byte of the packed item. For example, Figure 12-3 shows how -138 is converted from zoned decimal to packed decimal.

Notice that packed decimal data usually require less storage than zoned decimal data. For example, -138 in zoned decimal notation requires three bytes, while -138 in packed decimal form uses only two bytes.

If a zoned decimal item has an even number of digits, then converting to packed decimal requires special processing. For example, 2184 in zoned decimal is

$$11110010 \quad 11110001 \quad 11111000 \quad 11110100$$

or F2F1F8F4 in hexadecimal notation. In packed decimal form this becomes

$$00000010 \quad 00011000 \quad 01001111$$

or 02184F in hexadecimal notation. In converting to packed decimal form in this example, the bits 0000 have been added in the first four positions of the first byte. This is necessary when there are an even number of digits because the first byte must be used completely.

Boundary Alignment

When binary data is used in calculations, there are special restrictions on the locations where the data can be stored. Stated simply, these restrictions say that a binary item used in a calculation must begin at a storage location that is evenly divisible by the length of the item in bytes. Thus a half-word binary item must be stored beginning at an address that is evenly divisible by two. A full-word binary item

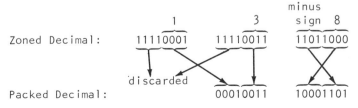

FIGURE 12-3. Converting -138 from Zoned Decimal Notation to Packed Decimal Form

must be stored so that the address of the first byte in the word is divisible by four. Similarly a double-word item must have an address divisible by eight.

These rules are called *boundary alignment* restrictions. If a binary item is not aligned on the appropriate boundary, when it is needed for calculation purposes it must be moved to a properly aligned boundary before the calculation can take place.

Boundary alignment does not apply to alphanumeric or packed decimal data. Such data may begin at any address in the computer's internal storage.

12-4. THE USAGE AND SYNCHRONIZED CLAUSES

Usually a COBOL programmer does not have to be concerned with the internal representation of the data used in his or her program. However, sometimes programs can be made more efficient if certain COBOL clauses are used in data descriptions. In this section we describe these clauses, and in the next section we discuss program efficiency.

In a data description entry, the USAGE clause can be used to specify the internal data representation or "usage" of an item. In ANS COBOL this clause has the general form:

$$[\text{USAGE IS}] \begin{Bmatrix} \underline{\text{DISPLAY}} \\ \underline{\text{COMPUTATIONAL}} \\ \underline{\text{COMP}} \end{Bmatrix}$$

For example, the following data description entry uses the USAGE clause:

```
05  A-AMOUNT      PIC 9(5)V99
                  USAGE IS COMPUTATIONAL.
```

The phrase USAGE IS is optional with the clause, but one of the three words DISPLAY, COMPUTATIONAL, or COMP must be used. (As we will see, some versions of COBOL have other words that can be used in the USAGE clause.)

If DISPLAY usage is specified then the item is stored as alphanumeric data. The COMPUTATIONAL usage specifies that the item is stored as numeric data. The word COMP is an abbreviation for COMPUTATIONAL.

With the IBM System/360 and System/370, DISPLAY usage means that the data is stored in the EBCDIC code. COMPUTATIONAL usage means that the item is stored as binary data. For packed decimal data another usage is needed. This is COMPUTATIONAL-3 which may be abbreviated COMP-3. (COMPUTATIONAL-1 and COMPU-TATIONAL-2 are used for floating-point data, which are not discussed in this book.) Other versions of COBOL may use other USAGE clauses for different types of data (see Appendix A for details).

A USAGE clause may appear with any item description in the data division. If it is used with a group item, then the usage specified applies to all elementary items in the group. If a USAGE clause is *not* used, then the DISPLAY usage is assumed. In fact, because of this characteristic, DISPLAY usage is rarely specified.

Usually, input and output fields are DISPLAY usage. This is required for card input and printer output. Magnetic tape and disk files sometimes use other forms of data representation for some fields. Working items used for intermediate results of calculations usually are specified as COMPUTATIONAL usage (or COMPUTATIONAL-3 on the IBM systems). If they are not specified otherwise, then they are assumed to be DISPLAY usage. Before such an item can be used in a calculation, it must be converted to an appropriate computational form.

To specify boundary alignment, the SYNCHRONIZED clause is used with the data description entry. This clause, which is just the word SYNCHRONIZED or the abbreviation SYNC, may be used with any internal data representation, but can only appear with an elementary item. However, it only has an effect if boundary alignment is significant with the item's representation. For the IBM System/360 and System/370, the SYNCHRONIZED clause has an effect only on COMPUTATIONAL usage items. (See Appendix A for the effect of the SYNCHRONIZED clause in other systems.) For example, the following data description entry specifies a binary item that is aligned on the appropriate boundary in internal storage:

```
05  A-AMOUNT       PIC 9(5)V99
                   USAGE IS COMPUTATIONAL
                   SYNCHRONIZED.
```

If the SYNCHRONIZED clause is not used, then the item is not aligned. Whenever such a nonaligned item is used in a calculation, it first is moved to a properly aligned area in storage.

12-5. PROGRAM EFFICIENCY

It is possible for a programmer with no knowledge of the computer's internal data representation to use COBOL. Programs coded by such a programmer may be as efficient as those coded by a very knowledgable programmer. However, a programmer who is experienced in the use of the USAGE and SYNCHRONIZED clauses and who is aware of the internal storage characteristics of the computer generally can write more efficient programs than the less experienced programmer.

In this section we discuss several basic rules for program efficiency. Efficiency rules depend largely on the internal structure of the computer being used. The rules presented in this section apply to the IBM System/360 and System/370. Appendix A discusses variations in these rules for other computers.

In an arithmetic calculation or comparison of numeric items, all fields should have the same internal representation if possible. If they do not, then extra processing is required to convert the fields to a common form. Numeric input items normally have DISPLAY usage and must be converted to a numeric form before they can be used in calculations. Moving such items to working storage fields with COMPUTATIONAL or COMPUTATIONAL-3 usage may save processing time if the fields are used in several calculations. In general, COMPUTATIONAL-3 usage should be used for all numeric working items. If COMPUTATIONAL usage is used, then extra processing is required to convert to and from DISPLAY usage. This processing is warranted only if the item being converted is used in at least eight to ten calculations with other items of the same usage.

The one place where COMPUTATIONAL usage always should be used is with subscripts (see Chapter 11). This produces more efficient table processing. If COMPUTATIONAL usage is specified for any item, then the SYNCHRONIZED clause should also be used. This forces boundary alignment of the item, which is required if the item is used in any form of calculation or numeric comparison.

If COMPUTATIONAL-3 usage is specified, then the item's picture should have an odd number of digits. The reason for this is that a half of a byte is wasted if an even number of digits are specified for packed decimal data. Thus the picture 9(7)V99 is better than 9(6)V99.

In an arithmetic operation or numeric comparison, the number of decimal places in the items used should be the same. For example, assume that A-DATA has the picture 9(5)V99. We wish to test this item to see if it is equal to 100. The relation condition in the test should use the numeric literal 100.00 rather than 100, since A-DATA has two decimal places. Thus, the condition should be

```
A-DATA IS EQUAL TO 100.00
```

and not

```
A-DATA IS EQUAL TO 100
```

Whenever a numeric item is specified, a sign (S) should be indicated in the item's picture unless it specifically is not wanted (see Section 9-4 for sign specification). The reason for this is that, when no sign is indicated, the computer purposefully removes any positive or negative sign if it appears. Thus, extra instructions and processing time are required when the sign specification is not used.

In general, the rules discussed in this section will increase the efficiency of a COBOL program. However, efficiency in computer programs comes in two forms. One is execution speed and the other is storage utilization. Usually the programmer must trade off between these two. That is, a fast program may require more storage than a slow one and vice versa. However, this is not always true and the efficiency rules discussed here usually will produce faster programs that use less storage.

Another factor that is important to remember when considering program efficiency is that most business data processing programs are *I/O bound*. This means that most of the time the CPU is waiting for an input or output device to complete its processing. The reason for this is that I/O devices are much slower than the central processing unit. Therefore, saving a few fractions of a second in internal calculation speed may not decrease the overall processing time.

Finally, program correctness is far more important than program efficiency. Because of this, the programmer should concentrate on the design of the program before he or she begins thinking about efficiency. In general, it is best to design, code, and test the program completely before worrying about matters of speed and storage utilization. The few rules presented in this section may be followed in the initial version of the program, as long as in so doing the programmer is not distracted from the basic goal of producing a correct program. After the program has been debugged thoroughly, the programmer can think about efficiency. It usually turns out that matters of speed and storage utilization are not important, and, therefore, the programmer need not worry about making the program more efficient. However, if these matters are significant, then changes can be made to increase the efficiency of the program. Thus, program efficiency should come after program correctness in priority in the programming process.

CHAPTER 13

Magnetic Tape and Disk Processing

There are many forms of input and output that are used in computerized data processing. In previous chapters we have considered mainly punched card input and printed output. In some data processing applications these are the sole forms of input and output. However, in many situations, other types of I/O are used in addition to these basic forms or as substitutes for them.

Two of the most commonly used input/output media are magnetic tape and magnetic disk. In this chapter we discuss these forms of I/O and describe the COBOL elements used to process them in a program.

13-1. MAGNETIC FILE CONCEPTS

Magnetic tape and magnetic disk are similar in that they both record data by magnetic means. As a result, some of the characteristics of tape and disk files are the same. However, as we will see, there are a number of important differences between tape and disk that result in different methods of file organization and processing. In this section we describe the physical characteristics of magnetic tape and disk and discuss the organization and processing of files stored on these media.

Magnetic Tape Characteristics

The magnetic tape that is used with computers is similar to tape recorder tape. Magnetic tape is made of a plastic material with a metallic coating on one side. Usually computer tape is one-half inch wide and comes in reels of various lengths. The most common length is 2400 feet. Figure 13-1 shows a reel of magnetic tape.

Data is recorded on the metallic surface of the tape by patterns of magnetic spots. Each character is represented by a unique pattern of spots just as hole patterns are used to represent characters in punched cards. The capacity of a tape is usually expressed in characters per inch of tape. One commonly used tape can store 800 characters per inch. However, some types of magnetic tape have a capacity of 1600 characters per inch and more.

A *magnetic tape drive* is used to record data on a magnetic tape and to retrieve data from a tape. Figure 13-2 shows a tape drive. A tape reel is mounted in the tape drive by the computer operator and the tape is fed past a mechanism called a *read/write head* (see Figure 13-3). This mechanism has the ability to read data from a tape and to write data on a tape. When data is read from a tape, the original

FIGURE 13-1. A Magnetic Tape Reel (Courtesy of IBM Corp.)

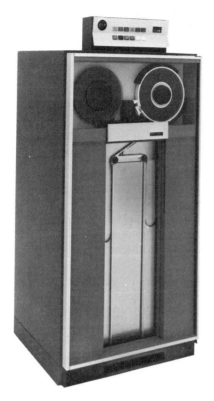

FIGURE 13-2. A Magnetic Tape Drive (Courtesy of IBM Corp.)

FIGURE 13-3. The Read/Write Mechanism of a Magnetic Tape Drive (Courtesy of IBM Corp.)

data on the tape is unchanged. However, during a write operation, any data that may be on the tape is erased and replaced with the new data.

To read or write data, the tape drive moves the tape past the read/write head. Usually data can be read or written in only one direction. We call a tape drive a *sequential access* device because data must be read or written in sequence starting at the beginning of the tape file. After the processing of a tape is completed, the tape drive rewinds the tape onto its original reel.

The speed with which data can be read or written depends on the tape drive. One common tape drive feeds the tape at 75 inches per second. With a tape capacity of 800 characters per inch, this tape drive can read or write at a rate of 60,000 characters per second.

Magnetic Disk Characteristics

A magnetic disk* is a flat, round metal surface, usually one to three feet in diameter. It is similar to a phonograph record, except that, instead of recording music in grooves, data are recorded on the surface of the disk in concentric rings called *tracks*. On one common type of disk there are 400 tracks on the disk surface. Tracks can be thought of as thin loops of magnetic tape along which characters of data are recorded by patterns of magnetic spots. Each track can store a certain number of characters. For example, one type of disk has a maximum capacity of 13,030 characters per track.

Usually disks are not used individually, but rather, several disks are stacked together to form a *disk pack*. For example, Figure 13-4 shows a disk pack with 11 disks. There are spaces between each disk in the pack. Data is recorded on the top and bottom of each disk in the disk pack except that the top of the top disk and the bottom of the bottom disk are not used. For the 11-disk pack illustrated in Figure 13-4 there are 20 recording surfaces, each with 400 tracks and each track with a capacity of 13,030 characters.

To use a magnetic disk for input or output, a disk pack is mounted in a *disk drive*. Figure 13-5 shows a disk storage unit with eight disk drives. In the disk drive, the disk pack is attached to a spindle that rotates the disks in the pack at a high speed. As the disks rotate, *read/write heads* move over the disk surfaces. There is usually one read/write head for each surface. These heads are connected to a mechanism that causes all read/write heads to move in unison (see Figure 13-6). A read/write head may be positioned over any track on any disk surface.

*The word "disk" is sometimes spelled "disc."

FIGURE 13-4. A Magnetic Disk Pack (Courtesy of IBM Corp.)

FIGURE 13-5. A Magnetic Disk Storage Unit with Eight Disk Drives (Courtesy of IBM Corp.)

To read or write data, the read/write head first must be positioned over the appropriate track. Then, as the disk rotates, the head can read data from the track or record data on the track. The read/write head can be positioned over any track on the disk surface. It is not necessary to begin reading with the first track and continue in se-

FIGURE 13-6. The Read-Write Heads of a Magnetic Disk Drive (Courtesy of IBM Corp.)

quence. The read/write mechanism can move forward or backward depending on the location of the track where the data are to be read or written. We call a disk drive a *direct access* device (or *random access* device) because data can be located directly without going through the disk file in sequence.

The time that it takes to read or write data depends on the time required to move the read/write head into position and on the rotational speed of the disk pack. On one common disk drive, it takes an average of 30 milliseconds (30/1000 seconds) to position the read/ write head. If the disk pack rotates at 60 revolutions per second, then 16.7 milliseconds are required to read all of the data from one track once the head is in position.

Magnetic File Organization

Files on magnetic media such as tape and disk are organized to some extent like card and printer files. Characters are recorded one after the other along the tape surface or the disk track. The characters are organized into fields, which in turn are grouped into records. One of the differences between magnetic files and card and printer files is that the former do not require a specific number of characters in each record. As we know, the length of a card record depends on the number of columns in the card. Similarly, printed output records are limited to the length of the print line. However, magnetic tape and disk records may be practically any length.

To show the layout of tape and disk records, a *proportional record layout form* often is used. This form serves the same purpose for magnetic files as the card layout form and print chart serve for card and printer files. Figure 13-7 shows a proportional record layout form with the layout of two records. Notice that the records are not limited to a specific length. The first record contains 43 characters and the second record has 118 characters. As shown in Figure 13-7, if more than 100 characters are included in a record, then the record layout continues onto the next line of the layout form.

On a tape or disk file, the records are stored one after the other. Between each record there is a space called an *inter-record gap* or *IRG*. (Sometimes this gap is called an *inter-block gap* or *IBG*.) On a magnetic tape each IRG is usually .6 inches in length. The gap is necessary because after reading each record on a tape the tape drive stops. The tape drive must have space to slow down after reading a record and space to speed up before reading the next record. A disk drive does not stop after reading a record. However, an IRG is still required between each record on a disk file.

Inter-record gaps are necessary in tape and disk files. However, the gaps result in wasted space because data cannot be recorded in the IRGs. In addition, extra processing time is required because of the IRGs. This is especially true with tape files in which the tape drive must stop and start between each record.

To overcome some of the problems associated with IRGs, records in tape and disk files often are *blocked*. When this is done several records are grouped together to form a *block*. Sometimes a block is called a *physical record* and the records within the block are called *logical records*. Gaps appear only between the physical records and not between the logical records. This arrangement is illustrated in Figure 13-8. The number of logical records that appear in each block is called the *blocking factor*. In Figure 13-8 the blocking factor is four.

There are two advantages to using blocked records. First, space is saved on the disk or tape because IRGs appear only between blocks and not between logical records. Thus fewer IRGs are required for the file. Second, processing time is usually decreased. The reason for this is that the computer reads or writes a complete block at one time rather than reading or writing individual logical records. For example, assume that the records in an input file are blocked as shown in Figure 13-8. When the first input instruction is executed, the first physical record is read into internal storage and the first logical record is made available for processing. When the second input instruction is executed,

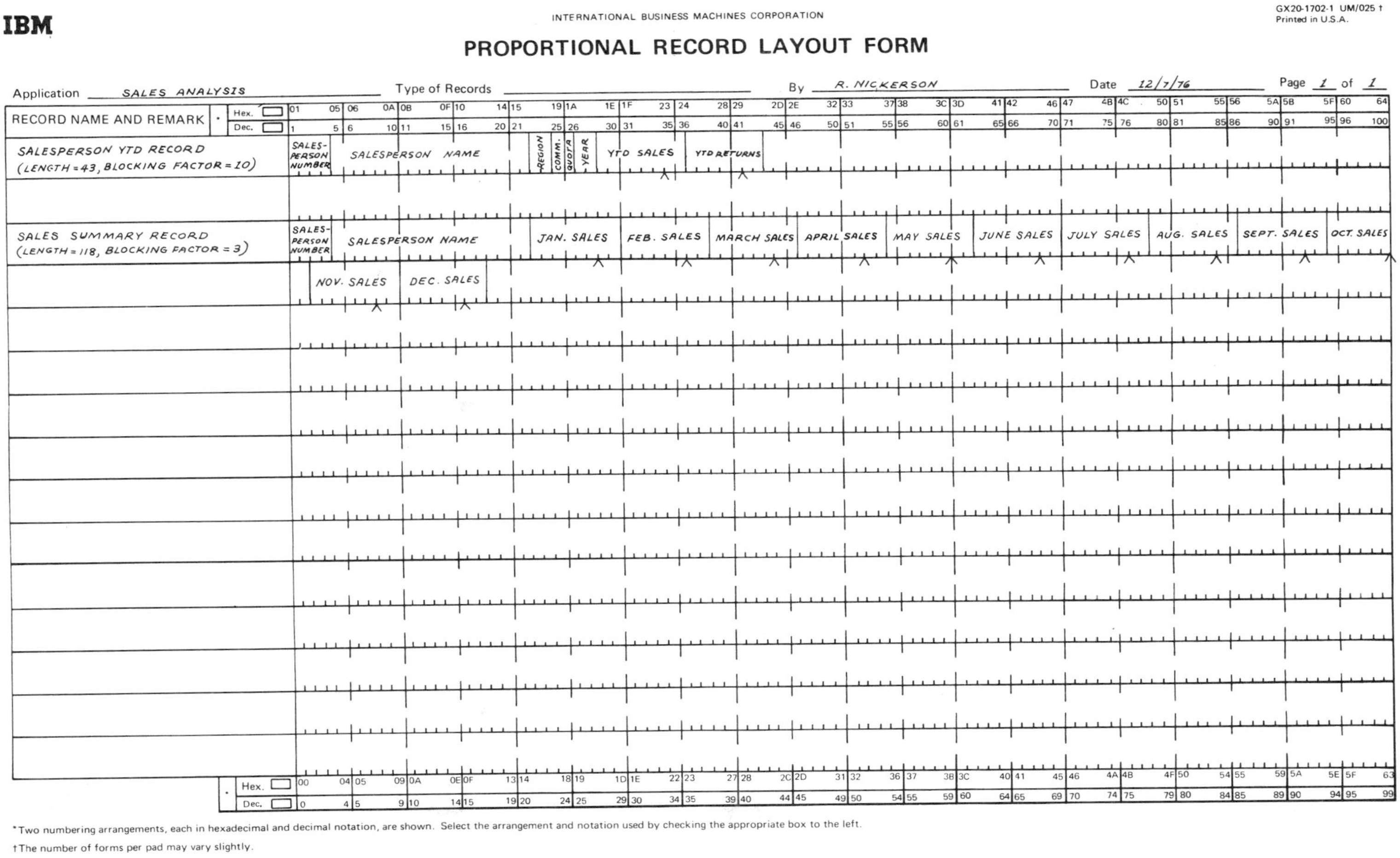

IBM

INTERNATIONAL BUSINESS MACHINES CORPORATION

PROPORTIONAL RECORD LAYOUT FORM

GX20-1702.1 UM/025 †
Printed in U.S.A.

Application ___SALES ANALYSIS___

By ___R. NICKERSON___ Date ___12/7/76___ Page ___1___ of ___1___

RECORD NAME AND REMARK · Hex. / Dec. Type of Records

SALESPERSON YTD RECORD
(LENGTH = 43, BLOCKING FACTOR = 10)

| SALES-PERSON NUMBER | SALESPERSON NAME | REGION | COMM. QUOTA | YEAR | YTD SALES | YTD RETURNS | JAN. SALES | FEB. SALES | MARCH SALES | APRIL SALES | MAY SALES | JUNE SALES | JULY SALES | AUG. SALES | SEPT. SALES | OCT. SALES |

SALES SUMMARY RECORD
(LENGTH = 118, BLOCKING FACTOR = 3)

| SALES-PERSON NUMBER | SALESPERSON NAME | NOV. SALES | DEC. SALES |

*Two numbering arrangements, each in hexadecimal and decimal notation, are shown. Select the arrangement and notation used by checking the appropriate box to the left.

†The number of forms per pad may vary slightly.

FIGURE 13-7. A Proportional Record Layout Form

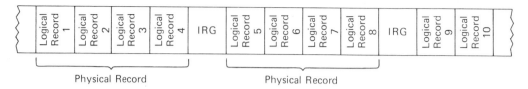

FIGURE 13-8. Blocked Records

the second logical record is already in internal storage. Hence, it is not necessary to read from the disk or tape file. It is only necessary to extract the second logical record from the physical record in internal storage. (This extraction process is called *unblocking* or *deblocking*.) The same process takes place for the third and fourth input instructions. When the fifth input instruction is executed, the second physical record is read from disk or tape. Thus far, fewer input operations actually are required when using blocked records. For output of blocked records, the opposite process takes place. Each output instruction puts a logical record in the physical record in internal storage. (This is called *blocking* the records.) Only after the entire physical record has been constructed is the data actually transferred to the output device.

There are two main disadvantages of using blocked records. First, special input/output routines are required to block and unblock logical records. For the COBOL programmer, the programming of these routines is not of concern. The routines are included automatically in the object program if blocked records are used. However, these special routines require extra internal storage space and processing time.

The second disadvantage of blocked records is that extra space is required in internal storage for the physical record. The entire physical record must be read into internal storage at one time. If a larger blocking factor is used, more space is required. The extra storage needed for blocked records means that less space is available for the instructions in the program. Whether or not this is critical depends on the size of the program.

One of the differences between card and printer files and magnetic files is that blocking is not used with the former. Another difference is the use of label records. These are special records stored with the magnetic file and used to identify the file. Usually there is a label record at the beginning of each file and another label record at the end of the file. The label records give information about the file such as the file name, when the file was created, and whether or not the file can be erased. Usually *standard* labels, designed by the computer manufacturer, are used. Sometimes special label records designed by the user are substituted for the standard labels.

When a file is to be read, the label records first must be checked to be sure that the proper tape or disk is available for processing. In COBOL this is done when the OPEN statement is executed. If, during the execution of this statement, it is determined that the wrong file is available, an error message is printed for the computer operator and the execution of the program is stopped. At the end of processing, the CLOSE statement causes the label record at the end of the file to be checked. For an output file, the label record at the beginning of the file is created when the OPEN statement is executed. When the CLOSE statement for the file is executed the label record at the end of the file is written.

The records in a magnetic file may be organized in several different ways. The simplest technique is called *sequential file organization*. In this approach, the records in the file are organized in sequence one after the other. Data is stored in the file in the order in which the records are written. When retrieving data from a sequential file the records must be read in the sequence in which they are stored.

Direct file organization is a second way in which magnetic files may be organized. In this approach each record in the file is stored at a specific location that can be determined in the program. For example, if a direct file is stored on magnetic disk then the track that contains each record in the file must be calculated by some means in the program that creates the file. To retrieve a specific record from the file, the location of the track containing the record must be determined again so that the disk drive can be instructed to move the read/write head to the appropriate track. Notice that direct file organization allows the program access to any record directly without going through the file in sequence as is required with a sequentially organized file.

The third way that magnetic files may be organized is called *indexed file organization*. (This also is called *indexed sequential file organization*.) Actually an indexed file consists of two files — a data file and an index file. The *data file* is organized as a sequential file in the manner that we have described previously. Each record in the data file must have some field that distinguishes it from the other records. This is called the *key field* or *record key*. For example, if data for the salespeople in a business are stored in an indexed file, the salesperson number may be used as the key field. The *index file*, or simply *index*, contains one record for each data record in the data file. This index record gives the key field of the data record and the location of the data record in the data file. To retrieve a record from an indexed file the index is searched for the appropriate key field. Then, using the record location given in the index, the data record is retrieved directly without going through the data file in sequence. If necessary, the data file can be processed sequentially without using the index.

Not every form of input/output can store files organized in all of the ways described here. Punched card and printer files are always organized sequentially. In addition, a magnetic tape file can have only a sequential organization. On a magnetic disk, sequential, direct, and indexed organization can be used.

In this chapter we discuss COBOL processing elements for magnetic tape files and for sequential and indexed disk files. Direct file organization is not used as extensively as the other file organization techniques and is not discussed in this book.

Magnetic File Processing

There are two basic file processing techniques — sequential processing and random (or direct) processing. *Sequential processing* involves reading or writing the records in a file in sequence. Input or output begins with the first record in the file and continues through the file one record at a time. In *random processing*, records are not necessarily processed in sequential order. Records are read or written randomly in whatever order is specified in the program.

Sequentially organized files can only be processed sequentially. Thus, sequential processing must be used for magnetic tape files and for sequential disk files. Indexed files can be processed either sequentially or randomly. This is one of the main advantages of this type of file organization. Direct files can only be processed randomly. To process a direct file sequentially, random processing techniques must be used to read or write each record in sequence.

Because magnetic tape files can only be organized sequentially, sequential processing must be used with such files. To create a magnetic tape file, records are read from some other file and written on a magnetic tape in sequence. To process the data in a magnetic tape file, the records are read back from the file in sequence. Sometimes it is necessary to change the data in a particular record of a file or to delete or add records to the file. This is called *updating* the file. To update a tape file an entirely new file must be created. It is not possible to change the data in a record of a tape file once the file has been created.

A sequential disk file is created in the same way that a tape file is created. Similarly, sequential processing is used to read data from a sequential disk file. However, unlike a tape file, it is possible to change the data in a sequential disk file. Thus, to update a sequential disk file, new data is written in the file in place of the old, out-of-date data.

An indexed disk file may be processed sequentially or randomly. Usually an indexed disk file is created in a sequential manner like a tape file or a sequential disk file. After the file is created, records may be read sequentially or randomly. An indexed disk file may be updated sequentially or updating may take place randomly.

13-2. TAPE FILE PROCESSING

The COBOL elements used for processing magnetic tape files are very similar to those needed for punched card input and printed output. This is because, like card and printer files, tape files are sequentially organized and must be processed sequentially. The only differences for tape file I/O are in the SELECT entry and the FD entry. The OPEN, READ, WRITE, and CLOSE statements are essentially the same for tape, card, and printed file processing.

The SELECT entry for a tape file must associate a file name with the name for the tape drive that contains the tape to be processed. Usually there are several tape drives available with the computer system. Each tape drive is identified by a unique name. The programmer must use the name of the tape drive on which the tape is mounted in the ASSIGN clause of the SELECT entry. For example, assume that the tape containing the year-to-date data for the salespeople in a business is mounted on a tape drive with the name TAPE-DRIVE-1. (The layout of the records in this file is shown in Figure 13-7.) Then the SELECT entry is of the form:

```
SELECT SALESPERSON-YTD-FILE
    ASSIGN TO TAPE-DRIVE-1.
```

(The names used for tape drives depend on the computer systems. Typical names for several common computers are illustrated in Appendix A.)

Several tape files may be processed in the same program. Usually a separate tape contains each file and the tapes are mounted on different tape drives. There must be one SELECT entry for each tape file, giving the name of the file and the name of the tape drive containing the tape.

The FD entry for a tape file contains clauses that describe special characteristics of the file. First, the fact that label records are used with the tape file must be indicated. For card and printer files, label records are always OMITTED. However, with tape files, STANDARD label records normally are used. To indicate this we use the clause

```
LABEL RECORDS ARE STANDARD
```

in the FD entry. If the tape records are blocked, then the blocking factor must be specified in the FD entry. This is accomplished in the BLOCK CONTAINS clause. For example, if the blocking factor is ten, then the following clause must be included in the FD entry:

```
BLOCK CONTAINS 10 RECORDS
```

If the records are not blocked (that is, if the blocking factor is one), then this clause is not needed. Finally, the RECORD CONTAINS clause specifies the number of characters in each logical record. This number is not fixed for tape files and depends on the record layout. The following is a complete FD entry for the SALESPERSON-YTD-FILE:

```
FD  SALESPERSON-YTD-FILE,
    LABEL RECORDS ARE STANDARD,
    BLOCK CONTAINS 10 RECORDS,
    RECORD CONTAINS 43 CHARACTERS,
    DATA RECORD IS SALESPERSON-YTD-DATA.
```

In the procedure division, the OPEN, READ, WRITE, and CLOSE statements are used to process a tape file. If a tape file is to be created, then the file is opened as an OUTPUT file. Records are created in the file by the WRITE statement. If data are to be read from an existing tape file, then the file is opened as an INPUT file. The READ statement is used to get records from the file.

If the tape file is a new file, then the OPEN statement causes label records at the beginning of the file to be created. For an existing file, the OPEN statement checks the labels to be sure that the correct tape is mounted on the tape drive.

After a file has been processed, the CLOSE statement must be used. When a new tape file is closed, the label record at the end of the file is created. For an existing tape file, the CLOSE statement causes the trailing label record to be checked. After label processing is completed, the tape is rewound automatically.

A tape file cannot be opened as both an input and an output file at the same time. However, in a single program a tape file can be first opened as, say, an output file, then closed, and then reopened as an input file. This is possible because the CLOSE statement rewinds the tape and thus makes the tape ready for further processing.

If a tape is an output file, then the WRITE statement is used to write records in the file. For example, the following WRITE statement might be used for the SALESPERSON-YTD-FILE:

```
WRITE SALESPERSON-YTD-DATA FROM SALESPERSON-YTD-RECORD.
```

Notice that the AFTER ADVANCING phrase is not used. Each time that a WRITE statement for a tape file is executed, a new record is written in the next logical position in the file. If the records are blocked, then the logical record is transferred to the appropriate position in the physical record in internal storage. After the physical record has been completely filled, it is transferred to the next available space on the tape. Thus, the process of blocking the records is handled automatically in the program.

For an input file, the READ statement is used to get records in sequence from the file. For example, the following statement might be used to read data from the SALESPERSON-YTD-FILE:

```
READ SALESPERSON-YTD-FILE INTO SALESPERSON-YTD-RECORD
    AT END . . .
```

Each time that a READ statement is executed for a tape file, the next logical record in the file is made available for processing. Any unblocking of records is handled automatically in the program. If the READ statement is executed and there are no more records in the file, then the AT END phrase in the READ statement is executed.

We can see from this discussion that processing magnetic tape files is practically the same as card and printer file processing. Because COBOL automatically handles such details as label record checking, and blocking and unblocking records, the programmer need only be concerned with the processing of the logical records in the file.

13-3. SEQUENTIAL DISK FILE PROCESSING

In this section we describe the COBOL elements used for sequential disk file processing. The 1968 and 1974 versions of ANS COBOL use somewhat different elements for this type of input and output. Most implementations of COBOL are based on the 1968 version. Therefore we mainly describe the elements from this version in this section. Appendix A discusses the 1974 standard and differences between various implementations of COBOL.

To some extent the COBOL elements used to process sequential disk files are very similar to those used in tape file processing. Most of the differences are found in the SELECT entry and in the WRITE statement. In addition, there are special features that are used for updating sequential disk files.

The SELECT entry for a sequential disk file must associate a file name with the name for the disk drive containing the disk file. The names used for disk drives depend on the computer system. (See Appendix A for typical disk drive names.) Two additional clauses must be included in the SELECT entry for a sequential disk file. These are ACCESS MODE IS SEQUENTIAL and PROCESSING IS SEQUENTIAL. (These clauses are optional in some versions of COBOL; see Appendix A.) The following is a typical SELECT entry that may be used for a sequential disk file:

```
SELECT SALESPERSON-YTD-FILE
    ASSIGN TO DISK-DRIVE-1
    ACCESS MODE IS SEQUENTIAL
    PROCESSING IS SEQUENTIAL.
```

The FD entry for a sequential disk file is exactly the same as the FD entry for a tape file. Label records are specified as STANDARD, the blocking factor is given in the BLOCK CONTAINS clause, and the RECORD CONTAINS clause gives the number of characters in the disk record.

In the procedure division, the COBOL elements that are used depend on whether the sequential disk file is to be used for input or for output, or is to be updated. If the file is used for input, then the OPEN, READ, and CLOSE statements are the same as those used with tape files. The OPEN statement must indicate that the file is an INPUT file. The READ statement causes the next logical record to be made available for processing. If no more records are in the file, then the AT END phrase is executed. After processing of the file is completed, the CLOSE statement for the file must be executed. All label record processing is handled automatically by the OPEN and CLOSE statements in the same manner as with tape files. In addition, unblocking of blocked records is performed when the READ statement is executed.

To create a sequential disk file, the OPEN statement must specify an OUTPUT file. The WRITE statement causes a logical record to be written in the next sequential position in the file. For most versions of COBOL, the WRITE statement must include an INVALID KEY phrase. This phrase includes one or more statements that are executed if no more space is available in the disk file. For example, the following WRITE statement might be used to write a record in a sequential disk file:

```
WRITE SALESPERSON-YTD-DATA FROM SALESPERSON-YTD-RECORD
    INVALID KEY
        PERFORM ERROR-ROUTINE-BEGIN
            THRU ERROR-ROUTINE-END.
```

If the file is full, so that the record cannot be written, then the PER-FORM statement in the INVALID KEY phrase is executed. (Not all versions of COBOL require the INVALID KEY phrase. See Appendix A for differences.)

To update a sequential disk file, the record to be changed must be read first and then the new record must be written. Thus, the file is used for both input and output. To indicate this, the OPEN statement must specify that the file is an I-O file. For example, assume that the file named SALESPERSON-YTD-FILE is to be updated. Then the OPEN statement for the file must be:

```
OPEN I-O SALESPERSON-YTD-FILE.
```

With an I-O file, each execution of a READ statement causes the next record in sequence to be read. When a WRITE statement is executed, the record is written in the file location where the record retrieved by the previously executed READ statement was found. The INVALID KEY clause must be used with the WRITE statement. Thus, to update a sequential disk file, the record to be changed must first be read using a READ statement. Then the data in the record is modified according to the requirements of the program. Finally, a WRITE statement is executed for the modified record. This causes the new record to be written in place of the old data. This process is summarized in Figure 13-9.

Some versions of COBOL use the REWRITE statement for updating a disk file (see Appendix A). This statement has the same form as the WRITE statement except that the first word is REWRITE and the INVALID KEY clause is not used. For example, the REWRITE statement for the program shown in Figure 13-9 is as follows:

```
REWRITE SALESPERSON-YTD-DATA FROM SALESPERSON-YTD-RECORD.
```

This statement causes a record to be written in the same disk location as the record read by the previous READ statement.

13-4. INDEXED DISK FILE PROCESSING

The 1968 version of ANS COBOL does not include elements for indexed file processing. Such elements were added to ANS COBOL in 1974. However, most implemented versions of the language do not as yet include the 1974 standard. Therefore, the COBOL elements used for indexed file processing vary considerably from one version of COBOL to another.

```
OPEN I-O SALESPERSON-YTD-FILE.
    .
    .
    .

READ SALESPERSON-YTD-FILE INTO SALESPERSON-YTD-RECORD
    AT END . . .
    .
    .
    .

(Update data in SALESPERSON-YTD-RECORD.)
    .
    .
    .

WRITE SALESPERSON-YTD-DATA FROM SALESPERSON-YTD-RECORD
    INVALID KEY
        PERFORM ERROR-ROUTINE-BEGIN
            THRU ERROR-ROUTINE-END.
    .
    .
    .

CLOSE SALESPERSON-YTD-FILE.
```

FIGURE 13-9. Updating a Record in a Sequential Disk File

In this section we describe the indexed file processing elements used in COBOL with the IBM System/360 and System/370 computers. In Appendix A we discuss some of the differences between the elements described in this section and those used with other versions of COBOL.

In Section 13-1 we discuss how indexed files can be processed sequentially or randomly. Indexed files are created in a sequential manner. Once created, records in an indexed file may be retrieved sequentially or randomly. Updating of records in an indexed file also may take place sequentially or randomly. In this section, we first describe sequential processing of an indexed file and then discuss random processing.

Sequential Processing of an Indexed File

Every record in an indexed file must have a field that uniquely identifies it. This is called the *key field* or *record key*. For example, if data about salespeople is stored in an indexed file, then the salesperson-number field might be used as the record key. The records in an indexed file must be stored in ascending numerical order by the record key. If this is not the case, then errors occur during processing.

The name of the field that is the record key is specified in the SELECT entry for the file. The clause RECORD KEY IS, followed by the name of the record key, is used for this specification. The data name given in this clause must appear in the description of the record in the FILE section. It must not refer to a field in the WORK-ING-STORAGE section. The SELECT entry for a sequentially processed indexed file also includes the clause ACCESS MODE IS SEQUENTIAL. For example, the following SELECT entry might be used for the SALESPERSON-YTD-FILE which is organized as an indexed file:

```
SELECT SALESPERSON-YTD-FILE
    ASSIGN TO DISK-DRIVE-2
    ACCESS MODE IS SEQUENTIAL
    RECORD KEY IS SY-RECORD-KEY.
```

(The device name used in the ASSIGN clause depends on the computer system. See Appendix A for details.) In this example, SY-RECORD-KEY is the name of the record key defined in the description of the disk record in the FILE section.

In the data division, the FD entry for an indexed file has the same form as the FD entry used for tape and sequential disk files. Label records usually are STANDARD, the blocking factor is given in the BLOCK CONTAINS clause, and the record length is specified in the RECORD CONTAINS clause.

With some systems, a record in an indexed file must have an extra character position at the beginning of the record. Usually this position is used for a special code that indicates whether a record contains active or inactive data. We will not use this code in examples in this chapter. However, since many systems make use of this extra character position, we will include it in all record descriptions. This is done by specifying a filler with a picture of X in the first position in the record. As a result, the records stored in indexed files usually are one character longer than equivalent records that appear in sequential files. For example, the record of the year-to-date sales data illustrated in Figure 13-7 would be 44 characters, instead of 43, if stored as an indexed file.

Figure 13-10 illustrates the elements used in the environment and data divisions for sequential processing of an indexed SALESPERSON-YTD-FILE. There are several things to notice in this figure. First, the RECORD KEY clause in the SELECT entry contains the name of a field defined in the record description in the FILE section. In this record description, the record key field occupies the positions reserved for the salesperson number. Thus, the salesperson number field is used to identify the records in the file. This field begins in the

```
ENVIRONMENT DIVISION.
        .
        .
        .
INPUT-OUTPUT SECTION.
FILE CONTROL.
    SELECT SALESPERSON-YTD-FILE
        ASSIGN TO DISK-DRIVE-2
        ACCESS MODE IS SEQUENTIAL
        RECORD KEY IS SY-RECORD-KEY.
        .
        .
        .
DATA DIVISION.
FILE SECTION.
FD  SALESPERSON-YTD-FILE,
        LABEL RECORDS ARE STANDARD,
        BLOCK CONTAINS 10 RECORDS,
        RECORD CONTAINS 44 CHARACTERS,
        DATA RECORD IS SALESPERSON-YTD-DATA.
01  SALESPERSON-YTD-DATA.
        05  FILLER                  PIC X.
        05  SY-RECORD-KEY           PIC XXXX.
        05  FILLER                  PIC X(39).
        .
        .
        .
WORKING-STORAGE SECTION.
        .
        .
        .
01  SALESPERSON-YTD-RECORD.
        05  FILLER                  PIC X.
        05  SY-NUMBER               PIC XXXX.
        05  SY-NAME                 PIC X(18).
        05  SY-REGION               PIC XX.
        05  SY-COMM-CLASS           PIC 9.
        05  SY-QUOTA-CLASS          PIC X.
        05  SY-YEAR                 PIC XX.
        05  SY-Y-T-D-SALES          PIC 9(6)V99.
        05  SY-Y-T-D-RETURNS        PIC 9(5)V99.
```

FIGURE 13-10. Environment and Data Division Elements for Sequential Processing of an Indexed Disk File

second position in the record, since the first position is reserved for other purposes as described previously. The remainder of the record in the FILE section is specified with a FILLER. The complete description of the disk record appears in the WORKING-STORAGE section. Notice that the first character position in this record description is also set aside. The total number of characters in the record in the FILE section and in the record in the WORKING-STORAGE section is the same and is specified in the RECORD CONTAINS clause in the FD entry.

In the procedure division, the elements used to sequentially process an indexed file depend on whether records in the file are being created, retrieved, or updated. To create records in an indexed file, the file is opened as an OUTPUT file. All label processing is handled when the OPEN statement is executed. The WRITE statement causes a record to be written in the next sequential position in the file. An INVALID KEY phrase must be included in the WRITE statement. The statements in this phrase are executed if the contents of the record key are not in ascending order or if a record with the same record key already exists in the file. For example, the following statement may be used to write a record in the SALESPERSON-YTD-FILE:

```
WRITE SALESPERSON-YTD-DATA FROM SALESPERSON-YTD-RECORD
      INVALID KEY
          PERFORM ERROR-ROUTINE-BEGIN
          THRU ERROR-ROUTINE-END.
```

Any blocking of records is performed automatically when the WRITE statement is executed. At the end of processing the file is closed; final label processing is performed at this time.

To retrieve records sequentially from an indexed file, the file is opened as an INPUT file. The READ statement is used to read the next sequential record from the file. For example, to read a record from the SALESPERSON-YTD-FILE we could use the following:

```
READ SALESPERSON-YTD-FILE INTO SALESPERSON-YTD-RECORD
     AT END . . .
```

The AT END phrase is executed if there are no more records in the file.

If records in an indexed file are to be updated sequentially, then the file is opened as an I-O file. Thus, the OPEN statement used if records in the SALESPERSON-YTD-FILE are to be updated is as follows:

```
OPEN I-O SALESPERSON-YTD-FILE.
```

As with sequential disk files, updating requires first reading the record to be updated and then writing the new record. The READ statement is used as before to retrieve the old record from the file. The REWRITE statement is used to write a new record in place of the old data. For example, assume that the record to be updated in the SALESPERSON-YTD-FILE has been retrieved and the necessary changes have been made in the record's data. Then the following statement may be used to update the data on the disk:

```
REWRITE SALESPERSON-YTD-DATA FROM SALESPERSON-YTD-RECORD
    INVALID KEY
        PERFORM ERROR-ROUTINE-BEGIN
        THRU ERROR-ROUTINE-END.
```

This statement must be executed after a READ statement. The RE-WRITE statement writes the new data in the location where the previously read record was found. The INVALID KEY phrase is executed if there has been an error such as a change in the value of the record key.

Random Processing of an Indexed File

For random processing of an indexed file, the SELECT entry must specify that the ACCESS MODE IS RANDOM. A record key must be indicated as with sequential processing. In addition, a *nominal key* must be specified in the SELECT entry. The purpose of the nominal key is to indicate which record in the file is to be read or written. The nominal key's description must appear in the WORKING-STORAGE section. The nominal key must have the same picture as the record key. For example, the following SELECT entry may be used when randomly processing the indexed SALESPERSON-YTD-FILE:

```
SELECT SALESPERSON-YTD-FILE
    ASSIGN TO DISK-DRIVE-2
    ACCESS MODE IS RANDOM
    RECORD KEY IS SY-RECORD-KEY
    NOMINAL KEY IS WK-NOMINAL-KEY.
```

The nominal key is WK-NOMINAL-KEY. In the WORKING-STORAGE section this item's description might appear as follows:

```
77  WK-NOMINAL-KEY        PIC XXXX.
```

Notice that the picture of WK-NOMINAL-KEY is the same as SY-RECORD-KEY in Figure 13-10. The nominal key need not be an independent item; it could be a field in an input or output record's description.

The nominal key is used in the procedure division to specify the key field of the record that is to be read or written in the file. Before a READ, WRITE, or REWRITE statement is executed, the nominal key must be given a value equal to the key field of the input or output record. If a record is being read, the computer searches the file's index for the nominal key value and finds the location of the desired record in the file. For an output record, the nominal key value is added to the index along with the location in the data file where the record is stored.

To read a record from an indexed file, the file is opened as an INPUT file. The nominal key is assigned the value of the key field in the record that is to be read. Usually this value comes from some other form of input such as a punched card. For example, we may have punched a salesperson's number in a card. We wish to retrieve the record for the salesperson with this number from the indexed SALESPERSON-YTD-FILE. If the field in the punched card is called SP-NUMBER, then we would assign the value to the nominal key with a MOVE statement as follows:

```
MOVE SP-NUMBER TO WK-NOMINAL-KEY.
```

After this is accomplished, the READ statement is used to retrieve the appropriate record from the file. However, when using a READ statement for random retrieval of records in an indexed file, the AT END phrase is not used. Instead, an INVALID KEY phrase is included. The statements in this phrase are executed if a record with a record key equal to the nominal key cannot be found in the file. For example, to randomly retrieve a record from the SALESPERSON-YTD-FILE, the following READ statement may be used:

```
READ SALESPERSON-YTD-FILE INTO SALESPERSON-YTD-RECORD
    INVALID KEY
        PERFORM ERROR-PROCESS-BEGIN
            THRU ERROR-PROCESS-END.
```

To add a record to an indexed file, the WRITE statement is used. First, the file must be opened as an I-O file. The nominal key must be given the value of the key field of the record to be added to the file. Then a WRITE statement must be executed to add the record to the file. Notice that no READ statement is required before the WRITE statement, even though the file is an I-O file. The INVALID

KEY phrase is required in the WRITE statement. The statements in this phrase are executed if there already is a record in the file with a key field value equal to the nominal key.

If an indexed file is to be updated randomly, then the file is opened as an I-O file. The nominal key must be assigned the value of the record to be updated. A READ statement is used to get the appropriate record. Again, the INVALID KEY phrase is needed in case the record with the given nominal key is not in the file. After the record has been retrieved, modifications in the record are performed and then the REWRITE statement is executed. This causes the updated record to be written in the file in place of the record retrieved by the previous READ statement. In the REWRITE statement the INVALID KEY phrase is executed if an error condition occurs.

As we have seen in this section there are a number of ways of processing indexed disk files. Often the details vary from one version of COBOL to another. Additional features are also available with some versions. It is best to refer to the appropriate reference manual when coding COBOL programs for indexed file processing.

APPENDICES

APPENDIX A

COBOL Implementation Differences

Before 1968 there was wide variation in the versions of COBOL implemented by various computer manufacturers. In 1968 the American National Standards Institute (ANSI) published the first standards for the COBOL language. Subsequently, most manufacturers attempted to implement a version of COBOL that closely adhered to the ANSI standard. In 1974 ANSI published a new standard version of COBOL with many new features and some modifications to the old (1968) features. At the time that this book was researched and written the most commonly used implementations of COBOL had not yet been modified to reflect the changes in the 1974 standard. The common versions of COBOL are more closely related to the 1968 standard. However, we can expect that changes will be made during the next few years.

To adhere to the ANSI standards, a version of COBOL need not implement all of the features of the standard. Various subsets of the language are allowed. The subsets that are acceptable are discussed in detail in the appropriate ANSI publications. (See the list of references at the end of this book for titles of ANSI and IBM publications.) By using subsets of the language, computer manufacturers can implement versions of the language on small as well as on large computers.

All of the subsets of COBOL have the most useful elements of the language in common. In this text we have presented the most common and useful elements of COBOL. The more advanced features, and those that are found only in a particular version of the language, can be understood best by studying the appropriate reference manual. The text material adheres most closely to the 1974 ANSI standards. Differences between the 1968 and 1974 standards and between the ANSI standards and some of the most commonly used implementations are explained in this appendix.

The following abbreviations are used in the explanations of implementation differences:

ANS-68	ANS COBOL, 1968 version
ANS-74	ANS COBOL, 1974 version
OS	IBM System/360–370 OS Full ANS COBOL
DOS FULL	IBM System/360–370 DOS Full ANS COBOL
DOS SUBSET	IBM System/360–370 DOS Subset ANS COBOL
S/3	IBM System/3 Subset ANS COBOL
1130	IBM 1130 COBOL

Publications that describe each of these versions are listed in the references. Differences are listed by the chapter in which the first reference to the COBOL element was made.

CHAPTER 2

Character set differences

ANS-68, ANS-74. The character set listed in Section 2-1 is correct for these versions.

OS, DOS FULL, DOS SUBSET. The character set is the same as listed in Section 2-1 except that the apostrophe (') is included. The apostrophe must be used instead of the quotation mark ('') unless a special control record is used at the time of compilation.

S/3. The character set is the same as listed in Section 2-1 except that the semicolon (;), greater than symbol (>), and less than symbol (<) may not be used. In addition, the apostrophe (') is included. The apostrophe must be used instead of the quotation mark ('') unless a special control record is used at the time of compilation.

1130. The character set is the same as listed in Section 2-1 except that the semicolon (;), greater than symbol (>), and less than symbol ($<$) cannot be used. In addition, the apostrophe (') is included. It may be used in place of the quotation mark ("). If a quotation mark is used in printed output, however, an apostrophe will be printed.

CHAPTER 3

Program name differences

ANS-68. The program name may be any user-defined word. It need not contain any alphabetic characters.

ANS-74. The program name may be any user-defined word containing at least one alphabetic character.

OS, DOS FULL, DOS SUBSET. The program name may be any user-defined word. It need not contain any alphabetic characters. However, if the first character is numeric, it is converted to an alphabetic character according to the following rules:

0 becomes J
1 becomes A
2 becomes B
3 becomes C
4 becomes D
5 becomes E
6 becomes F
7 becomes G
8 becomes H
9 becomes I

Any hyphen within the first eight characters is converted to a zero. Then only the first eight characters are used to identify the program.

S/3. The rules are the same as for OS except that only the first six characters are used to identify the program.

1130. The rules are the same as for OS except that only the first five characters are used to identify the program.

Computer name differences

ANS-68, *ANS-74*. The selection of a computer name is left up to the computer manufacturer.

OS, *DOS FULL*, *DOS SUBSET*. The name IBM-360 or IBM-370 is used.

S/3. The name IBM-S3 is used.

1130. The name IBM-1130 is used.

Input/output device name differences

ANS-68, *ANS-74*. The selection of I/O device names is left up to the computer manufacturer.

OS. The device name that is used depends on what type of input and output devices are available. Typical names are of the following form:

For card input:	UR-2540R-S-SYSIN
For printer output:	UR-1403-S-SYSPRINT

DOS FULL, *DOS SUBSET*. Typical I/O device names are of the following form:

For card input:	SYS005-UR-2540R-S
For printer output:	SYS007-UR-1403-S

S/3. Typical I/O device names are of the following form:

For card input:	UR-5424P-RD
For printer output:	UR-1403-3

1130. Typical I/O device names are of the following form:

For card input:	RD-1442
For printer output without carriage control:	PR-1132
For printer output with carriage control:	PR-1132-C

Carriage control is discussed in Chapter 7.

Punctuation differences

ANS-68, OS, DOS FULL, DOS SUBSET. A period, comma, or semicolon must not be preceded by a space. A left parenthesis must not be followed by a space. A right parenthesis must not be preceded by a space. The semicolon and comma are not always interchangable; refer to the appropriate reference manual for details.

ANS-74. Spaces may optionally appear before a period, comma, or semicolon, after a left parenthesis, and before a right parenthesis. The semicolon and comma may be used interchangably.

S/3, 1130. The rules are the same as for ANS-68 except that semicolons are not permitted.

CHAPTER 4

DIVIDE statement differences

ANS-68, ANS-74, OS, DOS FULL, DOS SUBSET. All forms of the DIVIDE statement discussed in Section 4-1 are valid.

S/3, 1130. All forms of the DIVIDE statement discussed in Section 4-1 are valid except those containing the REMAINDER option.

Relational operators

ANS-68, ANS-74, OS, DOS FULL, DOS SUBSET. All forms of relational operators discussed in Section 4-4 are valid.

S/3, 1130. All forms of relational operators discussed in Section 4-4 are valid except those using the greater than symbol ($>$) or the less than symbol ($<$).

Collating sequence differences

ANS-68, ANS-74. The selection of a collating sequence is left up to the computer manufacturer.

OS, DOS FULL, DOS SUBSET. The collating sequence is as follows (listed in order from lowest to highest):

1.		space or blank
2.	.	period or decimal point
3.	<	less than symbol
4.	(	left parenthesis
5.	+	plus sign
6.	$	dollar sign
7.	*	asterisk
8.	)	right parenthesis
9.	;	semicolon
10.	-	minus sign or hyphen
11.	/	slash
12.	,	comma
13.	>	greater than symbol
14.	'	apostrophe
15.	=	equal sign
16.	"	quotation mark
17-42.		A through Z
43-54.		0 through 9

S/3, 1130. The collating sequence is as follows (listed in order from lowest to highest):

1.		space or blank
2.	.	period or decimal point
3.	(	left parenthesis
4.	+	plus sign
5.	$	dollar sign
6.	*	asterisk
7.	)	right parenthesis
8.	–	minus sign
9.	/	slash
10.	,	comma
11.	'	apostrophe
12.	=	equal sign
13.	"	quotation mark
14-39.		A through Z
40-49.		0 through 9

CHAPTER 5

All features discussed in this chapter are standard for all versions of COBOL.

CHAPTER 6

Differences in placement of 01-level items in working storage

ANS-68, OS, DOS FULL, DOS SUBSET, S/3, 1130. All 77-level items must come before any 01-level items in the WORKING-STOR-AGE section.

ANS-74. There is no restriction on the order of 77-level items and 01-level items in the WORKING-STORAGE section.

CHAPTER 7

AFTER ADVANCING phrase differences

ANS-68. There is no maximum value specified for the number of lines that can be skipped at one time. Only the plural LINES may be used. There is no requirement that the AFTER ADVANCING phrase must be used with all WRITE statements if it is used at all. There is no requirement that the first character in the output record must be set aside for forms control.

ANS-74. There is no maximum value specified for the number of lines that can be skipped at one time. Either LINE or LINES may be used. There is no requirement that the AFTER ADVANCING phrase must be used with all WRITE statements if it is used at all. There is no requirement that the first character in the output record must be set aside for forms control.

OS, DOS FULL, DOS SUBSET, 1130. The maximum number of lines that can be skipped at one time is 100. Only the plural LINES may be used. The AFTER ADVANCING phrase must be used for all WRITE statements if it is used at all. The first character of the output record must be set aside for forms control.

S/3. The maximum number of lines that can be skipped at one time is 100. Either LINE or LINES may be used. There is no requirement that the AFTER ADVANCING phrase must be used with all WRITE statements if it is used at all. There is no requirement that the first character in the output record must be set aside for forms control.

Special names differences

ANS-68, ANS-74. The selection of codes to be used in the SPECIAL-NAMES paragraph is left up to the computer manufacturer.

OS, DOS FULL, DOS SUBSET, 1130. The codes used in the SPECIAL-NAMES paragraph are as follows:

CSP - suppress spacing
C01-C12 - skip to channel 1 through 12

S/3. The codes used in the SPECIAL-NAMES paragraph are as follows:

CSP - suppress spacing
C01 - skip to next page

CHAPTER 8

Debugging feature differences

ANS-68. There are no special debugging features in this version of COBOL.

ANS-74. There are special debugging features in this version of COBOL but they have not been widely implemented. Refer to the ANSI reference manual for details.

OS, DOS FULL, S/3. The READY TRACE, RESET TRACE, and EXHIBIT statements may be used with these versions. When the trace feature is used, the computer prints the compiler-generated number of each paragraph as it is executed.

DOS SUBSET. The READY TRACE, RESET TRACE, and EXHIBIT statements may be used with this version. When the trace feature is used, the computer prints the name of each paragraph as it is executed.

1130. The READY TRACE and RESET TRACE statements may be used with this version. When the trace feature is used, the computer prints the computer-generated number of each paragraph as it is executed.

Identification division differences

ANS-68. The DATE-COMPILED and REMARKS paragraphs may be used.

ANS-74. The DATE-COMPILED paragraph may be used but the REMARKS paragraph may not.

OS, DOS FULL, DOS SUBSET. The DATE-COMPILED and REMARKS paragraph may be used.

S/3, 1130. The REMARKS paragraph may be used, but the DATE-COMPILED paragraph may not.

Differences in the use of source program comments

ANS-68. An asterisk in column 7 may not be used for comments in the source program. In the procedure division, the NOTE sentence may be used. This sentence always begins with the word NOTE and contains any comments that the programmer wishes to include. If NOTE is the first word in a paragraph, then the entire paragraph is taken as a comment. The comment ends at the beginning of the next paragraph. If NOTE is not the first word of a paragraph, then the comment ends with a period.

ANS-74. An asterisk in column 7 is used for comments anywhere in the source program.

OS, DOS FULL, DOS SUBSET, S/3, 1130. An asterisk in column 7 may be used for comments anywhere in the source program. In addition, the NOTE sentence may be used in the procedure division as described above under ANS-68.

CHAPTER 9

Date editing differences

ANS-74. Date editing as described in Section 9-4 is valid.

ANS-68, OS, DOS FULL, DOS SUBSET, S/3, 1130. Date editing is not valid.

Differences in the ALL figurative constant

ANS-68, ANS-74, OS, DOS FULL, DOS SUBSET. The literal in the ALL figurative constant is not limited to a single character. In addition, any other figurative constant may be used instead of a literal.

S/3, 1130. The literal in the ALL figurative constant must be a single character nonnumeric literal.

CHAPTER 10

Card punch device name differences

ANS-68, ANS-74. The selection of all I/O device names is left up to the computer manufacturer.

OS. The following is a typical card punch device name for this version of COBOL:
UR-2540P-S-SYSPUNCH

DOS FULL, DOS SUBSET. The following is a typical card punch device name for these versions of COBOL:
SYS006-UR-2540P-S

S/3. The following is a typical card punch device name for this version of COBOL:
UR-5424S-PU

1130. The following is a typical card punch device name for this version of COBOL:
PU-1442

Console typewriter I/O differences

ANS-68, ANS-74. The selection of the name used in the SPECIAL-NAMES paragraph to identify the console typewriter is left up to the computer manufacturer.

OS, DOS FULL, DOS SUBSET, S/3, 1130. The name CONSOLE

is used in the SPECIAL-NAMES paragraph to identify the console typewriter.

Unary plus sign differences

ANS-74, OS, DOS FULL, DOS SUBSET. The unary plus sign is allowed.

ANS-68, S/3, 1130. The unary plus sign is not allowed.

Spacing differences in arithmetic expressions

ANS-74. A space is required between a left parenthesis and a unary operator.

ANS-68, OS, DOS FULL, DOS SUBSET, S/3, 1130. No space is allowed between a left parenthesis and a unary operator.

Nested IF statement differences

ANS-68, ANS-74, OS, DOS FULL, DOS SUBSET. Nested IF statements are allowed in these versions of COBOL.

S/3, 1130. Nested IF statements are not allowed in these versions of COBOL.

GO TO/DEPENDING statement differences

ANS-74. The word TO is optional in the GO TO/DEPENDING statement.

ANS-68, OS, DOS FULL, DOS SUBSET, S/3, 1130. The word TO is required in the GO TO/DEPENDING statement.

EXAMINE and INSPECT statement differences

ANS-74. The INSPECT statement is valid in this version of COBOL, but the EXAMINE statement is not valid.

ANS-68, OS, DOS FULL, DOS SUBSET, S/3, 1130. All of these versions of COBOL allow the EXAMINE statement, but not the INSPECT statement.

STRING and UNSTRING statement differences

ANS-74, OS. The STRING and UNSTRING statements are available in these versions.

ANS-68, DOS FULL, DOS SUBSET, S/3, 1130. The STRING and UNSTRING statements are not available in these versions.

Library feature differences

ANS-74. The COPY statement may be used anywhere in the source program.

ANS-68, OS, DOS FULL, DOS SUBSET, S/3, 1130. The COPY statement is restricted to the uses listed in Figure 10-9.

CHAPTER 11

Spacing differences in subscripts

ANS-74. Unrestricted spacing may be used in subscripted table names.

ANS-68, OS, DOS FULL, DOS SUBSET, S/3, 1130. Spacing requirements in subscripted table names are as described in Section 11-2.

Differences in the use of commas in two and three level table subscripts

ANS-74, DOS FULL. Commas between subscripts are optional.

ANS-68, OS, DOS SUBSET, S/3, 1130. Commas between subscripts are required.

CHAPTER 12

Internal data representation differences

ANS-68, ANS-74. The standard versions of COBOL do not specify how data must be represented internally. This is left up to the computer manufacturers.

OS, DOS FULL, DOS SUBSET. The internal data representation discussed in Section 12-3 is used in these versions of COBOL.

S/3. The internal structure of the IBM System/3 is essentially the same as the structure of the IBM System/360 and System/370. The basic storage unit is the eight bit byte. Alphanumeric data is stored using the EBCDIC code. Numeric data can be stored as binary numbers in two, four, or eight bytes as described in the text. In addition, packed decimal form may be used for storage of numeric data. However, all calculations are done using data in zoned decimal form. Thus, binary and packed decimal data are used only to reduce storage requirements and not for calculations.

1130. The internal structure of the IBM 1130 is somewhat different from the structure described in the text. The basic storage unit in the 1130 is the 16 bit word; bytes are not used. Each word is given a unique address. Alphanumeric data is stored with one character per word using the EBCDIC code. The character is stored in the right-hand eight bits of the word; the remaining bits to the left are all zero. A numeric item is stored as a binary number using one, two, or four words depending on the item's length. If the item contains one to four decimal digits, then one word is used. Two words are used to store an item with five to nine decimal digits. Four words are required if the item has ten to 18 decimal digits.

USAGE clause differences

ANS-68, ANS-74. In the standard versions of COBOL, DISPLAY usage refers to the basic data format used for input and output. COMPUTATIONAL usage specifies that the item must be represented in a form suitable for numeric calculation.

OS, DOS FULL, DOS SUBSET. The forms of the USAGE clause discussed in Section 12-4 are applicable in these versions of COBOL.

S/3. For the IBM System/3, DISPLAY usage refers to alphanumeric data. COMPUTATIONAL usage identifies zoned decimal data. Packed decimal form is specified with COMPUTATIONAL-3 usage. For binary numbers, COMPUTATIONAL-4 usage must be indicated.

1130. With the IBM 1130, DISPLAY usage refers to alphanumeric data. COMPUTATIONAL usage identifies binary numbers. COM-

PUTATIONAL-4 may be used in place of COMPUTATION and means the same thing.

SYNCHRONIZED clause differences

ANS-68, ANS-74. The general description of the SYNCHRO-NIZED clause in Section 12–4 applies to these standard versions of COBOL.

OS, DOS FULL, DOS SUBSET. The SYNCHRONIZED clause only affects items of COMPUTATIONAL usage as discussed in Section 12–4.

S/3, 1130. The SYNCHRONIZED clause has no effect on any internal data representation used with the IBM System/3 and IBM 1130. However, it may be included with an item's picture, but it is always treated as a comment.

Program efficiency differences

ANS-68, ANS-74. Program efficiency, as discussed in Section 12–5, is dependent on the computer's internal data structure.

OS, DOS FULL, DOS SUBSET. The efficiency rules discussed in Section 12–5 are applicable in these versions of COBOL.

S/3. With the IBM System/3, COMPUTATIONAL usage should be indicated for numeric working items. However, for subscripts, COMPUTATIONAL-4 usage will result in more efficient table processing. The rule regarding the use of an odd number of digits in numeric items is not applicable. The SYNCHRONIZED clause has no effect. All other rules discussed in Section 12–5 are applicable.

1130. COMPUTATIONAL usage should be specified for all numeric working items, including subscripts, on the IBM 1130. The rule that an odd number of digits should be used with numeric items is not applicable. The SYNCHRONIZED clause has no effect. All other rules discussed in Section 12–5 are applicable.

CHAPTER 13

Tape drive name differences

ANS-68, ANS-74. The selection of device names for tape drives is left up to the computer manufacturer.

OS. The following is a typical tape drive name used in this version of COBOL:

UT-2400-S-TPFILE

DOS FULL, DOS SUBSET. The following is a typical tape drive name used in these versions of COBOL:

SYS020-UT-2400-S

S/3. The following is a typical tape drive name used in this version of COBOL:

UT-3400-F-TPFILE

1130. Magnetic tape processing is not available in IBM 1130 COBOL.

Disk drive name differences for sequential files

ANS-68, ANS-74. The selection of device names for disk drives is left up to the computer manufacturer.

OS. The following is a typical device name used for sequential disk files in this version of COBOL:

UT-3330-S-SDFILE

DOS FULL, DOS SUBSET. The following is a typical device name used for sequential disk files in these versions of COBOL:

SYS010-UT-3330-S

S/3. The following is a typical device name used for a sequential disk file that is opened as an input or output file in this version of COBOL:

UT-5444-S-SDFILE

If the file is opened as an I-O file the device name has the form:

UT-5444-S-SDFILE-U

1130. The following is a typical device name used for sequential disk files in this version of COBOL:

DF-20-1000-X

SELECT entry differences for sequential disk files

ANS-74. The clause PROCESSING IS SEQUENTIAL is not used in the SELECT entry for a sequential disk file. Instead, the clause ORGANIZATION IS SEQUENTIAL is included. Thus, a typical SELECT entry is of the following form:

```
SELECT file-name
    ASSIGN TO device-name
    ORGANIZATION IS SEQUENTIAL
    ACCESS MODE IS SEQUENTIAL.
```

The ORGANIZATION and ACCESS MODE clauses are optional. If they are left out, SEQUENTIAL organization and SEQUENTIAL access mode are assumed.

ANS-68. The form of the SELECT entry for sequential disk files described in Section 13-3 is correct for this version of COBOL. The ACCESS MODE clause and the PROCESSING clause are required.

OS, DOS FULL, DOS SUBSET, S/3, 1130. The form of the SELECT entry for sequential disk files described in Section 13-3 is correct for these versions of COBOL. The ACCESS MODE clause is optional. If it is left out, SEQUENTIAL access mode is assumed. The PROCESSING clause is optional and serves only as documentation.

WRITE statement differences for sequential disk files

ANS-74. The INVALID KEY phrase is not used with the WRITE statement in this version of COBOL.

OS. The INVALID KEY phrase is optional with the WRITE statement in this version of COBOL.

ANS-68, DOS FULL, DOS SUBSET, S/3, 1130. The INVALID KEY phrase is required with the WRITE statement in these versions of COBOL.

Differences in updating sequential disk files

ANS-74. The REWRITE statement must be used to update a sequential disk file.

OS. Either the WRITE or REWRITE statements may be used for updating sequential disk files.

ANS-68, DOS FULL, DOS SUBSET, S/3, 1130. The WRITE statement must be used for updating sequential disk files.

Disk drive name differences for indexed files

ANS-74. The selection of device names for disk drives is left up to the computer manufacturer.

OS. The following is a typical device name used for indexed files in this version of COBOL:

DA-3330-I-IDFILE

DOS FULL, DOS SUBSET. The following is a typical device name used for indexed files in these versions of COBOL:

SYS011-DA-3330-I

S/3. The following is a typical device name used for an indexed file that is opened as an input or output file in this version of COBOL:

DA-5444-I-IDFILE

If the file is opened as an I-O file the device name has the form:

DA-5444-I-IDFILE-U

ANS-68, 1130. Indexed file organization is not available in these versions of COBOL.

Indexed disk file processing differences

ANS-74. The SELECT entry for an indexed file has the following form:

```
SELECT file-name
    ASSIGN TO device-name
    ORGANIZATION IS INDEXED
    ACCESS MODE IS  {SEQUENTIAL}
                    {RANDOM    }
    RECORD KEY IS data-name.
```

SEQUENTIAL access mode is used if the file is processed sequentially. If random processing is used, RANDOM access mode must be specified. The data name in the record key clause must be alphanumeric. A nominal key is not specified.

All of the other elements for sequential and random processing of indexed files described in Section 13-4 are correct in this version of COBOL except for the use of the nominal key. A nominal key is not used. Instead, the record key must be assigned the value of the key field for the record to be read or written before a READ, WRITE, or REWRITE statement is executed.

OS, DOS FULL, DOS SUBSET, S/3. The COBOL elements described in Section 13-4 are valid in these versions of COBOL.

ANS-68, 1130. Indexed file organization is not available in these versions of COBOL.

APPENDIX B

COBOL Reserved Words

The words listed in this appendix are reserved in most versions of COBOL. They should not be used when a programmer-supplied word is required. The following keys appear before some words:

(74)   Words that are reserved in the 1974 ANSI standard but not in the 1968 standard.

(68)   Words that are reserved in the 1968 ANSI standard but not in the 1974 standard.

(IBM) Words that are reserved in one or more of the IBM implementations discussed in Appendix A but do not appear in either the 1968 or 1974 standard.

	ACCEPT	(74)	ALSO
	ACCESS		ALTER
(68)	ACTUAL		ALTERNATE
	ADD		AND
(68)	ADDRESS	(IBM)	APPLY
	ADVANCING		ARE
	AFTER		AREA
	ALL		AREAS
	ALPHABETIC		ASCENDING

283

	ASSIGN		CONTROL
	AT		CONTROLS
	AUTHOR		COPY
		(IBM)	CORE-INDEX
(IBM)	BASIS		CORR
	BEFORE		CORRESPONDING
(68)	BEGINNING	(74)	COUNT
	BLANK	(IBM)	CSP
	BLOCK		CURRENCY
(74)	BOTTOM	(IBM)	CURRENT-DATE
	BY	(IBM)	CYL-INDEX
		(IBM)	CYL-OVERFLOW
(74)	CALL	(IBM)	C01
(74)	CANCEL	(IBM)	C02
(IBM)	CBL	(IBM)	C03
(74)	CD	(IBM)	C04
	CF	(IBM)	C05
	CH	(IBM)	C06
(IBM)	CHANGED	(IBM)	C07
(74)	CHARACTER	(IBM)	C08
	CHARACTERS	(IBM)	C09
	CLOCK-UNITS	(IBM)	C10
	CLOSE	(IBM)	C11
	COBOL	(IBM)	C12
	CODE		
(74)	CODE-SET		DATA
(74)	COLLATING	(74)	DATE
	COLUMN		DATE-COMPILED
(IBM)	COM-REG		DATE-WRITTEN
	COMMA	(74)	DAY
(74)	COMMUNICATION		DE
	COMP	(IBM)	DEBUG
(IBM)	COMP-1	(74)	DEBUG-CONTENTS
(IBM)	COMP-2	(74)	DEBUG-ITEM
(IBM)	COMP-3	(74)	DEBUG-LINE
(IBM)	COMP-4	(74)	DEBUG-NAME
	COMPUTATIONAL	(74)	DEBUG-SUB-1
(IBM)	COMPUTATIONAL-1	(74)	DEBUG-SUB-2
(IBM)	COMPUTATIONAL-2	(74)	DEBUG-SUB-3
(IBM)	COMPUTATIONAL-3	(74)	DEBUGGING
(IBM)	COMPUTATIONAL-4		DECIMAL-POINT
	COMPUTE		DECLARATIVES
	CONFIGURATION	(74)	DELETE
(IBM)	CONSOLE	(74)	DELIMITED
	CONTAINS	(74)	DELIMITER

	DEPENDING		FIRST
(IBM)	DEPTH		FOOTING
	DESCENDING		FOR
(74)	DESTINATION	(IBM)	FREE
	DETAIL		FROM
(74)	DISABLE		
(IBM)	DISP		GENERATE
	DISPLAY		GIVING
(IBM)	DISPLAY-ST		GO
	DIVIDE	(IBM)	GOBACK
	DIVISION		GREATER
	DOWN		GROUP
(74)	DUPLICATES		
(74)	DYNAMIC		HEADING
			HIGH-VALUE
(74)	EGI		HIGH-VALUES
(IBM)	EJECT		
	ELSE		I-O
(74)	EMI		I-O-CONTROL
(74)	ENABLE	(IBM)	ID
	END		IDENTIFICATION
(74)	END-OF-PAGE		IF
(68)	ENDING		IN
	ENTER		INDEX
(IBM)	ENTRY		INDEXED
	ENVIRONMENT		INDICATE
(74)	EOP	(74)	INITIAL
	EQUAL		INITIATE
	ERROR		INPUT
(74)	ESI		INPUT-OUTPUT
	EVERY	(IBM)	INSERT
(68)	EXAMINE	(74)	INSPECT
(74)	EXCEPTION		INSTALLATION
(IBM)	EXHIBIT		INTO
	EXIT		INVALID
(74)	EXTEND		IS
(IBM)	EXTENDED-SEARCH		
			JUST
	FD		JUSTIFIED
	FILE		
	FILE-CONTROL		KEY
(68)	FILE-LIMIT	(68)	KEYS
(68)	FILE-LIMITS		
	FILLER		LABEL
	FINAL	(IBM)	LABEL-RETURN

	LAST		OMITTED
	LEADING		ON
(IBM)	LEAVE		OPEN
	LEFT		OPTIONAL
(74)	LENGTH		OR
	LESS	(74)	ORGANIZATION
	LIMIT	(IBM)	OTHERWISE
	LIMITS		OUTPUT
(74)	LINAGE	(74)	OVERFLOW
(74)	LINAGE-COUNTER		
	LINE		PAGE
	LINE-COUNTER		PAGE-COUNTER
	LINES	(IBM)	PASSWORD
(74)	LINKAGE		PERFORM
	LOCK		PF
	LOW-VALUE		PH
	LOW-VALUES		PIC
			PICTURE
(IBM)	MASTER-INDEX		PLUS
	MEMORY	(74)	POINTER
(74)	MERGE		POSITION
(74)	MESSAGE	(IBM)	POSITIONING
	MODE		POSITIVE
	MODULES	(IBM)	PRINT-SWITCH
(IBM)	MORE-LABELS	(74)	PRINTING
	MOVE		PROCEDURE
	MULTIPLE	(74)	PROCEDURES
	MULTIPLY		PROCEED
		(68)	PROCESSING
(IBM)	NAMED	(74)	PROGRAM
(74)	NATIVE		PROGRAM-ID
	NEGATIVE		
	NEXT	(74)	QUEUE
	NO		QUOTE
(IBM)	NOMINAL		QUOTES
	NOT		
(68)	NOTE		RANDOM
(IBM)	NSTD-REELS		RD
	NUMBER		READ
	NUMERIC	(IBM)	READY
		(74)	RECEIVE
	OBJECT-COMPUTER		RECORD
	OCCURS	(IBM)	RECORD-OVERFLOW
	OF	(IBM)	RECORDING
	OFF		RECORDS

	REDEFINES		SET
	REEL		SIGN
(74)	REFERENCES		SIZE
(74)	RELATIVE	(IBM)	SKIP1
	RELEASE	(IBM)	SKIP2
(IBM)	RELOAD	(IBM)	SKIP3
	REMAINDER		SORT
(68)	REMARKS	(IBM)	SORT-CORE-SIZE
(74)	REMOVAL	(IBM)	SORT-FILE-SIZE
	RENAMES	(74)	SORT-MERGE
(IBM)	REORG-CRITERIA	(IBM)	SORT-MESSAGE
	REPLACING	(IBM)	SORT-MODE-SIZE
	REPORT	(IBM)	SORT-RETURN
	REPORTING		SOURCE
	REPORTS		SOURCE-COMPUTER
(IBM)	REREAD		SPACE
	RERUN		SPACES
	RESERVE		SPECIAL-NAMES
	RESET		STANDARD
	RETURN	(74)	STANDARD-1
(IBM)	RETURN-CODE	(74)	START
	REVERSED		STATUS
	REWIND		STOP
(74)	REWRITE	(74)	STRING
	RF	(74)	SUB-QUEUE-1
	RH	(74)	SUB-QUEUE-2
	RIGHT	(74)	SUB-QUEUE-3
	ROUNDED		SUBTRACT
	RUN		SUM
		(74)	SUPPRESS
	SAME	(IBM)	SW0
	SD	(IBM)	SW1
	SEARCH	(IBM)	SW2
	SECTION	(IBM)	SW3
	SECURITY	(IBM)	SW4
(68)	SEEK	(IBM)	SW5
(74)	SEGMENT	(IBM)	SW6
	SEGMENT-LIMIT	(IBM)	SW7
	SELECT	(IBM)	SW8
(74)	SEND	(IBM)	SW9
	SENTENCE	(IBM)	SW10
(74)	SEPARATE	(IBM)	SW11
(74)	SEQUENCE	(IBM)	SW12
	SEQUENTIAL	(IBM)	SW13
(IBM)	SERVICE	(IBM)	SW14

(IBM)	SW15		(IBM)	TRACKS
(74)	SYMBOLIC		(74)	TRAILING
	SYNC		(IBM)	TRANSFORM
	SYNCHRONIZED			TYPE
(IBM)	SYSIN			
(IBM)	SYSIPT			UNIT
(IBM)	SYSLST		(74)	UNSTRING
(IBM)	SYSOUT			UNTIL
(IBM)	SYSPCH			UP
(IBM)	SYSPUNCH			UPON
(IBM)	S01		(IBM)	UPSI-0
(IBM)	S02		(IBM)	UPSI-1
(IBM)	S03		(IBM)	UPSI-2
(IBM)	S04		(IBM)	UPSI-3
(IBM)	S05		(IBM)	UPSI-4
(74)	TABLE		(IBM)	UPSI-5
(68)	TALLY		(IBM)	UPSI-6
	TALLYING		(IBM)	UPSI-7
	TAPE			USAGE
(74)	TERMINAL			USE
	TERMINATE			USING
(74)	TEXT			
	THAN			VALUE
(IBM)	THEN			VALUES
	THROUGH			VARYING
	THRU			
(74)	TIME			WHEN
(IBM)	TIME-OF-DAY			WITH
	TIMES			WORDS
	TO			WORKING-STORAGE
(74)	TOP			WRITE
(IBM)	TOTALED		(IBM)	WRITE-ONLY
(IBM)	TOTALING		(IBM)	WRITE-VERIFY
(IBM)	TRACE			
(IBM)	TRACK			ZERO
(IBM)	TRACK-AREA			ZEROES
(IBM)	TRACK-LIMIT			ZEROS

APPENDIX C

Keypunch Operation

A keypunch is operated in much the same manner as a typewriter — one character is recorded with each depression of a key. However, special operating procedures are needed to move the cards through the machine and to perform other functions. This appendix describes the main features of the IBM 29 keypunch and the procedures for its operation. A more detailed description of this machine may be found in the IBM publication *Reference Manual IBM 29 Card Punch* (A24-3332).

GENERAL FEATURES

The main features of the keypunch are (see Figure C–1):

MAIN LINE SWITCH. The main line switch turns on the power for the keypunch. The machine may be used immediately once the switch is turned on. When all punching is finished, the switch should be turned off.

CARD HOPPER. Blank cards are placed in the card hopper, face forward, with the 9-edge down. A pressure plate holds the cards in place. The cards are fed from the front of the deck, down to the card bed.

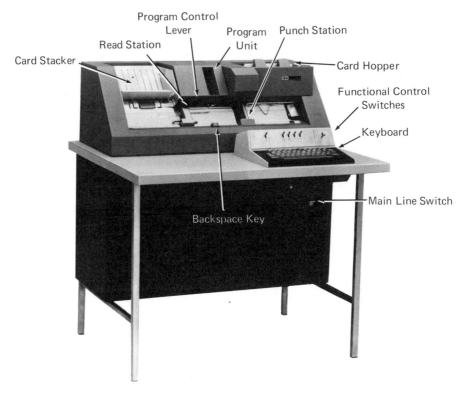

FIGURE C-1. The IBM 29 Keypunch (Courtesy of IBM Corp.)

PUNCH STATION. Punching is performed at the punch station as the card moves from right to left.

READ STATION. After a card leaves the punch station it passes through the read station. If a card is in the read station and another is in the punch station then the two cards move simultaneously. Data may be duplicated from the first card to the second. (See discussion of the DUP key.)

CARD STACKER. After a card leaves the read station it is fed into the card stacker. If the stacker becomes full, a switch is operated that locks the machine. Removing excess cards from the stacker releases the switch.

BACKSPACE KEY. The backspace key causes the cards at the read and punch stations to be moved back as long as the key is held down.

PROGRAM UNIT. The program unit controls certain automatic

features of the machine. The unit is accessed by lifting the back of the cover over the unit. Since punching can be performed without the use of the program unit, no further discussion of it is included here. See the IBM reference manual mentioned above for a complete description of program unit use and operation.

PROGRAM CONTROL LEVER. The program control lever is located above the card bed between the read station and the punch station. The normal position for this lever for punching without the use of the program unit is depressed to the right.

COLUMN INDICATOR. The column indicator is located at the bottom of the program unit. It shows the number of the column that is ready to be punched.

PRESSURE-ROLL RELEASE LEVER: The pressure-roll release lever is at the right of the column indicator. Pressing this lever releases cards at the read and punch stations. This is used when it is necessary to remove a card manually.

KEYBOARD

The keyboard consists of a set of punching keys, a space bar, and a number of functional keys. (See Figure C-2.) Each depression of a punching key causes one character to be punched and the card to advance one column. Depression of the space bar causes the card to advance one column without a character being punched. The important functional keys are:

NUMERIC (Numeric Shift). When this key is pressed, the keyboard is shifted into numeric shift. As long as this key is held down, depression of a punching key causes the upper character on the key to be punched. With the numeric shift key released, the lower character on the punching key is punched.

MULT PCH (Multiple Punch). When this key is pressed, the keyboard is in numeric shift and depression of a punching key does not cause the card to advance. This feature may be used to punch a unique code in a column.

DUP (Duplicate). When this key is held down, the data in the card in the read station is duplicated in the card in the punch station. This is accomplished column-for-column and may be stopped by releasing the DUP key.

FIGURE C-2. Keyboard Elements for IBM 29 Keypunch (Courtesy of IBM Corp.)

REL (Release). When this key is pressed, the cards at the read and punch stations are released and moved to the next station.

FEED. When this key is pressed, one card moves from the hopper down to the card bed just before the punch station. A second depression of this FEED key causes the card to be moved into the punch station and another card to come down from the hopper.

REG (Register). When this key is pressed, the card that is next to enter the punch station is moved into the punch station. Similarly, any card that is just before the read station is moved into the read station. An additional card is not fed from the card hopper when this key is pressed.

FUNCTIONAL CONTROL SWITCHES

The important functional control switches located above the keyboard are (see Figure C-2):

AUTO FEED. When this switch is on and a card is released by depression of the REL key, another card is fed automatically from the card hopper.

PRINT. When this switch is on, any character that is punched is also printed above the column in which it is punched.

CLEAR. When this switch is activated, all cards in the card bed are cleared and stacked. No additional cards are fed from the card hopper.

OPERATING PROCEDURES — BATCH PUNCHING

When a group of cards is to be punched, blank cards are placed in the card hopper and fed automatically. Make sure the auto feed switch is on. The procedure is:

1. Place a group of blank cards in the card hopper.
2. Press the feed key twice.
3. Punch the first card.
4. Press the release key.
5. Repeat Steps 3 and 4 for each succeeding card.
6. After all punching is completed remove all cards from the stacker and the hopper and turn off the main line switch.

OPERATING PROCEDURES — INSERTING INDIVIDUAL CARDS

Sometimes it is necessary to insert individual cards into the machine. This is often done when correcting an error using the duplicating feature. A card can be inserted to the right of the punch station. Do not insert cards manually to the right of the read station. The procedure is:

1. Remove the cards from the card hopper or turn off the auto feed switch.
2. Insert a card in the card bed at the right of the punch station.
3. Press the register key. The card may now be punched, or if it contains errors it may be moved to the read station by pressing the release key.

4. Repeat steps 2 and 3 for the next card. If the first card contains errors, this second card is a blank card into which correct data from the first card may be duplicated.

REMOVING JAMMED CARDS

Sometimes a card jams at the read or punch station. When this happens, push the pressure-roll release lever with one hand while gently pulling the jammed card with the other hand. If small torn pieces are caught at either station, push them out with another card or blow them away.

APPENDIX D

Programming Problems

This appendix contains 28 programming problems. All of the problems are related to the sales analysis application discussed in the text. Input for most of the problems is the file of salesperson records with the layout shown in Figure 1-9. Test data should be punched exactly as shown in Figure 2-3. Additional test data may be made up if desired.

In general the problems are arranged in order of increasing difficulty. The minimum prerequisite reading for each problem is given in parentheses following the problem number.

PROBLEM 1. (CHAPTER 2)

The program shown in Figure 2-1 is complete and can be run on a computer. In order to become familiar with the basic elements of COBOL, along with the coding format, control records, deck set-up, and other aspects of running a program, this program should be processed on an actual computer. Punch the program into cards exactly as it is coded in Figure 2-1. (It is necessary first to modify the entries in the SOURCE-COMPUTER and OBJECT-COMPUTER paragraphs and the SELECT entries for the specific computer that is used.) The resulting source deck should appear as in Figure 2-2. Punch an input data deck exactly as shown in Figure 2-3. Combine the source deck and the data deck with the proper control records. The general deck set-up is shown in Figure 2-4 but the specific control records depend on the computer that is used. Run the program on the computer and obtain the print-out. Any errors that occur are the result of keypunching mistakes. Correct any errors and rerun the program until the program is error-free. The source listing should appear as in Figure 2-5. Check the output to be sure that it is the same as Figure 2-6.

PROBLEM 2. (CHAPTER 3)

Prepare a program that prints one line for each salesperson, giving the person's number, name, region, year-to-date sales, and year-to-date returns. The output should appear as shown in the print chart in Figure D-1.

PROBLEM 3. (CHAPTER 4)

Prepare a program that calculates the average monthly sales for each salesperson. The average monthly sales is calculated by dividing the current month minus one into the year-to-date net sales. Assume that the current month field may be any value from 2 through 12. The year-to-date net sales is found by subtracting the year-to-date returns from the year-to-date sales. The output should list the salesperson's number, name, and average monthly sales in the format shown in Figure D-2.

PROBLEM 4. (CHAPTER 4)

Assume that the commission paid a salesperson is based on the commission classification code (column 26 of the input record). If this code is less than four, then the commission is 4.5 percent of the net current sales. If the code is four or greater, then the commission is 6 percent of the net current sales. The net current sales is calculated as in the illustrative program in Chapter 4. In addition, there is a bonus of $250 that should be added to the commission if the commission code is six or greater but no bonus if the code is less than six.

Prepare a program to calculate the commission for each salesperson. The output should list the salesperson number, name, commission classification code, and commission for each salesperson. The output format is shown in Figure D-3.

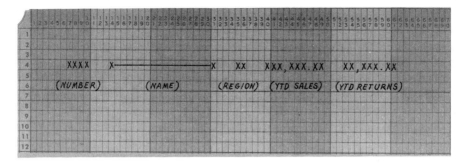

FIGURE D-1. The Print Chart for Problem 2

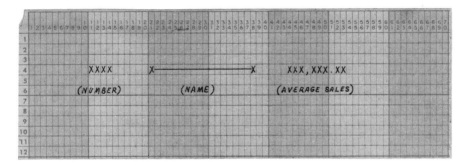

FIGURE D-2. The Print Chart for Problem 3

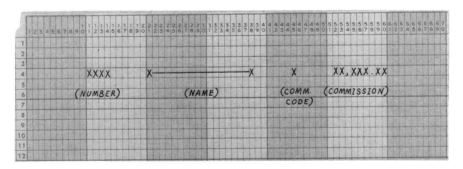

FIGURE D-3. The Print Chart for Problem 4

PROBLEM 5. (CHAPTER 4)

The quota for each salesperson is based on the quota classification
code (column 25 of the input record). If the quota classification
code is A then the quota is 110 percent of the average monthly sales.
If the code is B then the quota is 105 percent of the average monthly
sales. A quota classification code of C indicates a salesperson with
no quota. (The calculation of the average monthly sales is given in
Problem 3.)

Prepare a program that calculates the quota for each salesperson. The output should list the salesperson number, name, quota classification code, and quota for each salesperson. If the salesperson does not have a quota, print .00 for the salesperson's quota. The output should appear as shown in Figure D-4.

PROBLEM 6.   (CHAPTER 5)

Do Problem 4 as a modular program. Draw a module hierarchy diagram for the program.

PROBLEM 7.   (CHAPTER 5)

Do Problem 5 as a modular program. Draw a module hierarchy diagram for the program.

PROBLEM 8.   (CHAPTER 5)

Do Problem 5 with the modification that the output should list data for a salesperson only if the current month's net sales is greater than the quota. The current month's net sales is found by subtracting the current returns from the current sales. If the salesperson has no quota (i.e., the quota classification code is C), then no output should be printed. The output format should be the same as in Figure D-4 with the addition of a field for the current month's net sales. This program should be a modular design. All tests to determine whether

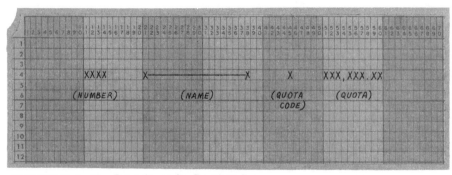

FIGURE D-4. The Print Chart for Problem 5

output should be printed should be in the control module. Draw a module hierarchy diagram and a set of modular flowcharts for the program.

PROBLEM 9. (CHAPTER 7)

Do the program specified in Problem 8 with the output format as shown in Figure D-5. This output includes a report title and column headings. Do not worry about line counting in this problem. Draw a module hierarchy diagram for the program.

PROBLEM 10. (CHAPTER 7)

Do the program specified in Problem 9 with the modification that only 15 detail lines are printed on each page of output. In addition, headings should be printed at the top of each page and totals should be included for the quota and current net sales. Draw a module hierarchy diagram for the program.

PROBLEM 11. (CHAPTER 7)

Develop a modular program that finds the percent increase or decrease of the current net sales over the average monthly sales. The average monthly sales is calculated as in Problem 3. The current net sales is found by subtracting the current returns from the current sales. If the current net sales are greater than the average monthly sales, then

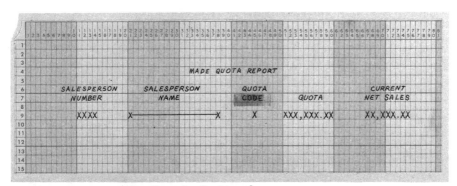

FIGURE D-5. The Print Chart for Problem 9

the percent increase is calculated as follows:

$$\text{percent increase} = \frac{\text{current net sales} - \text{average monthly sales}}{\text{average monthly sales}} \times 100$$

If the average monthly sales are greater than the current net sales then the percent decrease is calculated as follows:

$$\text{percent decrease} = \frac{\text{average monthly sales} - \text{current net sales}}{\text{average monthly sales}} \times 100$$

If the average monthly sales equals the current net sales, then there is a 0 percent increase in sales. If the average monthly sales is zero, then no output should be printed for the salesperson.

The output should list the salesperson number, name, average monthly sales, current net sales, and percent increase or decrease in sales as shown in Figure D-6. Twenty detail lines should be printed per page.

PROBLEM 12.   (CHAPTER 7)

Arrange the input data so that the records are in numerical order by region number. Within each region, the records should be in order by salesperson number. Prepare a modular program that finds the current net sales for each salesperson, the total current net sales for each region, and the overall total for all regions. The output should list each salesperson's number, name, and current sales. After processing the records for a region, the total should be printed before going on to the first salesperson in the next region. The final total should be printed at the end of the output. Headings should be supplied. The output format is shown in Figure D-7.

The output from this program is an example of a common type

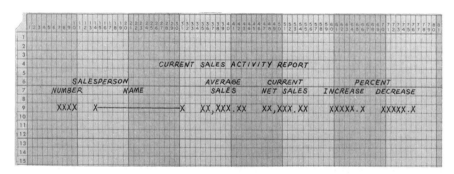

FIGURE D-6. The Print Chart for Problem 11

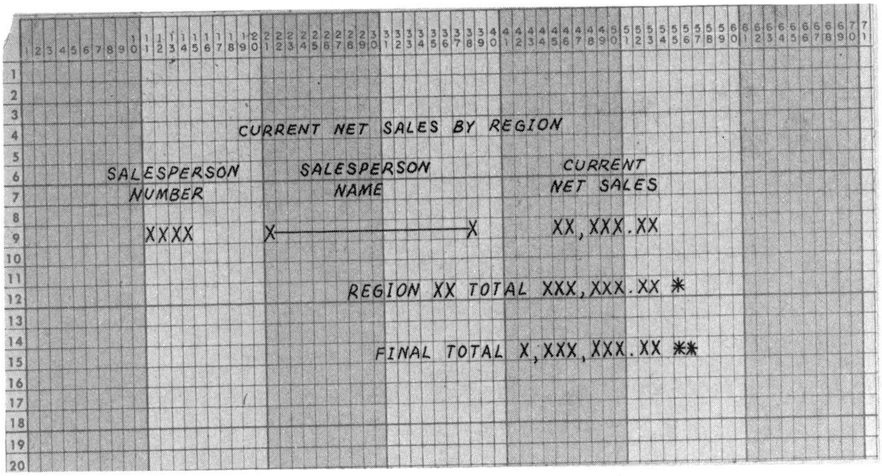

FIGURE D-7. The Print Chart for Problem 12

of report that is used in business data processing. In this type of report, totals are produced for groups of records within the input file. The group is identified by some field that has the same value for each record in the group. This field often is called a *control field*. In this problem the control field is the region number. A group of records in which each record has the same value in its control field is called a *control group*. During processing, the control field must be examined as each record is read. When the control field's value changes, then the end of the control group has been reached. This is called a *control break*. When a control break occurs, totals are printed for the previous control group and then processing continues with the first record in the next control group. When the end-of-file condition is reached, no control break is sensed, but the totals for the last control group must be printed before the final totals are printed.

PROBLEM 13. (CHAPTER 7)

Prepare a set of program flowcharts for the sample program discussed in Section 7-5. The source program listing is shown in Figure 7-6.

PROBLEM 14. (CHAPTER 8)

Prepare complete program documentation as discussed in Section 8-5 for the program written for Problem 10, Problem 11, or Problem 12.

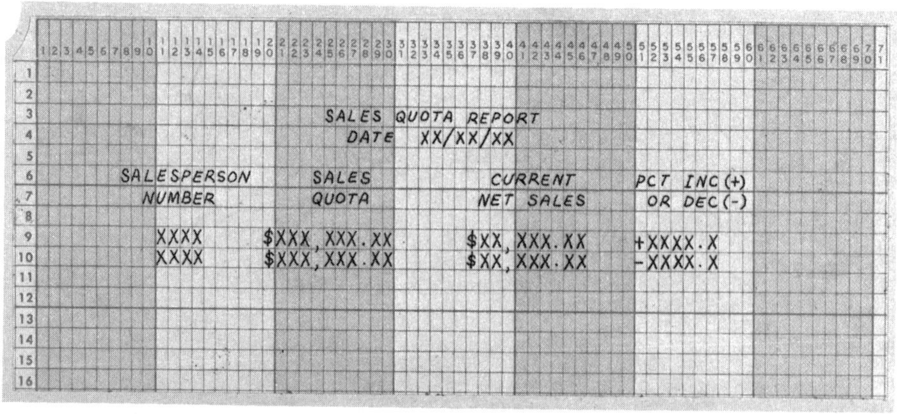

FIGURE D-8. The Print Chart for Problem 15

PROBLEM 15.   (SECTIONS 9–3 AND 9–4)

Prepare a program that calculates the sales quota for each salesperson, as in Problem 5. However, use condition names for the quota classification codes. Calculate the current net sales for each salesperson and the percent change in the current net sales over the sales quota. The percent change is calculated as follows:

$$\% \text{ change} = \frac{\text{current net sales} - \text{sales quota}}{\text{sales quota}} \times 100$$

If there is an increase in sales over the quota, then the percent change is positive; if there is a decrease, then this quantity is negative. If there is no sales quota (quota classification code C), do not perform this calculation and do not print any output for the salesperson.

Add a date card to the input data deck. This card should be the first card in the deck and should be punched with 091576 in the first six columns. (This represents the date September 15, 1976.)

The output from the program should appear as shown in Figure D-8. Notice that the date is included in the heading in edited form. The sales quota and current net sales are edited with floating dollar signs. The percent change is edited with a plus or minus sign depending on whether there is an increase or decrease in current net sales over the sales quota.

PROBLEM 16.   (SECTION 10–4)

Prepare a program to validate the salesperson data file. The validation process should check for the following errors:

1. Region number is not numeric
2. Region number is not in the range 01 to 12
3. Salesperson number is not numeric
4. Salesperson name is not alphabetic
5. Quota classification code is not equal to A, B, or C
6. Commission classification code is not numeric
7. Commission classification code is not in the range 1 to 8
8. The year-to-date sales is not numeric
9. The year-to-date returns is not numeric
10. The current sales is not numeric
11. The current returns is not numeric
12. The current month is not equal to 08
13. The current year is not equal to 76
14. The year-to-date sales is not greater than or equal to the year-to-date returns
15. The year-to-date sales plus the current sales is not greater than or equal to the year-to-date returns plus the current returns

If an error is found in any record, then the entire record should be printed. Following this print-out there should be a list of the error codes for all errors found in the record. Use the numbers for the errors listed above as error codes.

To test the program, punch cards with the data shown in Figure D-9. Intersperse these cards with the valid sales data. Additional valid and invalid test data may be included if desired.

PROBLEM 17. (SECTION 11-2)

The commission rate is based on the commission classification code. The rates vary from time to time, but the current rates are shown in the table in Figure 11-1. Write a program that reads the commission rate table from an input record. Then process the sales data file. Cal-

```
051A37ANDERSON RICHARD CAT147213000213500087500567000250000
170425JACKSON MARY      D40825671000D789958760AW0350178900
P347599SOKEL N K        67000479800125000A87602366010G69B0
071478JONES, MARTIN P.  C917C294000892317087T4793100167890
0683W6MAHLER ANTHONY    B00010000001000000876000000000000
119789CHANEY H          A104500000440000008760000000150000
```

FIGURE D-9. Additional Test Data for Problem 16

culate the commission for each salesperson by multiplying the current net sales by the appropriate rate from the rate table. The output should list the salesperson number, name, commission classification code, commission rate, current net sales, and commission.

PROBLEM 18.   (SECTION 11-2)

Figure D-10 shows a table of region numbers and names. Prepare a program that looks up and prints the name of the region for each salesperson. The program should define the table in WORKING-STOR-AGE. Output should consist of one line for each salesperson, giving the person's number and name, and the region number and name.

Region Number	Region Name
01	NORTH EASTERN A
02	NORTH EASTERN B
03	SOUTH EASTERN A
04	SOUTH EASTERN B
05	NORTH CENTRAL A
06	NORTH CENTRAL B
07	NORTH CENTRAL C
08	SOUTH CENTRAL
09	NORTH WESTERN
10	SOUTH WESTERN A
11	SOUTH WESTERN B
12	SOUTH WESTERN C

FIGURE D-10. The Region-Name Table for Problem 18

PROBLEM 19.   (SECTION 11-2)

Write a program that calculates the percent of the salespeople whose current net sales are greater than or equal to their quota in each commission classification. The quota calculation is given in Problem 5. One way of writing this program is to use three tables, each with eight elements. One table is needed to count the number of people in each commission classification. The second table is required to count the number of people in each classification that make their quota. Do not count salespeople who do not have a quota in either table. The third table is used to store the percents that are calculated for each commission classification after all sales records are processed. The output should list the commission classification codes and the percent of the salespeople in each classification who made their quota.

PROBLEM 20.   (SECTION 11-3)

Write a program that creates a two-level table giving the total number of salespeople in each combination of quota classification and commission classification. Since there are three quota classifications (A, B, and C) and eight commission classifications (1 through 8), a three-row, eight-column table is required. After the table is created from the sales data file, print the table in an appropriate format. To make this problem more realistic, additional input data should be used.

PROBLEM 21.   (SECTION 11-3)

Prepare a program that builds a three-level table giving the total number of salespeople in each combination of quota classification and commission classification within each region. This requires a "3-by-8-by-12" table, since there are three quota classifications, eight commission classifications, and 12 regions. Print the output in an appropriate format. Supply additional input data to make the problem more realistic.

PROBLEM 22.   (SECTION 11-3)

Write a program that builds the three-level table described in Problem 21. From this table, build the two-level table described in Problem

20. From this two-level table, create a one-level table giving the number of salespeople in each quota classification. Print all tables in appropriate formats.

PROBLEM 23.   (SECTION 13-2)

Write a program that creates a tape master file of salesperson year-to-date data in the format shown in Figure 13-7. Use the card file of sales data as input.

PROBLEM 24.   (SECTION 13-2)

Write a program to update the tape master file created in Problem 23 with current sales data. Input for this program is the tape master file and a card file of current sales data. The card file contains records with the salesperson number, current sales, and current returns. Use the data in Figure D-11 for this file. Output is a new, updated master file and an error listing. To create the updated file, add the current data from the card file to the year-to-date data from the tape master file. The error listing is necessary because not all records in the card file match records in the tape file. Those records that do not match should be printed in the error listing. If it is not practical to create a new updated file with the computer used to test the program, print the updated file.

This problem demonstrates an important technique in data processing. The problem is to sequentially update a sequential file. The technique that is used is sometimes called *matching records*. In this technique, the computer must determine whether records in the *transaction file* (in this case, the card file) match the records in the *master file* (that is, the tape file). The matching is done on some field such as the salesperson number. The records in both files must be in increasing numerical order with respect to this field.

The records in each file are read in sequence. Three conditions can occur during processing:

1. The transaction record matches a master record.
2. The transaction record does not match any master record. Such a record is called an unmatched transaction record.
3. A master record does not match any transaction record. Such a record is called an unmatched master record.

Salesperson Number	Current Sales	Current Returns
0005	1,600.35	12.50
0239	26,000.00	1,000.00
0429	4,302.00	152.00
1060	12,350.00	.00
1111	.00	.00
1185	425.00	62.50
1374	25.00	125.00
1642	4,635.21	125.16
1703	5,700.00	1,235.00

FIGURE D-11. Test Data for Problems 24, 26, and 28

If the first condition occurs, the master record is updated with the transaction data. If condition two occurs, an error message is printed. Condition three indicates a master record that should be copied into the updated master file without any changes.

PROBLEM 25. (SECTION 13-3)

Prepare a program that creates a sequential disk file of salesperson year-to-date data in the format shown in Figure 13-7. Use the card file of sales data as input, or if a tape master file of sales data exists as described in Problem 23, use this as input.

PROBLEM 26. (SECTION 13-3)

Write a program to update the sequential disk file created in Problem 25 with current sales data. Use the technique discussed in Problem

24, except that a new file need not be created; the records in the sequential disk file may be updated in place. The test data in Figure D-11 may be used for this program. If it is not practical to modify the disk file with the computer used to test the program, print the updated file.

PROBLEM 27. (SECTION 13-4)

Write a program that creates an indexed disk file of salesperson year-to-date data. The format shown in Figure 13-7 may be used for the records in this file, except that an extra character position should be added at the beginning of each record. Use the figurative constant LOW-VALUES to assign a value to this extra position. (With some systems, if this character position contains the equivalent of the figurative constant HIGH-VALUES then the record is considered deleted and is not processed during sequential retrieval.) For input use either the card file of sales data, the tape master file created in Problem 23, or the sequential disk master file created in Problem 25.

PROBLEM 28. (SECTION 13-4)

Prepare a program to update the records in the indexed disk file randomly. Use the card data in Figure D-11 to update the year-to-date sales and returns with the current data. If a record in the card file does not match any record in the disk file, add the record to the disk file. The record added should have the new salesperson's number from the card record, but the other fields should be blank. In addition, print an error message indicating that a record has been added; give the salesperson's number in this error message. If it is not practical to modify the disk file with the computer used to test the program, print the updated records along with the error messages for records that should be added to the file.

References

COBOL REFERENCES

The following references may be used to answer questions regarding details of particular versions of COBOL.

American National Standard COBOL, X3.23-1968. New York: American National Standards Institute, Inc., 1969.

American National Standard Programming Language COBOL, X3.23-1974. New York: American National Standards Institute, Inc., 1974.

IBM OS Full American National Standard COBOL, GC28-6396. International Business Machines Corporation, 1972.

IBM DOS Full American National Standard COBOL, GC28-6394. International Business Machines Corporation, 1973.

IBM System/360 Disk Operating System Subset American National Standard COBOL, GC28-6403. International Business Machines Corporation, 1971.

IBM System/3 Subset American National Standard COBOL Reference Manual, GC28-6452. International Business Machines Corporation, 1973.

IBM 1130 COBOL Language Specifications Manual, SH20-0816. International Business Machines Corporation, 1971.

OTHER READINGS

There are numerous references that deal with various aspects of the programming process. The following have been selected because they should be understandable and useful to the reader of this book.

ACM Computing Surveys, 6, 4 (December 1974). This issue contains five good articles on the programming process. The articles by Brown and Yohe are very general and are easy reading. The articles by Wirth and Knuth require more concentration. The Kernighan and Plauger article contains much of the same material as their book listed in this bibliography.

American National Standard Flowchart Symbols and Their Usage in Information Processing, X3.5-1970. New York: American National Standards Institute, Inc., 1970. This is the "official" description of the ANS flowchart symbols and their usage.

Armstrong, Russel M. *Modular Programming in COBOL*. New York: John Wiley & Sons, 1973. This book contains an extensive discussion of modular programming for COBOL programmers. Note especially Chapter 4 on documentation, Chapters 5 and 6 on modularity, and Chapter 8 on program constructs.

Aron, Joel D. *The Program Development Process: The Individual Programmer*. Reading, Mass.: Addison-Wesley Publishing Co., 1974. This volume contains a good discussion of the programming process for the individual programmer. There is a proposed companion volume dealing with programming teams.

Bohl, Marilyn. *Flowcharting Techniques*. Chicago: Science Research Associates, Inc., 1971. This is a very complete description of flowcharting with many examples. Modular flowcharting is discussed briefly in Chapter 10.

Conway, Richard and David Gries. *An Introduction to Programming: A Structured Approach Using PL/1 and PL/C-7*. 2nd ed. Cambridge, Mass.: Winthrop Publishers, Inc., 1975. This is a good text on structured programming emphasizing PL/1 and PL/C. Note especially Part II on program structure, Part III on program development, Part V on program testing, and Part VIII on confirmation of program correctness.

Datamation, 19, 12 (December 1973). This issue contains a number of good articles on structured programming. There is also an article by Baker and Mills on "chief programmer" teams, an approach to team programming.

Dijkstra, E. W. "Notes on Structured Programming." In O. J. Dahl, E. W. Dijkstra, and C. A. R. Hoare, *Structured Programming*. New York: Academic Press, 1972. This is one of the "classic" works on structured programming by the person who is often credited with "inventing" the approach.

IBM DOS Full American National Standard COBOL Programmer's Guide, GC28-6398. International Business Machines Corporation, 1972. This manual contains a section on programming techniques including coding conventions and modular programming. Similar manuals are available for other versions of COBOL.

Kernighan, Brian W. and P. J. Plauger. *The Elements of Programming Style*. New York: McGraw-Hill Book Co., 1974. This is a good discussion of style and structure in programs. Examples are in FORTRAN and PL/I but many of the principles apply in COBOL.

Polya, G. *How to Solve It*. Princeton, N. J.: Princeton University Press, 1945, 1957. Although this book does not mention computer programming, it still should be read by all programmers. It deals with problem solving and gives many hints that are applicable in programming. A background in geometry is necessary to understand some of the examples.

Stevens, W. P.; G. J. Myers; and L. L. Constantine. "Structured Design," *IBM Systems Journal*, 13, 2 (1974): 115-139. This is a good discussion of modularity in program design.

Van Tassel, Dennie. *Program Style, Design, Efficiency, Debugging, and Testing*. Englewood Cliffs, N. J.: Prentice-Hall, Inc., 1974. This book contains many ideas related to the topics listed in the title. Some examples are in COBOL; others are in FORTRAN, PL/I, and ALGOL W.

Weinberg, Gerald M. *The Psychology of Computer Programming*. New York: Van Nostrand Reinhold, 1971. This is the first major work on this subject. It should be read by all programmers.

Index

312